Built-ins
& Storage

STANLEY®

Built-ins
& Storage

David Schiff

The Taunton Press

To Doris Schiff, who encouraged me in whatever path I wished to take.

The Taunton Press
Inspiration for hands-on living®

The Taunton Press, Inc.
63 South Main Street
PO Box 5506
Newtown, CT 06470-5506

Email:tp@taunton.com

Editor: Peter Chapman
Copy Editor: Diane Sinitsky
Indexer: Cathy Goddard
Cover and Interior Design: Stacy Wakefield Forte
Layout: Jennifer Willman
Photographer: David Schiff, except for photos: p. 4 (right): Steve Cory; p. 4 (left), p. 6 (bottom left), p. 9 (left and top right), p. 10 (bottom), p. 11 (top left): courtesy Stanley; p. 67 (bottom right), p. 125 (bottom left, bottom right), p. 131 (bottom): ©2015 Merrillat® Cabinetry; p. 144: courtesy Rev-A-Shelf®; p. 145: (bottom): courtesy Delta Children; p. 148 (bottom): courtesy EasyCloset®

The following names/manufacturers appearing in *Built-ins & Storage* are trademarks: Accuride®; DeWalt®; EasyCloset®; Floetrol®; Grizzly®; Kreg®; Merillat®; Rev-A-Shelf®; Walmart®

Library of Congress Cataloging-in-Publication Data

Names: Schiff, David, 1955- author.
Title: Stanley built-ins & storage : a homeowner's guide / David Schiff.
Other titles: Stanley built-ins and storage
Description: Newtown, CT : The Taunton Press, Inc., [2016] | Includes index.
Identifiers: LCCN 2015050183 | ISBN 9781631861321
Subjects: LCSH: Built-in furniture. | Cabinetwork. | Storage in the home.
Classification: LCC TT197.5.B8 S33 2016 | DDC 684.1/6--dc23
LC record available at http://lccn.loc.gov/2015050183

Printed in the United States of America
10 9 8 7 6 5 4 3 2 1

FIRST, I'D LIKE TO THANK THE STAFF OF THE
Taunton Press for their creativity and profession-
alism. From graphic artists and photo editors
to illustrators, copyeditors, and administrative
staff, it takes a complex combination of talents
to create a how-to book that empowers read-
ers to advance their skills. I've worked with the
folks at Taunton on and off for about 15 years,
and everyone I have encountered has always cheerfully advanced the cause
of bringing you the best book we can.

In particular, I thank my editor, Peter Chapman. He is that rare editor
who has the knack for improving a writer's work while inflicting as little
pain as possible.

I would also like to thank my ever-patient photo models Cathy Neu,
Quinn Kimble, and Rennie Bradner, who would stand holding a circular
saw or chisel just so, sometimes until their arms ached while I searched for
the perfect shot. And a special thanks to Shana and Michael Sandor and
Ingela and Daniel Grant-Noren, two couples who not only modeled for me
but also graciously let me drag tons of photo equipment and construction
tools into their homes so I could build projects for this book.

Most of all, I thank my dear wife, Beth Kalet, who would interrupt her
own work whenever I was ready to take a photo. And finally, thanks and
an apology to my daughter, Hannah Schiff, who had no idea she would be
roped into modeling for the utility shelves project when she was expecting
a relaxing weekend at the old homestead.

CONTENTS

STANLEY

Introduction

Chances are, you have already flipped through these pages and found some projects you'd like to build for your home. Otherwise, this book would already be back on the shelf. Some of the projects look pretty sophisticated, so now you might be wondering if you have the skill to pull them off. Rest assured, you don't need to be a professional woodworker to build any of the projects here. There's nary a dovetail nor mortise-and-tenon joint in sight.

Every project in this book is designed to be built in the home shop. The simplest ones can be accomplished with basic tools and are a great way to break the ice if you are new to carpentry and woodworking. The spice rack, wine rack, utility shelves, garden tool rack, overhead garage storage, and attic shelves are all great projects to start with.

You may have noticed that some of the larger projects have dozens of steps. That's because we want to offer complete guidance. You'll find that each step is easy to accomplish. Read through the step-by-step instructions before you start a project. Study the drawings—they'll make it clear how the parts fit together, and they label each part so you'll know exactly what "front cleat" refers to in the text.

And, while you don't need pro skills to accomplish these projects, you do need time and patience. So take your time and work safely. The process will be fun and the results will be custom-made to fit your space, your needs, and your taste.

1

TOOLS AND MATERIALS

YOU DON'T NEED A SHOP FULL OF PROFES-SIONAL woodworking tools to build the projects in this book—they are designed with the home shop in mind. And, of course, you don't need every tool listed here for every project, so before beginning to build, read through the step-by-step instructions (always a good idea anyway). Alternative tools are often mentioned.

Buy tools as you need them so you don't end up with tools you never use. When you do decide to purchase a new tool, it's generally a good idea to buy the best tool you can afford. However, the best tool for your needs is not always the most expensive version. Some professional power tools are built to stand up to daily job-site or shop use. There's no need to pay for super durability when a lighter-duty tool will provide a lifetime of occasional use.

And while it would be nice to have pro shop equipment like a stationary cabinetmaker's tablesaw and a planer and joiner, you probably aren't planning on investing thousands of dollars in these kinds of tools. We want to make sure you can accomplish every project with tools you can store on a shelf and a portable tablesaw you can push against the wall when not in use. For that reason, these projects don't use rough-sawn hardwoods or other exotic materials. You can buy all the lumber and nearly all the hardware at any lumberyard or home center.

Power Tools

Once upon a time, some of the projects in this book would have required expensive machinery and complex joinery techniques that take years of practice to master. But these days, you don't need to cut dovetails to make drawers for the Rolling Kitchen Cart on p. 102 or the Window Seat on p. 77. Even pros are likely to reach for a pocket-screw jig to construct drawers that are just as strong in a fraction of the time. And the advent of the biscuit joiner eliminates the need for mortise-and-tenon joints in face frames and door frames in projects such as the Cabinet with Bookcase on p. 34.

Tablesaw

The tablesaw is the one stationary power tool you really can't do without for many of the projects in this book. Tablesaws fit into three roughly defined types: tabletop, contractor, and cabinetmaker.

Tabletop models often have 8-in. blades and are handy because you can stow them away and easily lift them onto a bench when you need them. However, building storage projects often involves ripping large pieces of plywood. A small saw may not allow wide enough rips, and a short rip fence makes it difficult to make accurate long rips.

A cabinetmaker's saw is an extremely accurate tool with a 10-in. blade that will handle large pieces, but it is also extremely heavy and expensive. If your shop and budget are relatively modest, a contractor model or a larger tabletop model (the definitions overlap) such as the ones shown below with a 10-in. blade may be your best choice. Many come with slide-out extension tables that extend the ripping capacity up to 24 in. Designed to be transported to job sites, contractor saws usually come with a stand that folds up, sometimes with wheels, making them a good choice if you need to move your saw around your work space.

A portable contractor's saw with a sliding extension table and a sturdy stand is a good compromise that will allow you to make accurate cuts up to 24 in. wide and still be able to move the tool out of the way when not in use. Two popular models are shown here.

Miter saw

You can make perfectly accurate crosscuts with a hand miter saw (see p. 12), with the miter gauge on your tablesaw, or with the circular saw with crosscutting jig described on p. 22. But for making quick, accurate crosscuts, you can't beat a power miter saw. Some models take 8-in. blades, others take 10-in. blades, and some take 12-in. blades. The bigger the blade diameter, the thicker and wider the stock you can cut. In some models, the blade just pivots straight down; in others, the blade slides on rails to extend the cutting-width capacity, so a sliding 8-in. blade may cut wider stock than a pivoting 12-in. blade. As a result, cutting-width capacities vary from less than 5 in. to more than 12 in. Some models can cut compound miters—meaning they can cut at an angle across the face of the board while cutting a bevel on the edge—a feature you won't need for the projects in this book. The model shown at right is a sliding compound miter saw with a 12-in.-dia. blade.

Circular saw

When it comes to bang for your tool buck, there's no better investment than a circular saw. You'll use yours for many of the projects in this book. You don't need a heavy-duty worm-drive saw, but look for a saw with

A power miter saw makes quick, accurate crosscuts. This model has a 12-in. blade that tilts and slides on two rails. As a result, it can make compound miter cuts on stock up to 12 in. wide.

well-machined parts that operate smoothly. Try out the levers that set the height and angle to make sure they operate easily so you can make accurate settings. Avoid buying a circular saw—or any other tool for that matter—that is made of stamped steel with rough edges.

Many of the projects in this book use birch plywood, and it's well worth buying a fine-finish blade to reduce splintering when cutting this material. A framing blade has fewer teeth and will make faster, rougher cuts in lumber.

TIP Is there a power tool you'd really like to get your hands on for a project in this book—perhaps a power miter saw to speed making the 72 core pieces, cleats, and rails for the Built-in Shelves on p. 64? If you can't justify buying the tool, check out your local rental center. Many home centers rent tools as well.

A good-quality circular saw with adjusting mechanisms that operate smoothly is one of the best investments you can make for your shop.

The Right Circular Saw Blade for the Job

There are several kinds of specialized blades you can buy for your circular saw, including blades designed just for ripping or just for crosscutting, and even abrasive blades with no teeth for cutting masonry, tile, or steel. For the projects in this book, you'll do fine with just the two shown here. At left is a fine-finish blade that will help you avoid splintering when cutting plywood (see "How to Prevent Splintering" on p. 23). At right is a framing blade that has fewer teeth and will make faster, rougher cuts in lumber when you are making projects like the Utility Shelves on p. 202.

The blades shown here have carbide tips on each tooth. This feature can triple the cost of a blade, but carbide blades stay sharp a lot longer than blades of plain steel. They also provide a cleaner, straighter cut.

Drill/Driver

Today's cordless drill/drivers are powerful enough to handle any drilling task in this book. They come with two batteries so you are unlikely to run out of juice. However, corded drills still offer more torque, and it is worth having one around if you will be drilling a lot of large-diameter holes or driving many long screws.

A sabersaw (also known as a jigsaw) is used to cut curves and notches. Use a thin blade like the one shown above for cutting curves.

Sabersaw

Some projects require you to make notches or curved cuts. You can cut notches with a handsaw and curves with a coping saw, but a sabersaw—also called a jigsaw—is the best tool for this job. Use a thin fine-cutting blade for curves and a wider blade for straight cuts such as notches.

Today's good-quality cordless drills are powerful tools and come with two batteries (so you can use one while the other charges). They also have keyless chucks for quick bit changes.

A full index of drill bits means you'll always have the right bit on hand when you need it.

Drill bits

It makes sense to have a complete set (or "index") of drill bits, so you won't find yourself having to run out to buy a bit you need. The bit shown here has 29 bits from 1⁄16 in. to 1⁄2 in. dia. For holes wider than 1⁄2 in. or so, use a paddle-shaped spade bit. You'll also want a countersink bit for some projects (see "Countersinking and Counterboring" on p. 27)

Router

Routers are capable of all kinds of joinery and shaping tasks. For the projects in this book, you'll need one mainly for making dadoes and rabbets for constructing cabinets and doors. A fixed-based router is all you need for these jobs. The only time you'll need a plunge router is if you decide to make the optional keyhole slots for hanging the Spice Rack (see p. 132). A plunge router allows you to start the motor and plunge the bit straight down into the workpiece. Many router motors, including the one shown at left below with a plunge base, are designed to fit into a fixed or plunge base. You can start out with a fixed base and buy a plunge base later if you need it, or buy the motor and both bases as a kit.

Router bits

There are, of course, many types of router bits, but you'll need only three types for the projects in this book. You'll need a straight-cutting bit for making dadoes and rabbets, a piloted rabbeting bit for fitting panels into frames, and a keyhole bit if you want to make keyhole slots for the hanging Spice Rack project.

The three router bits used for the projects in this book include, from left, a straight-cutting bit, a piloted rabbeting bit, and a keyhole bit.

A router plays a key role in modern woodworking practice. This router motor is shown installed in a plunge base; it also comes with a fixed base.

Biscuit joiner

Also called a plate joiner, a biscuit joiner is the tool that makes it possible to build strong cases and doors without mortises and tenons or other complicated joinery. The tool cuts crescent-shaped slots in mating parts, into which you glue football-shaped "biscuits" of compressed wood. The top and bottom surfaces of the mating parts are automatically aligned, while the biscuits allow side-to-side adjustment during glue-up. The biscuits come in several sizes.

A pocket-hole jig is the fastest, easiest way to make strong joints when one side of the joint will be hidden.

A biscuit joiner cuts slots for football-shaped biscuits that create strong joints.

Pocket-hole jig

If only one side of a joint will be visible, screws driven into pocket holes are even faster than biscuit joints and just as strong. A pocket-hole jig itself is not powered; rather, it guides a power drill/driver to make holes at the proper depth and angle. The jig shown above sets up quickly and has a built-in clamping mechanism that automatically cuts the holes at the right depth and angle. Stored on the side of the jig are two drill bits of different lengths with square heads to fit the specialized pocket-hole screws (see "Pocket-Hole Screws" on p. 16).

Finish nailer

You can use a small hammer and a nailset for any of the nailing tasks in this book. But a powered finish nailer will greatly speed the work, driving and setting a nail instantly with the pull of a trigger. Some models work with an air compressor; others are electric.

A finish nailer powered by an air compressor (shown here), or by an electric power cord or battery, instantly inserts and sets finish nails with the pull of a trigger, eliminating the need to use a hammer and nailset. It also requires only one hand to use, leaving the other hand free to hold the work.

Hand Tools

The hand tools you'll need for the projects in this book are pretty basic—in fact, there's a good chance you own most of them already. As with power tools, there's no need to purchase a new hand tool until you need it. When you do, it's always a good idea to get the best tool you can afford. Quality hand tools help you do your best work, and they last a lifetime.

Hammer and nailsets

Hammers are designed for various purposes, but the only style you'll need for the projects in this book is a claw hammer, which has a flat surface on one side of the head for striking nails and a claw on the other for pulling nails. Claw hammers come in a range of sizes that are described by the weight of the head. The heaviest, up to 28 oz., are designed for framing. You'll need a small claw hammer— 7 oz. is an ideal size—for driving the finish nails used in some of the projects. An inexpensive set of three nailsets will ensure you have the right one for nails of any size.

A 7-oz. claw hammer is just the right tool for driving finish nails. Nailsets come in three sizes for nails of different sizes.

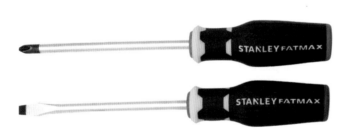

Even if you have a power drill/driver, you'll still need two hand drivers—a Phillips head (top) and a flat blade (bottom).

Screwdrivers

Most of the screws you'll drive will have a Phillips head, and most of the time you'll drive them with a Phillips bit in a power drill/driver. Still, you'll need a hand Phillips screwdriver for tasks such as installing small hinge screws. And a flathead screwdriver is indispensable for jobs like removing electric outlet covers and opening paint cans.

Wrenches

You won't need a wrench for most of the projects in this book, but you will need one to drive the lag screws that attach ledgers to studs in the Overhead Storage project in the Garages chapter on p. 207, and, depending on the installation method you choose, the Closet Tower on p. 142. A socket wrench is the best tool for driving lag screws, but a box wrench does the job just as well and almost as quickly.

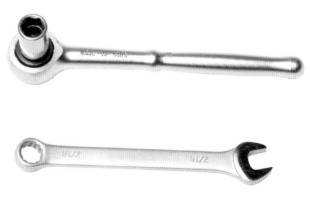

For driving lag screws, you'll need either a socket wrench (top) or a box wrench (bottom).

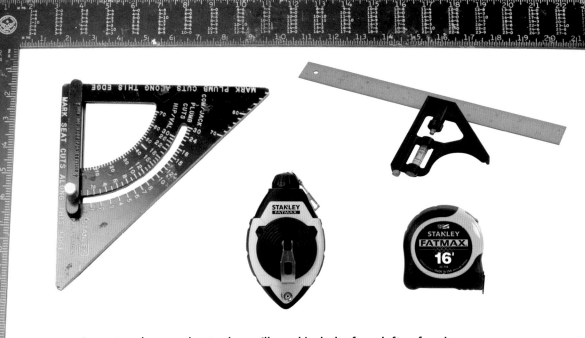

Layout and measuring tools you'll need include, from left, a framing square, an angle square, a chalkline, a combination square, and a tape measure.

Layout and measuring tools

A small collection of well-made layout and measuring tools is essential for accurately marking the locations of cuts. Look for layout tools with markings that are crisp and easy to read.

You'll need a framing square for laying out wide 90° cuts, an angle square for quickly laying out shorter cuts at any angle, a chalk line for laying out long cuts, a combination square for scribing mortises and other tasks, and a tape measure. Tape measures come in various lengths—16 ft. is convenient for storage projects. A wide blade lets you extend the tape several feet before it collapses under its own weight, which is helpful for measuring spaces when you're working solo.

Levels

You'll need a level whenever you need to check that a surface is plumb and/or level. For greatest accuracy, use the longest level that will fit into the space—a 4-ft. level and a 2-ft. level will do the trick for the storage projects in this book. A torpedo level is not essential but can come in handy in tight spots.

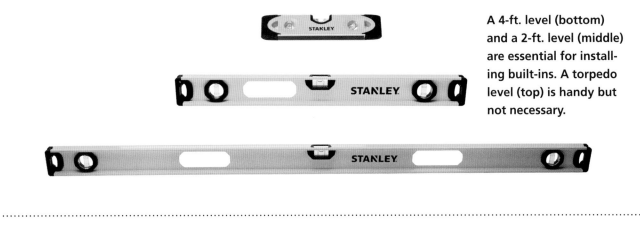

A 4-ft. level (bottom) and a 2-ft. level (middle) are essential for installing built-ins. A torpedo level (top) is handy but not necessary.

A utility knife is a simple tool you'll reach for to make cuts and layout lines and to trim edge veneer on plywood. Shown here are a well-used older knife and a more up-to-date version.

Utility knife

A utility knife is aptly named and is the tool you'll use for a wide variety of tasks from cutting edge veneer to scribing cuts to sharpening your pencil. There are a few different styles of utility knives: Some close by folding, in some the blade retracts, and in others the blade folds and retracts. The most common and versatile is an inexpensive nonfolding knife that retracts the blade when you slide back a button on the top. This slips easily into an apron or tool pouch and has convenient storage in the handle for extra blades. Make sure the retracting mechanism operates smoothly—it will get lots of use.

Block plane

When you need to make something just slightly smaller—such as trimming a door width to fit—nothing does the job faster and more accurately than a few strokes of a sharp block plane. Block planes have a knob on front for adjusting the opening for the blade (called the throat), and high-quality planes like the one shown below have a lever under the front knob to facilitate fine adjustments. There's another lever on top for clamping the cap to the blade and a knob at back for adjusting how far the blade extends under the base. When buying a block plane, make sure all the surfaces are smooth and flat and the mechanisms work easily and smoothly.

With the advent of power tools, in particular the router, you don't need a rack full of specialized planes. But no power tool can beat the handy block plane when you need to take a few licks off the edge of a board.

Chisels

You'll need chisels for various tasks, including squaring the corners of rabbets routed into frames, squaring stopped dadoes, and generally cleaning up joints made with the router or tablesaw. A set of four ranging in size from ¼ in. to 1 in. will handle all the jobs in this book.

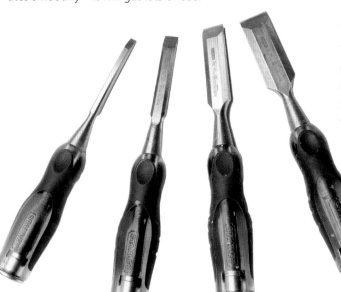

A set of four chisels ranging in size from ¼ in. to 1 in. will handle most woodworking tasks.

Hand miter saw

A hand miter saw is lighter, quieter, and makes less saw-dust than a power miter saw. As a result, even if you own a power version, you'll find yourself reaching for the hand miter saw when you have just a few cuts to make, especially in situations where you are cutting final pieces of molding to fit on site.

This fine-toothed hand miter saw runs on guides to provide clean, accurate crosscuts at any angle.

Clamp It Down

When using a hand miter box, or a power miter saw for that matter, it is important to secure the saw to your work surface. You'll work more accurately and, more important, more safely. Most saw bases have holes for screwing or bolting the tool in place, but unless you are making a permanent installation, you'll probably want to use a couple of clamps. If clamps won't fit properly, another alternative is to screw the tool to a piece of plywood and then clamp the plywood to the work surface.

Aptly named, "quick clamps" can be held in position and tightened with one hand. You'll need clamps to span various lengths. The longest one here can span 35 in., the shortest up to 6⅛ in.

Clamps

There are various types of clamps in common use, including bar clamps, pipe clamps, and C-clamps. A more recent innovation that can handle most clamping jobs is a clamp that is often referred to as a quick clamp. These are easy to use because they can be held in position and tightened with one hand and they have pads to protect the surfaces of your project.

Mallets

You can use a hammer to tap parts together during glue-up, as long as you put a scrap against the workpiece to protect it from denting. A rubber mallet makes the job easier by eliminating the need for the protective scrap. And while most chisels have a metal cap that allows you to strike them with a hammer, a well-balanced wooden mallet has just the right heft for the job.

A rubber mallet is the tool of choice for "persuading" parts to go together during glue-up. (As you can tell by looking at the one on top, it's also handy for seating paint can lids.) A wooden mallet, below, has just the right heft for tapping a chisel.

The plywood used in the projects in this book includes, from left, CDX grade, AC grade, cabinet-grade birch, and beadboard panels.

Plywood

Most of the projects in this book are built of plywood, and with good reason. Plywood comes in flat 4-ft. x 8-ft. sheets that are dimensionally stable—which means that parts won't expand, contract, or warp significantly with humidity changes as solid wood sometimes does. There are two broad categories of plywood: panels that are performance rated by the American Plywood Association (APA) and "cabinet-grade" plywood that is not actually subject to any formal system of grading. Only four types of plywood are used in this book.

CDX plywood

CDX is a sturdy, inexpensive grade of plywood that is most often used for house sheathing. In this book, it's used for utility projects like the Utility Shelves and Attic Shelves. The face veneer on one side is rated C, which means it contains knots. The other side is rated D, which means there can be voids in the face veneer. The X means the plywood is suitable for temporary exposure to the weather such as sheathing before it is covered with siding.

AC plywood

A step up from CDX plywood, AC plywood has an A side that is sanded smooth; it will take paint well, although it won't result in a painted surface that is as smooth as birch plywood (discussed next). The A side can have football-shaped repairs called "sleds"—you can see one near the middle of the example in the photo above. The

C side looks like the good side of CDX. AC plywood is approved for permanent outdoor use. It's used for the Fold-Up Worktable/Tool Cabinet project.

Birch plywood

Many projects in this book use plywood with birch face veneers. Birch is the only cabinet-grade plywood used in the book, because it takes paint and clear finish very well, is relatively inexpensive, and is readily available at lumberyards and home centers.

Because there is no formal standard for cabinet-grade plywood, your best bet is to check each sheet before you buy it. An occasional small void in the layers along the edges is okay, but make sure the layers aren't separating. Also make sure the face veneers aren't chipping. Look closely at the face veneers and run your hand over them to make sure they are flat and not wavy.

Beadboard panels

Beadboard is designed to be used as paneling on walls and ceilings as a less expensive alternative to individual solid-wood tongue-and-grooved beaded boards. Made from southern yellow pine, it's approved by the APA for permanent outdoor use. In this book, it's used for the door and back panels in the Cabinet with Bookcase project.

The solid wood used in the projects in this book includes, from left, maple, clear pine, and #2 pine, which has knots. Douglas fir 2x4s, not shown, are also used.

Solid Wood

The only projects in this book that use hardwood lumber are the Rolling Kitchen Cart and the Spice Rack. Maple is used for the cart's false drawer fronts and for the sides of the spice rack. The cart has poplar legs. You'll find both of these hardwoods, in addition to oak, at lumberyards and home centers. To get planed boards of other hardwood species, you'll most likely have to order online. Local saw mills usually sell only rough-sawn boards, so you'll need a thickness planer if you want to use this stock.

Many of the projects in this book use clear or #2 pine boards, which are available at lumberyards and home centers. Clear pine is used for parts that will be seen such as face frames and shelf edges, whereas #2, which has knots, should be reserved for hidden parts such as cleats. For projects that will be painted, you could save money by coating #2 knots with shellac or a stain-blocking primer that contains shellac, but the reality is that sometimes the knots bleed through anyway. Given that the projects don't use a lot of pine, you might decide that springing for the clear stuff is insurance worth the price.

The only other softwood lumber used is Douglas fir 2x4s, also available at any lumberyard or home center.

This lumber is used for the utility projects in the garage and attic chapter.

Edge veneer

In most cases when using plywood, you'll need to cover the edges with veneer to achieve a finished look. This veneer comes in rolls and is designed to cover the edges of matching species of hardwood plywood that is ¾ in. or less thick. One side is coated with a glue that is heat-activated by a household clothes iron.

Applying iron-on edge veneer is an easy way to cover the edges of hardwood plywood.

Dealing with Glue Squeeze-Out

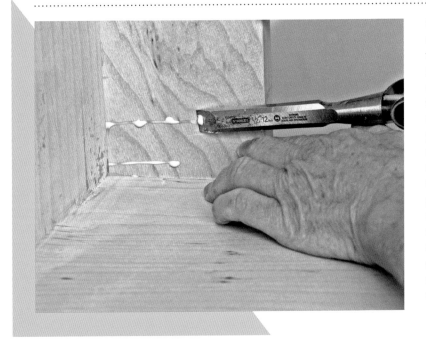

Squeeze-out is inevitable when you are assembling a project with glue. In fact, if there isn't a little squeeze-out, you may not have used enough glue. The easiest way to get rid of the squeezed-out glue is to simply wipe it away with a wet sponge while the glue is wet. This works fine for projects that will be painted. But it can cause a problem if the project will be stained or given a clear finish, because the water from the sponge dilutes the glue and some may soak into the wood, sealing the pores. This can cause an uneven, blotchy finish. To prevent this, let the glue dry for about 15 minutes until it starts to harden and darken around the edges. Then carefully skim the glue off the surface with a chisel.

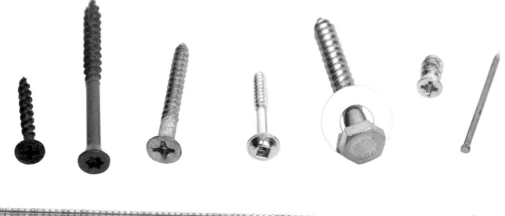

Fasteners you'll need for the projects in this book include, from left above, all-purpose screws, deck screws, flat-head wood screws, pocket-hole screws, lag bolts, Euro screws, finish nails, and, at left, finish nails for a power nailer.

Fasteners and Finishes

Modern fasteners have evolved into a wide range of screws and nails, each type designed to do a specific task very well. Each of the projects in this book specifies exactly which fastener to use for each purpose.

Conversely, improvements in paints and finishes have made them more versatile. You can still buy oil finishes, shellac, and wax. For an old-fashioned patina on solid wood, you might choose a few coats of boiled linseed oil or tung oil followed by hand-rubbed wax. However, for the projects in this book, we chose to use polyurethane or latex paint, two finishes that are durable, easy to clean, and easy to apply.

Here's a rundown of the fasteners and finishes used in this book.

ALL-PURPOSE SCREWS. These fasteners have a Phillips head and are sometimes called drywall screws. Some are black (as shown above), while others are metal-colored; they come coarse- or fine-threaded. Either will work for the projects in this book, but the coarse-threaded screws drive in more quickly and don't require predrilling in softwood unless you are close to the edge and worried about splitting.

DECK SCREWS. These screws can be galvanized or ceramic-coated like the one shown above. Some, as shown, have a star head that never strips out—the matching bit is usually

included in a box of screws. The coarse screw threads stop about halfway from the bottom. As a result, the screws drive quickly without predrilling and the top piece is drawn toward the bottom piece. Though coated for outdoor use, deck screws are an excellent choice any time you are assembling parts of 1½-in. or thicker lumber.

FLAT-HEAD WOOD SCREWS. These screws have a tapered Phillips head. You'll need to predrill and countersink holes for these screws. Brass versions like the one shown in the photo above look good when left exposed, but the heads strip easily because brass is soft.

POCKET-HOLE SCREWS. These screws have a square-drive head and are designed to fit the pockets made by pocket-hole jigs. The heads have flat bottoms to prevent splitting and, like deck screws, are threaded only halfway to draw the parts together.

LAG BOLTS. These fasteners have a flat-bottomed hex head and are used with a washer when you need a very strong connection—such as the ledger on the Overhead Storage project or the Closet Tower.

EURO SCREWS. These short, 5mm-dia. screws have a blunt bottom and are designed specifically for use in holes drilled for European-style hinges and for accessories installed in shelf-pin holes such as those in the Closet Tower project. They have a Pozi-drive head, which is similar to a Phillips head but with a blunt, nontapered tip. It's best to install these screws with a Pozi-head driver, which won't strip the head, but because the predrilled holes are shallow, you can get by with a Phillips-head driver.

FINISH NAILS. These thin nails have a small head designed to be set below the surface and hidden with wood putty. Lengths used in this book are 3d (1¼ in.), 4d (1½ in.), and 8d (2½ in.). Finish nails that are 1 in. or shorter are called brads.

POWER FINISH NAILS. These come in strips, and you need to buy ones that are designed to fit your specific brand of nailer. They are driven below the surface with a pull of the nailer trigger.

GLUE. Aliphatic resin glue, more commonly known as yellow glue or carpenter's glue, is the glue of choice for bonding wood. When used along the grain, it creates a bond that is stronger than the natural bond between wood fibers.

WIPE-ON POLYURETHANE. You can buy polyurethane finish that is designed to be applied with a brush. But for the projects in this book, we chose to use wipe-on polyurethane, which is essentially a thinned-down version that can easily be wiped on with a rag. Because it is thinned, you may need more coats, but the finish soaks in better and you won't have to worry about trapped air bubbles or brushstrokes.

Both types of polyurethane finishes are available in satin, semi-gloss, and gloss sheens.

SHELLAC. Shellac is a time-honored finish that consists of the shell of the lac beetle dissolved in alcohol. It's less durable than polyurethane—alcoholic drinks can mar it, for example, so it's not used for exposed parts of projects in this book. However, a coat of shellac is your best hope for preventing resin from pine knots from bleeding through paint. It is also used on the interior of the drawers for the Window Seat and Rolling Kitchen Cart projects. That's because shellac has little odor and cures quickly. By

contrast, polyurethane will continue to produce a faint odor for months. This odor won't be noticeable on an exposed surface but can collect inside a closed drawer to become very noticeable when you open it.

WOOD FILLER. There are several variations on wood fillers; for example, some come tinted for filling holes and gouges in surfaces that are already finished. There are epoxy formulations designed to fill large gaps and holes. In this book, wood filler is used to cover nails and screws driven below the surface, to fill small gaps in joints, and to fill voids in plywood. You can use filler that's designated for interior or exterior use—just make sure it is designated as sandable, stainable, and paintable.

PAINT. Interior latex acrylic paint is used for the projects in this book. You can choose your level of gloss, from flat through high gloss. Semi-gloss was used most often for the projects here.

From left, wipe-on polyurethane is an easy finish to apply, wood filler is used to cover nail holes and gaps, and aliphatic resin wood glue is used for interior wood joinery.

CHAPTER TWO

BASIC TECHNIQUES AND JIGS

THERE'S A RICH DIVERSITY OF STORAGE
projects in this book, but many of them
are built with similar techniques. In this
chapter, you'll find step-by-step instructions for techniques and simple jigs that
you'll use often for the projects here.
The instructions should also prove help-
ful for other woodworking jobs you'll undertake in the future.

As with all the techniques in the book, the ones in this chapter are
designed to help you work as accurately as possible and, more important,
as safely as possible. Some of the techniques and jigs will also speed your
work, but that's just a side benefit. In fact, there are sometimes faster but
less accurate and/or less safe ways to accomplish some of these tasks.

But you are in no hurry. Building these projects is fun—take your time
and enjoy the ride. If, for example, you take the time to make sure cabinet
sides are exactly the same size, you'll get a little tingle of satisfaction when
the glue-up comes out perfectly square.

Work Safely

One important technique for safe, accurate, and enjoyable work isn't a step-by-step procedure at all—it's an ongoing process: Always take the time as you work to keep an orderly shop. As you become immersed in the work, it's a natural tendency to just put a tool aside, thinking you'll put it away later. Before you know it, your work surfaces will be cluttered and you won't be able to find what you need quickly.

Clean up and keep organized as you go. Roll up the extension cord so you can't trip on it—it's especially important to keep the floor clear around your tablesaw. Vacuum the sawdust after routing those dadoes. These "mindless" tasks have the bonus benefit of giving you a few minutes to think about the next procedure, sometimes preventing mistakes. You just might turn around and think, "Whoops, I was about to rout the wrong side of that!"

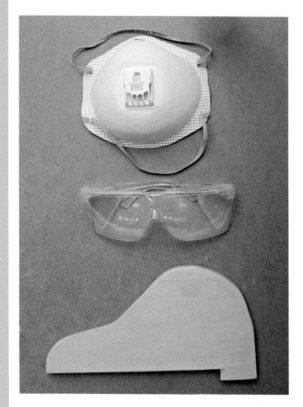

Three essential pieces of safety gear are, from top, a dust mask, safety goggles, and a push stick for the tablesaw.

USE SAFETY GEAR

There are three important pieces of safety gear you want to keep within reach at all times so you will never be tempted to skip using them.

Disposable dust mask. Even if you have a state-of-the-art dust-collection system in your shop, you need to protect your lungs with a dust mask when creating dust by sawing or sanding. It's even more crucial in the typical home shop that relies mostly on a shop vacuum. Use disposable masks with two straps and a metal strip that you pinch to fit the mask over the bridge of your nose. Replace the mask whenever it starts to look dirty.

As the name implies, a dust mask is to protect your lungs from dust, not from toxic fumes. You won't need protection from toxic fumes while making the projects in this book, but if you ever do, understand that you'll need a special filtering respirator for that job.

Safety goggles. Any power tool—including power saws, drills, biscuit joiners, and routers—has the potential to send particles or splinters toward your face. Hammering nails can, too. To protect your eyes, you need a pair of safety glasses or goggles that wrap around the sides of your head. Regular prescription glasses are no substitute. If you wear prescription glasses, you can put goggles over them, or, of course, you can have a pair of prescription safety glasses made.

Push stick. Always use a push stick to keep your hand away from the blade when making rip cuts of less than about 6 in. wide on the tablesaw. You can purchase a push stick from a woodworking catalog or make one yourself, like the one shown at left.

Although you'll use them less often, two other items you'll want to have on hand are a pair of work gloves and ear plugs or protectors. You'll need the gloves if you cut metal, as you will if you build the Window Seat project on p. 77. They are also a good idea when moving plywood and boards around to prevent splinters. Ear plugs, or better, protectors that cover the ears, are a good idea if you will be using a loud power tool such as a router or tablesaw for a long period of time.

Rough-Ripping Plywood

Because plywood comes in 4-ft. x 8-ft. sheets, it's ideal for building the boxes, shelves, and door panels that are the basic components of most storage projects. But those big sheets are unwieldy to handle in the home shop. If you don't have a panel saw or a large cabinetmaker's tablesaw with outfeed tables, it's difficult to safely cut full sheets accurately to size.

If you have a number of pieces that need to be ripped to the same width, the easiest solution is to have sheets ripped at the lumberyard or home center. Doing this also makes the plywood easier to transport if 4-ft.-wide sheets won't fit in your vehicle.

Sometimes it's not practical to have plywood ripped at the store—perhaps you are having sheets delivered or you want the luxury of cutting certain pieces to fit. In those cases, the best solution is to use a circular saw to make rough rips on the floor, as explained below.

Begin by placing a ½-in.-thick or ¾-in.-thick "sacrificial" piece of plywood on the floor to protect the floor and your sawblade. You can use two or three scraps instead, as long as the workpiece will be supported on both sides during the rip. Put the workpiece on the sacrificial piece. Measure across both ends to mark a width that's ⅛ in. to ¼ in. wider than the final width you need **(1)**.

With the saw unplugged, set your sawblade to cut about ⅛ in. deeper than the thickness of the workpiece—a depth of ⅞ in. for ¾-in.-thick plywood. Use a square to check the cutting depth **(2)**. You want the saw to cut through the workpiece and score the sacrificial piece. Make sure you have enough extension cord, then throw the cord over your shoulder and crawl along the plywood to make the cut **(3)**.

1 SNAP A LINE. With sacrificial scraps placed underneath the plywood, snap a line for a rip cut that will give you a piece slightly wider than the final dimension.

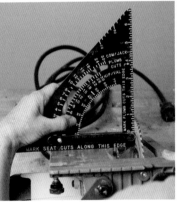

2 SET THE CUTTING DEPTH. Use a square to check the cutting depth of your circular saw and also to make sure the blade is perpendicular to the base.

3 MAKE THE ROUGH CUT. Crawl along the plywood to make the rough rip cut.

Making a Crosscutting Jig

The quickest way to make accurate straight cuts is with a power miter saw, but it's not a tool that all homeowners own. And even if you do, it may not be capable of making cuts wide enough for your project. A miter saw with a 10-in. blade can make a cut that's only about 6 in. wide. Even a sliding miter saw with a 12-in. blade will cut only a little over 12 in.

The crosscutting jig shown here takes about 30 minutes to construct and will make cuts up to 4 ft. wide. You can customize its length to fit your needs—it just needs to be long enough to clamp at both sides of your bench. With this jig, each cut takes a few minutes to set up, but the result is perfectly straight and accurate.

To make the base, start with a piece of ¼-in. plywood that's 48 in. long and at least 6 in. wider than the base of your saw. Glue and clamp a ¾-in. x 6-in. x 52-in. plywood guide flush to the outside edge of the base and overhanging about 2 in. on each side. When the glue dries, clamp the jig to your bench with enough of the base overhanging so that you can run your circular saw along the guide, trimming the base **(1)**.

Now you need to set the cutting depth on the circular saw. First, make sure the saw is unplugged, then set the blade depth to equal the thickness of the workpiece plus ¼ in. (for the thickness of the base) plus ⅛ in. You want the blade to score the sacrificial piece but not cut into your bench. For example, to cut through ¾-in. plywood, set the depth to 1⅛ in.

1 **ASSEMBLE THE JIG. Clamp the base to your bench, and run the circular saw against the guide to trim the base.**

Place a sacrificial piece of ½-in. or ¾-in. plywood on your bench, and position the workpiece on top so that it will be supported on both sides of the cut. Use a square to lay out the cut on the workpiece **(2)**.

To make the cut, position the jig on the non-waste side of the workpiece with the trimmed edge of the base just touching but not covering the layout line. Clamp the jig to the workpiece at both sides of the fence. If the workpiece is too narrow to do that, support the jig on the outfeed side with scrap equal in thickness to the workpiece, then clamp the workpiece in place with the scrap beneath as shown **(3)**.

CROSSCUTTING JIG

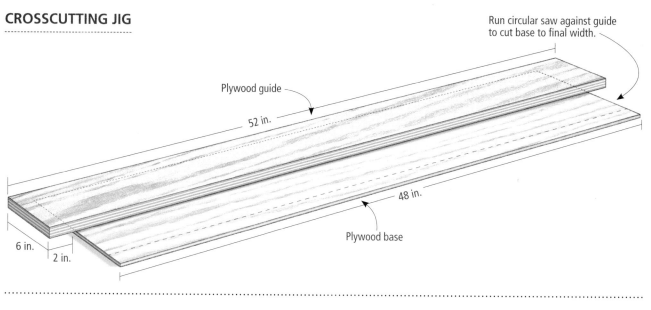

Run circular saw against guide to cut base to final width.

Plywood guide

52 in.

Plywood base

48 in.

6 in.

2 in.

STANLEY

2 **LAY OUT THE CUT.** Use a framing square to lay out the crosscut on the workpiece.

3 **MAKE THE CUT.** Clamp the workpiece and the jig to the bench. (If necessary, use a piece of scrap, as shown in the foreground, to support the jig.) Run the saw along the jig's plywood guide to make the cut.

How to Prevent Splintering

The thin face veneers on cabinet-grade plywood can splinter easily when plywood is cut, especially across the grain. You can minimize, but not prevent, splitting by using a fine-cutting blade when cutting plywood (see "The Right Circular Saw Blade for the Job" on p. 6.)

Saw teeth cut cleanly through veneer as they plunge into a piece, and they cause splintering on their way out. This means that if only one side of a cut will be seen in a finished product—for example, the ends of a cabinet side that's rabbeted to receive the top and bottom—you can simply make sure the blade will plunge into the good side and come out the unseen side. You should make cuts with the good side up on a power miter saw or tablesaw and with the good side down when using a circular saw or a sabersaw fitted with a standard woodcutting blade.

If both sides of a crosscut will be seen, you can prevent splitting by scoring the veneer along the cutline on the side the teeth will exit. Place a straightedge along the cutline and score with two or three passes of a sharp utility knife until you cut completely through the face veneer.

If the cut edge won't be seen on either side—perhaps it's a shelf end that will fit into a dado—splitting won't matter.

Making a Dado Jig

Cabinet-grade plywood is usually a little thinner than its nominal dimension. That means, for example, if you use a ¾-in.-dia. router bit to make dadoes for nominal ¾-in. plywood, the dadoes will be too loose. The solution is to rout the dadoes for a snug fit by making two overlapping passes with a ½-in.-dia. bit. For ½-in.-wide dadoes, use a ¼-in.-dia. bit. The simple dado jig shown here makes the job easy.

As shown in the drawing below, the jig is made from 2-in.-wide strips of ¾-in. plywood. Crosscut the fences to 4 in. longer than the width of the workpiece to be dadoed. To determine the length of the cleats, add 4¼ in. to the diameter of your router base.

The first step is to place the cleats against opposing sides of the workpiece to be dadoed. Use a clamp to hold the cleats snugly, but not tightly, against the sides. Put one fence in place across the workpiece, check that it is square to both cleats, and screw it to each cleat with three 1¼-in. all-purpose screws **(1)**.

Now place the bit you'll be using in the router and set it to the dado depth. Clamp the workpiece and the jig to your bench. With the router base against one fence, rout a groove partway through the cleat **(2)**.

For the next step, use a scrap of plywood that's the same thickness as the part that will fit into the dado. Place one face of this piece against the side of the groove that's closest to the installed fence and scribe a mark at the other side **(3)**. Use a square to extend this mark down the front edge of the cleat.

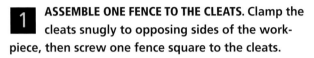
1 **ASSEMBLE ONE FENCE TO THE CLEATS. Clamp the cleats snugly to opposing sides of the workpiece, then screw one fence square to the cleats.**

2 **ROUT A GROOVE IN THE CLEAT. With the router bit set to the dado depth and working from left to right, rout a groove partway through the cleat.**

DADO JIG

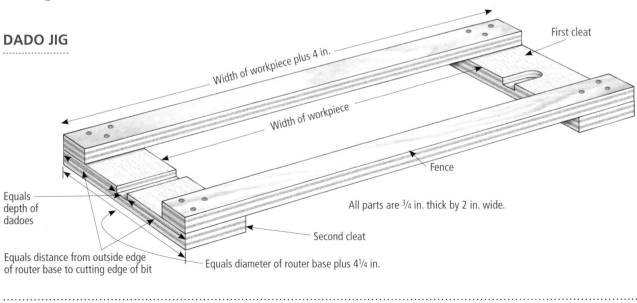

Width of workpiece plus 4 in.

Width of workpiece

First cleat

Fence

All parts are ¾ in. thick by 2 in. wide.

Equals depth of dadoes

Equals distance from outside edge of router base to cutting edge of bit

Equals diameter of router base plus 4¼ in.

Second cleat

3 **LAY OUT THE FINAL DADO WIDTH.** Use a scrap that's the same thickness as the part that will fit into the dado to scribe the width of the groove in the cleat.

4 **LAY OUT FOR THE SECOND FENCE.** Align the bit to the layout line on the cleat, then mark where the outside of the router base meets the cleat.

5 **SPACE AND ATTACH THE SECOND FENCE.** After screwing the second fence to the grooved cleat, cut a spacer to fit snugly between the guides at that cleat. Then use the spacer to gauge the distance between the fences at the other cleat before screwing the fences to that cleat.

6 **TEST THE FIT AND ROUT THE SECOND GROOVE.** Test-fit a piece of scrap into the first groove, make adjustments as necessary, and then rout the groove all the way across the second cleat.

Unplug the router. Align the outside edge of the router bit to the mark you made on the cleat. Then mark where the outside of the router base meets the cleat **(4)**. Screw the second fence to the grooved cleat at this line. From scrap stock, cut a spacer that fits snugly between the fences where they are attached to the grooved cleat. Use the spacer to gauge the space between the fences at the other cleat and screw the second fence to that cleat **(5)**.

Rout against the second fence to widen the groove you made in the first cleat. Then use a piece of plywood to test how your part will fit into the dado **(6)**. If necessary, re-position the second fence. If the fit is snug, rout a groove all the way across the second cleat. Do this in two passes, one against each fence.

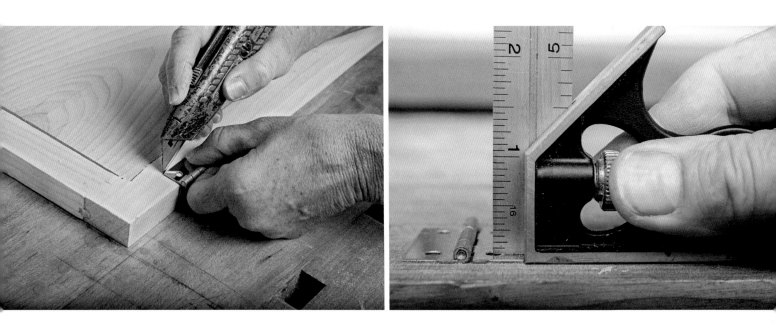

1 **SCRIBE THE MORTISES.** Scribe the outline of the hinge with a utility knife.

2 **MARK THE HINGE DEPTH.** Set a combination square to the thickness of the hinge and use it to scribe the depth of the hinge mortise on the sides of the door and cabinet stile.

Cutting Hinge Mortises

Most woodworking operations these days are done with power tools, and indeed, as you'll find later in this book, there are times when making hinge mortises with a router makes sense. But in most cases, it's quicker to cut a few hinge mortises with hand tools than it is to set up a router. Plus, it's a nice change of pace to grab a sharp chisel and cut out a neat little mortise.

Depending on the project, you'll have placed the door or lid in position to mark the location of the hinges on the door and cabinet or the lid and box. Now position the hinge at the mortise and scribe its outline with a utility knife **(1)**. Put a hinge leaf flat on your bench and set a combination square to its depth **(2)**. Then use the square to guide the knife as you scribe the hinge depth.

To avoid splitting the wood, make the cross-grain chops first, chopping straight down to the mortise depth scribe line **(3)**. Then chop along the grain. Keep the back of the chisel facing out for these cuts. Align your chisel flat to the mortise depth line with the flat side of the chisel down, and tap the chisel with a mallet or hammer to remove the waste **(4)**.

3 **CHOP THE MORTISE PERIMETER.** Chop the perimeter of the hinge mortise down to the depth you scribed in the previous step.

Countersinking and Counterboring

Countersinking and counterboring are both ways of drilling a depression into the wood so you can neatly drive a fastener below the surface. The difference is that a

From left: A lag bolt and washer in a counterbored hole, a paddle bit used to drill a counterbore, a screw in a countersunk hole, and a countersink bit.

countersink tapers inward to match the shape of a flat-head screw, whereas a counterbore has a flat bottom to match a bolt or screw with a head that is flat underneath.

You can countersink a screw just flush with the surface for a neat but exposed appearance. Or you can counter-sink deeper so the hole can be covered with wood putty or a wood plug to hide the screw. It is a good idea to pre-drill and countersink holes for screws near the edges of a board to prevent splitting. Do this with a countersink bit. This consists of a conventional bit held into a countersink by a setscrew that lets you adjust the drilling depth. Using this bit, you predrill and countersink in one operation.

Counterboring is usually done to get a bolt or screw head out of the way so something can be attached over it. For example, in the Closet Tower project (see p. 142), the towers are attached to a ledger that is lag-bolted to the wall. The screw holes are counterbored so the back of the towers can sit against the ledger. Counterbores are usually drilled with a paddle-shaped spade bit. Counterbore with a bit of the same diameter as the washer you are using with the lag bolt.

A stud finder makes it easy to locate studs in the wall. Move the finder over the surface of the wall and a red light will shine when the finder passes over wall framing.

TIP As a first step in zeroing in on the locations of framing behind drywall, try pounding lightly along the wall with the side of your hand. You may notice that the wall becomes stiffer and the sound changes when you pound over a stud or other framing member.

Finding Wall Studs

To attach built-ins to a wall, you'll need to locate the studs behind the drywall or plaster. With drywall, you can sometimes locate the studs through careful observation: You might find faint evidence of where a column of drywall nails or screws was covered with joint compound—the glancing beam of a work light held against the wall often reveals these connections. Or, you might notice slight dimples in the baseboard. If the dimples are at regular intervals—most commonly 16 in. apart—you likely have discovered where the baseboard was nailed into studs.

Studs in old plaster walls are often at irregular intervals and there are no nails or screws near the surface. Also, the old baseboards below may have many of layers of paint that hide the nails. To find studs behind plaster, you'll need an electronic stud finder. Even if you can observe stud locations in drywall, it's worth owning one of these inexpensive devices to confirm the locations before you start making holes in the wall.

A stud finder is easy to use. For the model shown above, you just place it on the wall and push a button on the side. A green light will come on. Move the device along the wall. When it detects the edge of the stud, it will beep and a red light will come on. When you reach the other side of the stud, the beep and red light will stop. Just mark the approximate center of the stud with a pencil.

Painting and Finishing

The projects in this book are either painted or finished with wipe-on polyurethane. In the case of the Toaster Caddy/Breadbox, both paint and finish are used.

Today's latex enamel interior paints create a beautiful, durable surface that looks great on furniture. They are easy to apply and clean up with soap and water. Latex enamel paint comes in several sheens from flat to high gloss. The projects in this book were painted with satin or semi-gloss paint, except for the white in the corner cabinet, which is a high-gloss paint. The sheen you choose is mostly an aesthetic decision—you might, for example, be matching the color and sheen of existing molding in the room. Keep in mind that flat paint is harder to clean than glossier paints.

Preparing for paint

Start by filling any holes from set nails with wood filler. The birch plywood used in many of the projects in this book is already smooth enough for paint without additional sanding. Use 80-grit sandpaper to smooth the solid pine used for the projects, being sure to remove the "mill marks"—shallow ripples left when the boards were milled to size.

Round all edges, at least slightly. Woodworkers call this "breaking the edges," a process that makes the edges more pleasing to the touch and to the eye. It also helps ensure that paint won't chip off the edges. Sand any holes you filled. Clean sanding dust off surfaces with a vacuum or by wiping with mineral spirits or a tack cloth—a sticky piece of cheesecloth you can buy at the hardware store. Don't use water—it can raise the grain.

Applying a wipe-on finish

Wood that will receive a clear finish needs to be sanded smoother than wood that will be painted. After filling nail

Round the edges slightly for a more pleasing look and to ensure that paint will adhere.

holes, sand any solid-wood parts with 80-grit sandpaper. Then sand all the parts, including plywood, with 120 grit and finally 220 grit. Vacuum all surfaces between coats and then wipe thoroughly with a tack cloth to make sure you remove all dust.

Wipe-on polyurethane finish is easy to apply. You simply pour a little finish on a rag and wipe it on. For larger areas, you can pour some finish directly on the wood and spread it with a rag. Bare wood will absorb a lot of finish on the first coat. When it dries, sand it lightly with 220 grit, vacuum, and use a tack cloth to pick up every last bit of dust. Add one or two more coats, sanding and cleaning between each.

Make a Match

It sometimes happens that you want to paint a built-in to match an existing element in the room but don't have a record of the color name, number, or brand. Or perhaps you are switching brands of paint so the name and number you have won't apply.

Paint stores or departments can mix a perfect match if you bring them a sample. If you have leftover paint, just apply some to a scrap. If you don't have the paint, take a sample from the room. For example, if you want the color of the Cabinet with Bookcase project on p. 34 to match the room trim, cut out a small piece of the baseboard that you'll be removing when you install the bookcase.

Wipe surfaces thoroughly with a tack cloth to remove all dust between coats of clear finish.

When using two colors, slightly overlap the first coats of each color.

Priming and painting

These days, you'll find some interior paints sold as "paint and primer in one" or "self-priming" that can be applied directly to bare wood without a separate primer. These paints adhere well to bare wood, and in some cases they will save you a step, although you might find yourself applying three coats of self-priming paint to get even coverage where a coat of primer and two coats of paint would have worked as well. If you are painting a small project in one color, it can be more convenient to buy a quart of self-priming paint than to buy primer and paint separately. For projects with two or more colors, it's easiest to prime the whole thing in one shot instead of priming in two colors.

Other reasons to use a separate primer: Bare wood sucks up a lot of paint, and self-priming paints are more expensive than regular paint and a lot more expensive than plain primer, so you can save significant money by using primer on bare wood on larger projects. And, if you want to prevent knots from bleeding through the paint, you can use a stain-blocking primer that contains shellac.

Brush it on

You can apply paint quickly with a paint roller or sprayer, but we used a brush for all the projects in this book. Here's why: With a roller, you'll need a brush anyway to get into corners, and while the slightly stippled texture left by a roller looks fine on walls, you may not like the way it looks on your project. And in many cases, the time you'll spend setting up and cleaning spray equipment or a roller will surpass the time you'll take brushing on a coat and wash-

> **TIP** When you pour paint from a can, or especially if you paint directly from the can, the gutter around the rim gets filled with paint that's hard to clean out. Then when you tap the lid back on, paint can squirt out and make a mess. The solution is simple. Use a hammer with a nailset or 8d common nail to make holes every few inches along the circumference of the gutter. This will allow paint to drip back into the can so the gutter never fills.

STANLEY

ing the brush under a faucet. And, of course, a top-of-the-line paintbrush is not a big investment.

You can buy paint additives such as Floetrol® that will make your brushstrokes disappear. On the other hand, neat and even brushstrokes lend a more traditional finish that you may prefer on your handcrafted piece. One technique is to alternate stroke directions between coats to create a subtle crossing pattern.

Cutting in

When a project will be painted two colors, start by applying a coat of one color, let it dry, then apply the other color. Let these first coats overlap a little and don't worry about getting a perfectly straight transition (see the photo on the facing page). Next apply a second coat to one of the surfaces—try to achieve a straight line, but make sure you are getting complete coverage. When that coat dries, apply painter's tape over it to create the transition line. Then paint the second coat of the second color.

Some projects in this book have flat panels set into frames. It's easier to neatly mask the panel than the narrow reveal of the frame (see the photo below). So, follow the strategy above, starting with the panel so the last coat will be on the frame with the perimeter of the panel taped.

> **TIP** Even if you use a stain-blocking primer, there is no guarantee knots will not eventually bleed through. That's why clear pine is specified for visible parts of the projects in this book. But if you do use pine with knots, you can increase the chance of preventing bleed-through by coating the knots with a coat or two of shellac before applying the stain-blocking primer.

For two-color jobs on panels set into frames, protect the final coat on the panel with painter's tape before applying the final coat on the frames.

CHAPTER THREE

THE LIVING ROOM

DESIGNING STORAGE FOR A LIVING ROOM is a two-fold challenge: The living room is the showpiece of your home—nowhere is it more important that your storage solutions blend beautifully into the décor. And, because we use the living room for so many purposes, including entertaining, family time, relaxing with a book, and perhaps watching TV, we typically need a variety of storage solutions.

So, start by thinking about what you'll want to store. Some items such as handsome books or a porcelain collection are decorative, and you'll want to display them prominently on open shelving or perhaps behind glass doors. Other items such as electronic equipment and games are better stashed out of sight in cabinets and drawers.

Custom built-in shelving and cabinetry like the Cabinet with Bookcase project that follows can add lots of style to a room and value to your home. And, of course, they use space more efficiently than freestanding units. A word of caution, though: Built-ins are permanent, so it's important to think about how your needs may change when planning them. For example, designing a space sized for your specific television is a great way to hide it or fit it into the décor. But had you done that for that square, deep 36-in. cathode-ray tube TV you had at the turn of the century, you'd be stuck with a large awkward space that doesn't work for the TV you own today.

CABINET WITH BOOKCASE

This built-in cabinet and bookcase was designed to provide versatile storage space with simple and elegant details that will fit in with any décor, whether it's a country home or the urban apartment shown here.

The apartment owner mentioned that she'd like to store board games in the bottom cabinet. To make this easier to do, the inset doors meet with an overlapping lip instead of closing on a center stile. In addition to increasing versatility, this feature makes the design less cluttered. For more versatility, the height of three of the bookcase shelves can be adjusted.

The cabinet doors are surprisingly easy to construct. The frames are joined with biscuits, and the panels are made of plywood beadboard paneling that is simply glued into rabbets routed into the backs of the frames. This same paneling was used for the cabinet and bookcase backs. The beads add a subtle texture to the design.

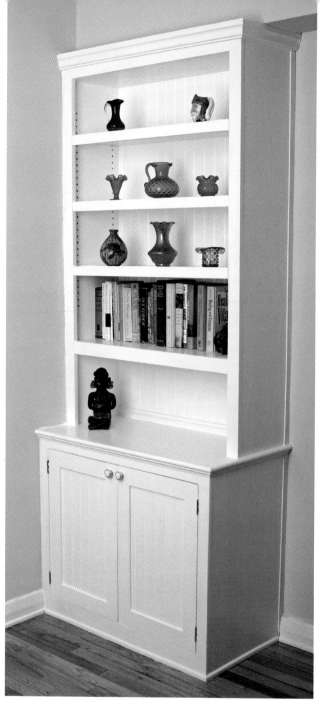

WHAT YOU'LL NEED

BASE CABINET

• 2 sides	¾ in. × 17¼ in. × 29⅝ in., birch plywood
• 1 top	¾ in. × 17⅝ in. × 36 in., birch plywood
• 1 shelf	¾ in. × 16⅛ in. × 35¼ in., birch plywood
• 1 bottom	¾ in. × 16⅞ in. × 35¼ in., birch plywood
• 1 back	⅜ in. × 29¾ in. × 35½ in., beadboard paneling
• 1 shelf facing	¾ in. × 1 in. × 34½ in., clear pine

- 2 stiles   3/4 in. × 2 in. × 29 1/4 in., clear pine
- 1 top rail   3/4 in. × 2 in. × 32 in., clear pine
- 1 bottom rail   3/4 in. × 3 in. × 32 in., clear pine

BOOKCASE

- 2 sides   3/4 in. x 11 1/4 in. x 56 1/4 in., birch plywood
- 1 top   3/4 in. x 10 7/8 in. x 35 1/4 in., birch plywood
- 1 fixed shelf   3/4 in. x 10 7/8 in. x 35 1/4 in., birch plywood
- 1 back   3/8 in. x 35 1/2 in. x 56 in., beadboard paneling
- 3 adjustable shelves   3/4 in. × 11 1/4 in. × 34 1/4 in., birch plywood
- 2 stiles   3/4 in. × 2 in. × 56 1/4 in., clear pine
- 1 top rail   3/4 in. × 3 in. × 32 in., clear pine
- 1 fixed shelf face   3/4 in. × 2 in. × 32 in., clear pine
- 3 adjustable shelf faces   3/4 in. × 1 1/2 in. × 31 7/8 in., clear pine

DOORS

- 3 stiles   3/4 in. × 2 1/2 in. × 24 1/8 in., clear pine
- 1 stile   3/4 in. × 2 7/8 in. × 24 1/8 in., clear pine
- 4 rails   3/4 in. × 2 1/2 in. × 10 15/16 in., clear pine
- 2 panels   3/8 in. × 11 11/16 in. × 19 7/8 in., beadboard paneling

TRIM

- 1 base cabinet nosing   3/4 in. × 1 3/8 in. × 56 in. (approx.), nose and cove molding, pine
- Bookcase crown molding   1 1/16 in. × 2 1/4 in. × 50 in. (approx.) solid crown molding, pine
- Shoe molding   56 in. (approx.)
- 1 top lattice   3/8 in. × 1 1/8 in. × 56 in. (approx.)
- 1 bottom lattice   3/8 in. × 1 1/8 in. × 28 5/8 in. (approx.)
- Transition molding   5/8 in. × 1 5/8 in. × 34 1/2 in., base cap molding

HARDWARE AND FASTENERS

- Wood glue
- 4d finish nails
- #0 joinery biscuits
- 2-in. all-purpose screws
- 3/4-in. panel nails or brads
- Shelf pegs
- Four cabinet hinges, 2 in. x 1 3/8 in.
- Two doorknobs
- Two magnetic catches

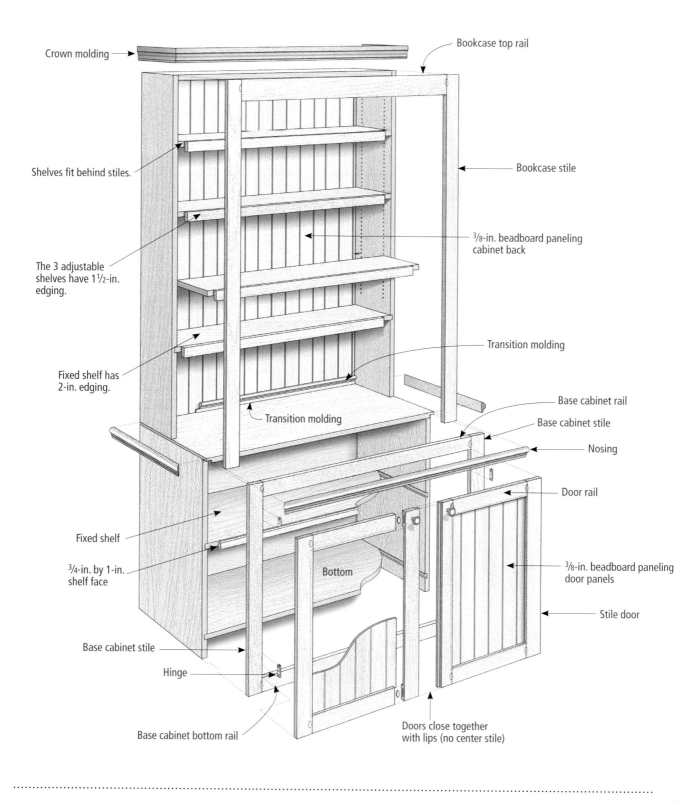

Crown molding

Bookcase top rail

Shelves fit behind stiles.

Bookcase stile

The 3 adjustable shelves have 1¹/₂-in. edging.

³/₈-in. beadboard paneling cabinet back

Transition molding

Fixed shelf has 2-in. edging.

Transition molding

Base cabinet rail

Base cabinet stile

Nosing

Door rail

³/₈-in. beadboard paneling door panels

Fixed shelf

Bottom

Stile door

³/₄-in. by 1-in. shelf face

Base cabinet stile

Hinge

Base cabinet bottom rail

Doors close together with lips (no center stile)

Prepare the Plywood Parts

The first step in building this project is to determine the height of the bookcase. Because ceiling heights vary, the length of the cabinet and bookcase sides listed in "What You'll Need" should be used only as a guide. To determine the length of the sides for your project, measure from floor to ceiling at the spot where one side of the cabinet will go and measure again where the other side will go **(1)**.

If the measurements differ, subtract ½ in. from the smaller measurement to get your total bookcase height. (The gap will be covered by the crown molding.) From this number, subtract the 30-in. height of the base cabinet. The result is the length of your bookcase sides. For the installation shown here, the cabinet fits under a soffit. The bottom of the soffit is 87½ in. at one side and 86¾ in. at the other. So the cabinet sides are 56¼ in. high.

Make rough cuts

Assuming the cabinet is no more than 8 ft. tall, you can make the base cabinet and the bookcase from two 4x8 sheets of plywood, as shown in the "Plywood Cutting Diagram" on p. 38. Start by making rough crosscuts (see "Rough-Ripping Plywood" on p. 21). Place sheet 1 on top of some scraps of sacrificial plywood. Set your saw to cut about ⅞ in. deep so it cuts through the plywood and into the scrap without hitting the floor **(2)**. Crosscut sheet 1 to your bookcase side length plus ½ in. (cut 1). Crosscut sheet 2 at 66 in. (cut 2). Use the same method to rough-rip both pieces of sheet 1 at 23 in. (cut 3) and the 66-in. piece of sheet 2 at 18 in. (cut 4).

1 **MEASURE BOTH SIDES. Ceilings and floors may not be level, so check the ceiling-to-floor height for both sides of the cabinet.**

Cut parts to final dimension

Now switch to the tablesaw and rip all of the ¾-in.-thick plywood parts to final widths **(3)**. Always make the first rip with the factory edge against the fence. This will ensure that both edges of the first piece are perfectly parallel and will also give you a straight edge to guide against the fence when cutting the second piece.

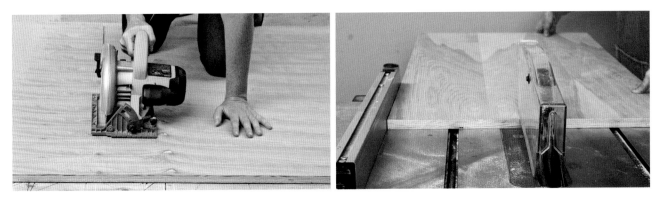

2 **MAKE ROUGH CUTS. Set the plywood sheet atop sacrificial scraps on the floor and make rough cuts with a circular saw.**

3 **CUT PARTS TO FINAL WIDTH. Make final-width cuts on the tablesaw, always starting with a factory edge against the saw fence.**

PLYWOOD CUTTING DIAGRAM

Sheet 1

Sheet 2

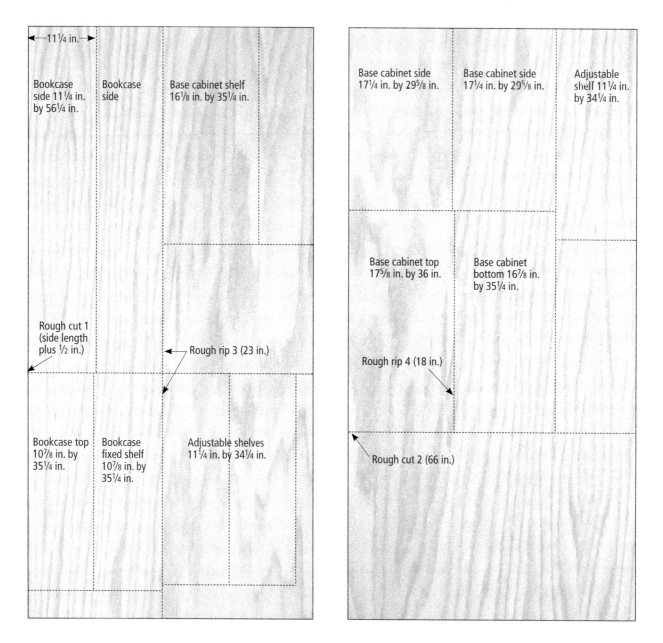

Sheet 1 labels:

← 11¼ in. →

Bookcase side 11¼ in. by 56¼ in.

Bookcase side

Base cabinet shelf 16⅛ in. by 35¼ in.

Rough cut 1 (side length plus ½ in.)

Rough rip 3 (23 in.)

Bookcase top 10⅞ in. by 35¼ in.

Bookcase fixed shelf 10⅞ in. by 35¼ in.

Adjustable shelves 11¼ in. by 34¼ in.

Sheet 2 labels:

Base cabinet side 17¼ in. by 29⅝ in.

Base cabinet side 17¼ in. by 29⅝ in.

Adjustable shelf 11¼ in. by 34¼ in.

Base cabinet top 17⅝ in. by 36 in.

Base cabinet bottom 16⅞ in. by 35¼ in.

Rough rip 4 (18 in.)

Rough cut 2 (66 in.)

4 **CUT THE PARTS TO FINAL LENGTH. Use the shop-made crosscutting jig to cut the plywood parts to final length.**

5 **CROSSCUT THE BACK PANELS. Use the crosscutting jig to cut the back panels to final length, using screws to anchor the jig to the sacrificial plywood.**

Use the circular saw with crosscutting jig (see "Making a Crosscutting Jig" on p. 22) to crosscut all of the ¾-in.-thick plywood parts to final length **(4)**. Support the workpiece with a sacrificial piece of plywood underneath so the offcut can't bind or fall off at the end of the cut.

Rough-cut the back panels

If the combined height of the base cabinet and bookcase is no more than 8 ft., you can get both cabinet backs and both door panels from a single sheet of ⅜-in.-thick 4x8 beadboard paneling, as shown in the "Beadboard Paneling Cutting Diagram" at right. Start by using the crosscutting jig on the floor to make a finish crosscut with the circular saw at 56 in. In lieu of clamps, screw the jig to the sacrificial piece as shown **(5)**. Then use the jig to make a finish crosscut 29¾ in. from the factory edge of the off-cut. You'll cut the door panels to size and the back panels to final width later to fit the cabinet and bookcase.

Make Dadoes and Rabbets

The base cabinet sides have dadoes to receive the bottom and the shelf, whereas the bookshelf sides have dadoes to receive the fixed shelf and the top. See "Dado Layout" on p. 41 for the positions of these dadoes.

Place the two base cabinet sides on the bench with their inside faces up and their front edges against each other. Make sure they are flush at top and bottom. Use a framing square to lay out the dadoes on both sides **(1)** (p. 40). Be sure to put an X on the side of the line where the dado will go. Repeat this procedure for the bookshelf sides.

BEADBOARD PANELING CUTTING DIAGRAM

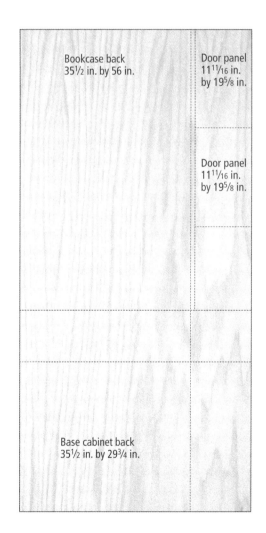

Bookcase back
35½ in. by 56 in.

Door panel
11¹¹⁄₁₆ in.
by 19⅝ in.

Door panel
11¹¹⁄₁₆ in.
by 19⅝ in.

Base cabinet back
35½ in. by 29¾ in.

Cut the dadoes

Cut the dadoes using a dado jig. If you are making a jig from scratch, see "Making a Dado Jig" on p. 24. For this project, we adapted an existing dado jig, as explained in the sidebar below. Fit the dado jig over one of the cabinet side pieces and align the routed guide grooves on the jig's cleats with one of the dado layout lines. Check for square and clamp the jig in place. Rout the dadoes against one of the jig's guides, moving from left to right, and then come back toward you with the router against the other guide **(2)**. Add another cleat to the jig positioned to fit the bookshelf sides, and rout those dadoes.

Cut the rabbets

The top of the base cabinet gets ¾-in.-wide by ⅜-in.-deep rabbets on each end to cover the top edges of the sides. As described in "Adapting Your Dado Jig" below, reposition a cleat on the dado jig to accommodate the greater width of the top. Align the guide cuts in the jig to the edge of the piece and check for square **(3)**. Rout the rabbets in the same way as you did the dadoes. Be careful to hold the router firmly on the plywood so it doesn't dip into the space between the plywood's edge and the outer guide.

1 **LAY OUT THE DADOES. To ensure that opposing dadoes will be at exactly the same level, lay them out on opposing cabinet sides at the same time.**

The base cabinet sides and the bookcase sides are rabbeted to hide the edges of the back panel. Put a ⅜-in. piloted rabbeting bit in the router and set the depth to ½ in. Clamp the workpiece, overhanging the bench enough to clear the clamps **(4)**. For extra insurance against workpiece slippage, clamp a piece of scrap across the bench abutting the workpiece. Working from left to right, cut a rabbet along the back inside edges of each of the four side pieces.

Adapting Your Dado Jig

There's no need to build a new dado jig to fit workpieces of different widths. Keep the two original cleats in place to preserve the carefully measured cleat spacing and add another cleat. To position the new cleat, put the jig in place, making sure it is square to the workpiece. Screw the fences to the new cleat. Clamp the jig over a scrap and rout a guide groove on the new cleat.

2 **CUT THE DADOES.** To rout dadoes using the dado jig, move the router from left to right against one fence and then bring it back against the other.

DADO LAYOUT

Bookcase

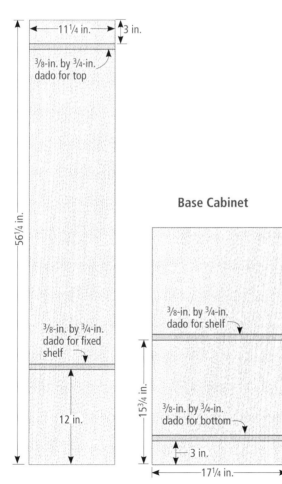

← 11¼ in. → | 3 in.

⅜-in. by ¾-in. dado for top

56¼ in.

⅜-in. by ¾-in. dado for fixed shelf

12 in.

Base Cabinet

⅜-in. by ¾-in. dado for shelf

15¾ in.

⅜-in. by ¾-in. dado for bottom

3 in.

← 17¼ in. →

3 **LAY OUT FOR THE TOP RABBETS.** To position the router jig for cutting rabbets in the top of the base cabinet, align the jig's guide grooves to the top of the workpiece.

4 **ROUT THE SIDE RABBETS.** Clamp the workpiece in place, slightly overhanging the workbench to rout the rabbet that will accept the back panel. The board clamped against the workpiece prevents slipping.

1 **BEGIN TO ASSEMBLE THE CABINET.** Put glue in the dadoes in one side of the base cabinet and insert the bottom and the shelf.

2 **SECURE THE SECOND SIDE OF THE CABINET.** Glue and nail the second side in place before flipping the cabinet to nail the other side.

3 **SQUARE THE CABINET.** Check that the cabinet is square, and then tack a scrap piece of plywood across the face to keep it that way while the glue sets.

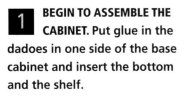

Assemble the Cases

To prepare for assembly, cut a scrap of wood that's long enough to span diagonally from a top corner to a bottom corner of the cabinet. You'll tack this across the cabinet to help keep it square while the glue sets.

Assemble the cabinet

To guide nailing, draw pencil lines on the outside of the sides to locate the center of the dadoes. Put one cabinet side on the bench, put glue in the dadoes, and insert the bottom and the shelf **(1)**. Make sure that the bottom shelf is flush to the front of the sides and the shelf is flush to the inside of the side's back rabbet.

4 **CUT THE DOOR PANELS TO SIZE.** With the lipped edge up and against the fence, rip the beadboard for the door.

Put glue on the edges that will go into the other side's dadoes. Put the second side in place and secure it with 4d finishing nails **(2)**. Turn the cabinet over and secure the other side with nails. Put glue in the rabbets on the top piece and put it in place, overhanging the front of the sides by ¾ in. Secure it with 4d finishing nails through the sides.

Use a framing square to check that the cabinet is square. Tack-nail the scrap strip diagonally across the front of the cabinet **(3)**.

5 **CUT THE BACK PANELS TO FINAL WIDTH.** Use the circular-saw jig on the floor to rip the back panels to final width.

Cut the beadboard panels

Check the distance between the back rabbets in the cabinet sides in case they vary from the parts list. The beadboard panels have lips along each long side designed to lap adjoining sheets when used as wall paneling. You can't set a tablesaw fence far enough from the blade to rip the back panels to final width, so set the fence at 12¼ in.—wide enough to make the door panels. For safety, make sure the lipped edge is facing up so it can't get jammed under the fence. Rip both pieces you crosscut earlier **(4)**.

Cut the back panels to final width

With the beaded face down, measure from the side you ripped in the last step and snap a line along a back panel. Use the circular-saw jig to cut the panel to final width **(5)**. The jig isn't long enough to span the length of the bookcase base, so you'll need to move it to finish that cut. Also for the bookcase back, you'll need to screw one end of the jig to the back panel—try not to screw all the way through. Repeat for the other panel.

Attach the back to the base cabinet

When the glue has set, remove the scrap piece and place the cabinet face down. Put glue in the rabbets and along the back edges of the top, shelf, and bottom. Put the back in place flush to the top of the top and secure it with ¾-in. panel nails or brads **(6)**. You can do this with a hammer (as shown) or with a power finish nailer if you have one. There will be a ¼-in. gap between the bottom of the back and the bottom of the sides, which allows for any irregularity in the floor.

Assemble the bookcase

Glue and nail the bookcase top and fixed shelf to the sides using the same techniques you used for the base cabinet **(7)**. Make sure the top and fixed shelf are flush to the front of the cabinet. Install the back flush to the bottom of the sides. In case your case width varies a bit from the plan, measure across the inside to confirm the length of the adjustable shelves. Cut the shelves to ¼ in. less than that measurement to allow room for the shelf support pegs.

Make and install the base cabinet shelf face

Cut pine stock to 1 in. wide. To scribe the piece to exact length, put one edge against the inside of the cabinet

6 **ATTACH THE BACK TO THE BASE CABINET. Put glue in the back rabbets, make sure the back is flush to the top of the cabinet, and then nail the back in place.**

7 **ASSEMBLE THE BOOKCASE. Use the same sequence you did for the base cabinet to assemble the bookcase. Make sure the fixed shelf and the top are flush to the front of the sides.**

8 **INSTALL THE BASE CABINET SHELF FACE. For best accuracy, scribe the shelf face to fit inside the cabinet.**

and use a utility knife to make a notch where the piece meets the other side **(8)**. On the bench, put the knife in the notch, and slide a square up to the knife. Scribe the cutline. Cut the piece to length, and then install it flush to the top of the shelf with glue and 4d finish nails.

1 CUT THE FACE FRAMES. Use a miter saw to accurately cut the face-frame parts to length.

2 LAY OUT THE BISCUIT JOINTS ON THE FACE FRAME. Use a combination square to mark the center of the joints.

3 MARK THE POSITION OF THE FIXED SHELF ON THE BOOKCASE STILES. While the face frame is clamped or tacked to the bookcase, mark where the top of the fixed-rail face meets the stiles.

Make and Install the Face Frames and Shelf Edges

Rip stock to the widths listed in "What You'll Need" for the base cabinet and bookcase face frames. Scribe and cut the base cabinet stiles to length to fit under the top. Temporarily clamp or tack the stiles in place. Then scribe and cut the top and bottom rails to fit between the stiles **(1)**.

Mark for the biscuit joints and cut the slots

The face frames are joined with biscuits. To mark for the biscuit joints, first clamp or tack the rails in place on the base cabinet. Use a combination square to mark where the center of each stile meets a rail **(2)**. Extend these lines across both pieces. It is particularly important that the mark is centered across the 2-in.-wide stiles to ensure that the biscuits don't protrude through one side.

Repeat this process for the bookcase: Scribe and cut the rails to length, clamp or tack them in place, and scribe and cut the top rail and fixed shelf rail to fit. Then lay out the biscuit joints.

While the stiles are clamped or tacked in place with the rails fitted between, draw a line across each stile to locate the top of the fixed shelf rail **(3)**. Draw an X on each stile to indicate the rail side of the line.

Set the biscuit joiner fence to $3/8$ in. and set the cutting depth for size #0 biscuits. Cut biscuit slots in each piece, making sure it is securely clamped to the bench **(4)**.

4 CUT THE BISCUIT JOINTS. Cut slots for the biscuits in the sides of the stiles and the ends of the rails. Be careful to keep the fence flat against the top of the workpiece as you cut.

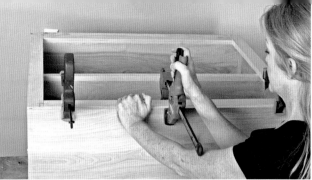

5 ASSEMBLE THE FACE FRAMES. After applying glue and inserting biscuits, use a clamp on each end of the frames to pull the stiles against the rails.

6 ATTACH THE FACE FRAMES. Glue and nail the face frames to the base cabinet and bookcase. When attaching the base cabinet face frame, put glue on the top of the top rail and clamp it in place under the cabinet top.

7 LAY OUT FOR THE SHELF FACES. Use a combination square set to 1³/₁₆ in. to mark where the faces will be positioned on the adjustable shelves.

Assemble and attach the face frames

For each face frame, put glue in the biscuit slots and on the ends of the rails, assemble the face frame, and then clamp the joints together along the rails **(5)**. Check that the face frame is square.

Secure the face frames with glue and 4d nails. When gluing up the base cabinet face frame, put glue on the top of the top rail where it meets the bottom of the cabinet top and clamp this joint **(6)**.

Attach faces to the adjustable shelves

The shelf faces stop 1³/₁₆ in. short of the shelf ends. After you paint the bookcase and shelves, there will be a barely visible gap between the shelf faces and the stiles—just enough to allow the shelves to be moved easily.

Clamp a shelf in a vise or to the side of your bench with the front edge facing up. Set an adjustable square to 1³/₁₆ in., and use it to lay out the position of both ends of the shelf face **(7)**. Then secure the edge with glue and 4d nails, making sure it is flush to the top of the shelf.

Make and Fit the Doors

The base cabinet opening should be 24¼ in. high and 32 in. wide. The door stiles are 24⅛ in. long and the rails are 10¹⁵/₁₆ in. long to allow ¹/₁₆ in. of clearance around the combined perimeter of the doors. Check the opening dimensions in case you need to adjust the stile and rail lengths from the lengths listed in "What You'll Need." The doors meet with ³/₈-in. overlapping lips that you will adjust with a block plane after the doors are hung. The overlapping lip is the reason why one inside stile is ³/₈ in. wider than the other.

Make the door frames

Cut the stiles and rails to width and length and join them with size #0 biscuits, gluing and clamping as you did the case frames. When the glue sets, use a ³/₈-in. piloted rabbeting bit to cut ³/₈ in. deep, and rout a rabbet around the inside edge of each door frame **(1)**. These rabbets will receive the door panels. Raise the frame off the bench with plywood to make room for the nut at the bottom of the bit. Keep the plywood edges back so the pilot bearing rides on the inside edges of the frame. Rout in a clockwise direction.

1 ROUT THE RABBETS FOR THE DOOR PANELS. Move in a clockwise direction as you rout the rabbet along the inside of each door frame.

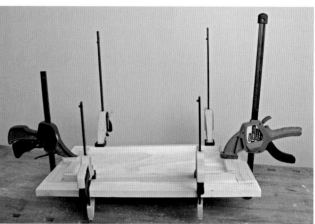

2 **CHOP THE RABBETS SQUARE. Use a chisel to square the corners of the rabbets in the door frames.**

3 **INSTALL THE DOOR PANELS. Use strips of wood to distribute the clamping pressure when you glue the panels into the doors. Make sure you are clamping against the frame on the front of the door and the panel on the back of the door.**

The corners of the rabbets will be rounded. Chop them square with a chisel **(2)**.

Cut and install the panels

Measure and cut ⅜-in. beadboard panels to fit in the frames. Use the tablesaw with fence to rip the pieces you set aside earlier to final width, then reset the fence to cut to length. The panels must be flush to the back of the frames so that the doors will close properly. If they are not flush, rout the rabbets slightly deeper. Put glue in the rabbets and clamp the panels in place **(3)**. Strips of pine protect the door surface and help distribute clamping pressure.

Set the ⅜-in. piloted rabbeting bit to cut ⅜ in. deep. Rabbet the front face of the wider stile and the back face of the stile that will overlap it **(4)**. Raise the door on pieces of plywood and support the router on a piece of pine as you did for the door frames (step 1 on p. 45).

4 **ROUT THE OVERLAPPING LIPS. Rout the lip on the front of the wider stile on one door. Rout the mating lip on the back of the other door.**

Mark and cut the hinge mortises

Place a door in its opening and shim it in place top and bottom. Business cards make good shims—stack equal numbers of cards to create equal spaces at the top and bottom of the door. Locate the hinges 2 in. from the corners of the door. Use a square to mark the top of each hinge across the door and the cabinet stiles at the same time **(5)**. Remove the door and extend this line around the edge of the door and the inside edge of the cabinet. Cut the mortises as described in "Cutting Hinge Mortises" on p. 26. Test-fit the doors. If necessary, use a block plane to take a shaving off one lipped edge and then the other until the doors close easily.

5 **MARK THE HINGE MORTISES. Use business cards to create even gaps at top and bottom, then mark the hinge positions on door and cabinet stiles.**

6 USE A SIMPLE TEMPLATE TO DRILL SHELF-PEG HOLES. **Drill the shelf-peg holes using a template made of pegboard and a depth gauge made of scrap wood.**

Drill shelf-peg holes

Drilling shelf-peg holes in the bookcase sides makes it easy to adjust the three shelves. Standard pegboard has ¼-in.-dia. holes spaced 1 in. on center apart, making it perfect to use as a peg-hole template. Make the length of the template about 6 in. less than the distance from the fixed

Commercial Drilling Templates

If you anticipate making a number of projects with adjustable shelf-peg holes, consider purchasing a drilling template. The one shown here comes with a drill bit and collar that makes holes of the right diameter and depth. After drilling the first set of holes, you insert a guide pin in the last hole, reposition the jig, and keep drilling. Shown here is a 6-in.-wide spacer that positions the first hole 6 in. from the top or bottom.

shelf to the inside of the bookcase top. For width, just use a circular saw to rip roughly through the third set of holes from one factory edge. You'll use the second row in as your template—mark the sixth hole up from the factory corner as the bottom starter hole.

Now prepare a block of wood as a drilling guide: Chuck a ¼-in.-dia. bit into your drill and measure the protruding length. Subtract the length of a peg plus ⁷⁄₁₆ in. from the bit length to get the length of your block. Drill a hole through the block. Drill the four sets of holes, flipping the template as necessary so that you always have the factory corner against the bookcase side and fixed shelf **(6)**.

Install the Base Cabinet and Bookcase

For this installation, the baseboard was cut away from behind the cabinet location—an operation that takes time and patience. Start by using a utility knife to scribe the cut-line and cut through the paint where the baseboard meets the wall. Cut through the baseboard with a small saw **(1)**. You may need a chisel to chop through the bottom of the cut. Then carefully pull the baseboard away with a pry bar.

1 REMOVE THE BASEBOARD. **Carefully cut out the sections of baseboard so the base cabinet can fit against the wall. Start with a small saw. To avoid damaging the wall, you may need to finish the cut with a chisel.**

TIP You'll need to do touch-up painting after installation, but it's usually easiest to paint the project before installing it. This project was primed and then given two coats of semi-gloss enamel latex paint (see "Painting and Finishing" on p. 28).

2 SHIM THE BASE CABINET. Use shims as necessary to make the base cabinet perfectly level across the front and from front to back.

3 INSTALL THE BASE CABINET. Predrill holes in the cabinet side using a countersink bit so you can cover the attachment screws with putty.

With the baseboard removed, put the base cabinet into position and then check that it is level across the front and from front to back. Use shims to level as necessary **(2)**.

Secure the base cabinet and bookcase

There should be studs at both sides of the corner of the wall. Use a stud finder to confirm this and to find other studs that will fall behind one side and the back of the cabinet and bookcase (see "Finding Wall Studs " on p. 28. Because the bookcase is only 12 in. deep, you may find only one stud at its side.

Use a countersinking bit to predrill holes for two 2-in. screws through one side of the base cabinet **(3)**. The bit has a conventional drill bit inserted into a wide countersink—it predrills the hole and then makes a wider, shallow cut for

the screw head. This allows you to sink the screw head below the surface and then cover it with wood putty.

Put the bookcase in place and secure it with four countersunk screws near the top—two through the back and one or two through one side.

Install the trim

With the cabinet and bookcase installed, all that remains is to trim them out with various moldings. Put a piece of nosing molding in place along the side of the cabinet butted against the wall and use a utility knife to scribe where it meets the corner **(4)**. Cut a 45° angle. Do the same for the molding that will go across the front. Secure the molding with 4d finish nails. Do the same for the crown molding.

Scribe and cut shoe molding to fit around the bottom of the base cabinet and install with 1-in. finish nails **(5)**. In this installation, the gap between the front of the cabinet and the wall was less than ¼ in.—small enough to fill with caulk. At the side, the gap was a bit bigger, so lattice molding was installed against the wall between the crown molding and the nosing and between the nosing and the shoe molding (you can see the lattice molding in the photo of the finished project on p. 34). Use ¾-in. brads to install the lattice.

TIP Some crown molding is designed to be nailed to the ceiling and the wall with a gap behind in case the wall and ceiling don't meet in a straight line. For this project, "solid crown" was used because the cabinet is deeper than the soffit, precluding attachment to the ceiling.

STANLEY.

4 **TRIM WITH NOSING AND CROWN.** Scribe the nosing and crown molding in place to cut to accurate length.

5 **INSTALL SHOE MOLDING.** Scribe and cut shoe molding to fit around the base cabinet.

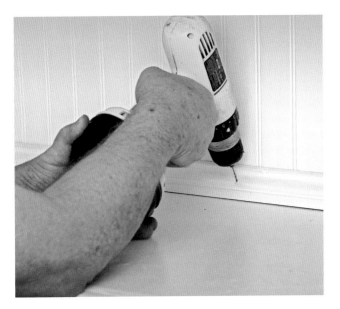

6 **INSTALL THE TRANSITION MOLDING.** Predrill holes for the 4d nails that will secure the transition molding to the cabinet.

Cut a piece of transition molding to cover the joint between the back of the bookcase and the top of the base cabinet. Install the molding with 4d finish nails in pre-drilled holes **(6)**. Finish by installing the doors. Install the

knobs 1 in. from the top of the doors and 1⅛ in. from the inside edges. Install magnetic catches as described on p. 63 of the Corner Cabinet project.

Another Way to Remove Baseboard

To save yourself from having to painstakingly cut baseboard in place (as explained on p. 47), it sometimes makes sense to remove full lengths of baseboard, install the cabinet, and then cut the baseboard to fit before reinstalling it.

That's a good strategy if the baseboard and walls don't have multiple coats of paint and the walls are drywall, not plaster. It also helps if you have some touch-up paint available in colors to match the baseboard and walls. Multiple layers of paint can make it tough to remove baseboard cleanly and plaster walls can crumble as you pull the baseboard away, leaving you with plaster repairs—both good reasons to cut the baseboard away in place.

CORNER CABINET

Corner cabinets are a time-honored way to make efficient use of space. This painted version is an elegant and streamlined take on an old idea. And while there are many steps involved, the contemporary look is achieved with materials and techniques that make this cabinet much easier to build than a more traditional design.

The cabinet itself is constructed of birch plywood faced in clear pine—both materials are easy to work with and are excellent surfaces for paint. The full-overlay doors are biscuit-joined frames with plywood panels—the easiest way to make and fit a panel door. The flat plywood panels won't expand, contract, or warp, and they contribute to the streamlined look.

A simple door casing is used to finish off the top instead of the more typical elaborate crown molding, further updating the look while simplifying construction.

WHAT YOU'LL NEED

- 2 cabinet sides   ¾ in. × 17 in. × 69 in., birch plywood
- 2 cabinet returns   ¾ in. × 4 in. × 69 in., birch plywood
- 5 shelves plus top and bottom   ¾ in. × dimensions in drawing (p. 52), birch plywood
- 2 cabinet stiles   ¾ in. × 1½ in. × 69 in., clear pine
- 1 top rail   ¾ in. × 3 in. × 20¾ in., clear pine

- 6 shelf faces — ¾ in. × ⅞ in. × 20¾ in., clear pine
- 5 foot sides — ¾ in. × 3 in. × 4 in., clear pine
- 1 rear foot side — ¾ in. × 3 in. × 3¼ in., clear pine
- 2 front footplates — ¾ in. × 2¾ in. × 4 in., plywood
- 1 rear footplate — ¾ in. × 3¼ in. × 3¼ in., plywood
- 1 front top molding — ½ in. × 1¾ in. × 25 in., pine door casing
- 2 side top moldings — ½ in. × 1¾ in. × 5½ in., pine door casing
- 4 door stiles — ¾ in. × 1½ in. × 23 in., clear pine
- 4 door rails — ¾ in. × 1½ in. × 9¼ in., clear pine
- 2 door panels — ½ in. × 10 in. × 20¾ in., birch plywood

HARDWARE AND FASTENERS

- Wood glue
- 4d finishing nails
- #0 joinery biscuits
- 6 all-purpose screws, 1¼ in.
- 4 brass butt hinges, ½ in. × 1½ in., with screws
- 2 magnetic catches

Cut the Sides and Returns

To begin this project, you'll prepare two pieces of plywood. Each piece will eventually be cut into one side and one return but not until after the dadoes and rabbets are cut.

Working with a circular saw and a sacrificial piece on the floor as described in "Rough-Ripping Plywood" on p. 21, rip two 22-in.-wide pieces from a full sheet of plywood. Then use the circular saw with the crosscutting jig (see "Making a Crosscutting Jig" on p. 22) to cut both pieces to a final length of 69 in. **(1)**. Again, support the workpiece with a sacrificial piece of plywood underneath so the offcut can't bind or fall off at the end of the cut.

Now you can rip the edges straight. Set up an outfeed table or rollers (or have a helper ready to catch the plywood as it comes off the tablesaw). Set the tablesaw fence 21⅞ in. from the blade (which is wide enough to yield one side and one return). With the factory edge of each piece against the fence, rip the rough-cut edge perfectly straight.

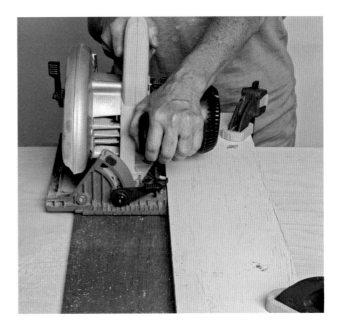

1 **CUT THE SIDES AND RETURNS. Use a circular saw with the crosscutting jig to cut the pieces to rough width and final length.**

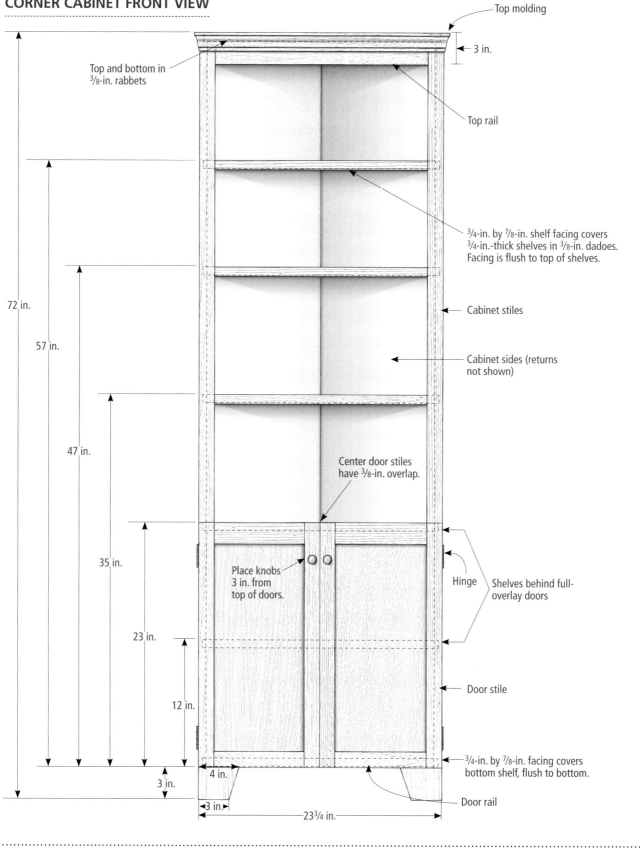

Top molding

3 in.

Top and bottom in ³/₈-in. rabbets

Top rail

³/₄-in. by ⁷/₈-in. shelf facing covers ³/₄-in.-thick shelves in ³/₈-in. dadoes. Facing is flush to top of shelves.

Cabinet stiles

Cabinet sides (returns not shown)

Center door stiles have ³/₈-in. overlap.

72 in.

57 in.

47 in.

35 in.

23 in.

12 in.

3 in.

Place knobs 3 in. from top of doors.

Hinge

Shelves behind full-overlay doors

Door stile

4 in.

3 in.

23³/₄ in.

³/₄-in. by ⁷/₈-in. facing covers bottom shelf, flush to bottom.

Door rail

2 **CUT THE RABBETS IN THE SIDES.** Clamp the dado jig to the ends of the side pieces to cut the rabbets for the top and bottom of the cabinet.

1 **CUT THE DADOES FOR THE SHELVES.** Use the dado jig to make each dado in two passes. Move the router from left to right so the cutter will scoop into the wood, ensuring a smooth, controlled cut.

Blade guard removed for clarity.

3 **CUT 45° ANGLES ON THE SIDES.** Lay out the angled cuts with the dadoes facing down on the saw.

Cut Dadoes, Rabbets, and Angled Edges

The first step is to cut the dadoes for the shelves. Place the factory edges of the two pieces against each other and make sure they are flush at top and bottom. Use a framing square to lay out the dadoes on both pieces, spaced as shown in the drawing on the facing page. Make an X to indicate which side of each line will receive a dado. Fit the dado jig (see "Making a Dado Jig" on p. 24) over the workpiece and align the routed cuts on both sides of the jig to the X side of the layout line. Check for square and clamp the jig in place. Rout the dadoes against one of the jig's guides, moving from left to right, then come back toward you with the router against the other guide **(1)**.

Now cut the rabbets for the top and bottom of the cabinet. Align the router cuts in the jig to the top or bottom edge of each side piece **(2)**. Rout the rabbets in the same way as you routed the dadoes. Be careful to hold the router firmly on the plywood so it doesn't dip into the space between the plywood's edge and the outer guide.

Make the angled cuts

The back edge of each side piece is mitered at 45° so that the sides meet at a 90° angle at the back corner. With dadoes facing down, lay out a 45° rip cut along the factory edge of one workpiece. Set the tablesaw blade to 45° and

4 **LAY OUT 22½° ANGLES ON THE SIDES.** Scribing from a tested scrap is an accurate way to lay out the 22½° angle on the side pieces.

align the layout line to the blade **(3)**. Then position the fence against the opposite side of the workpiece and lock it in place. Cut both pieces.

The sides will meet the returns at a 45° angle that requires 22½° angles on the meeting edges (see the drawing on p. 54). Crosscut a piece of scrap to test the angle (see "Checking the Angles" on p. 55). With the dadoes facing down, measure 17 in. from the outside of the 45° cut. Then use the test scrap to lay out the 22½° angle **(4)**. Cut both pieces. Label one side and one return "A" and the other pair "B." Hold onto the angled scrap—you'll use it again.

CORNER CABINET TOP VIEW (WITHOUT DOORS)

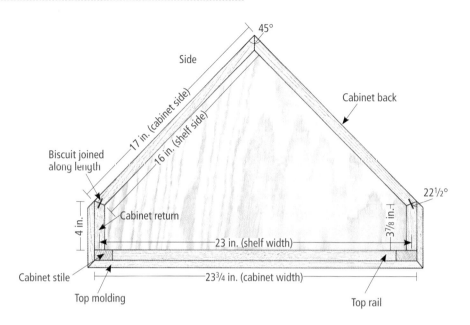

45°

Side

Cabinet back

17 in. (cabinet side)

16 in. (shelf side)

Biscuit joined along length

22½°

Cabinet return

4 in.

3⅞ in.

23 in. (shelf width)

Cabinet stile

23¾ in. (cabinet width)

Top molding

Top rail

After you've cut the 22½° angles on the sides, the long side of the 22½° cuts is currently on the dado face of the returns—it needs to be on the outside face. The blade on most tablesaws tilts the wrong way to make this cut, so you need to do it with the circular saw and crosscutting jig. Start by clamping the return to your bench with the edge to be cut overhanging about 1½ in. **(5)**. Position the clamp on the end away from where you will start cutting. Then clamp a board against the return to support the jig and keep the return from slipping sideways during the cut.

Align the crosscutting jig along the edge of the return and clamp it down at both ends. Set your saw blade to 22½° using the test piece you cut earlier (see "Checking the Angles" on the facing page) **(6)**. Make the cut until you run out of jig, then reposition the jig and clamps. Make sure the edge of the jig is perfectly flush to the part of the return edge you just cut, then continue cutting.

With all the angles cut, you can cut the returns to final width **(7)**. Set the tablesaw for a 4-in.-wide rip. For safety, make the cut with the dadoes down on the table. This will prevent the angled edge from jamming under the fence.

5 **SET UP FOR THE 22½° ANGLE CUTS ON THE RETURNS. Clamp the return piece overhanging the bench (right) with the dadoes facing down. Clamp a plywood offcut to the bench (left) to support the crosscutting jig and keep the return from sliding when you rip the angled edge.**

TIP When you used the crosscutting jig to make the 22½° cut in the returns, you also ripped an angled slice off the base of your crosscutting jig. Now you can only align the base to layout lines for 22½° cuts and you'll need to make a new jig the next time you need one for 90° cuts.

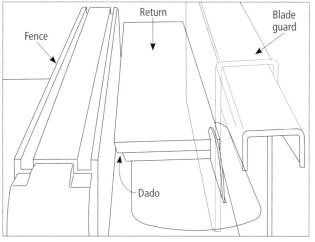

6 MAKE THE ANGLED CUTS ON THE RETURNS. Clamp the jig in place and make the 22½° cut along the edge of each return.

7 CUT THE RETURNS TO FINAL WIDTH. With the dadoes down, rip both returns to final width.

Checking the Angles

Many tablesaws don't have a positive stop for a 22½° angle, so it is a good idea to make a test cut to check the angle. First, crosscut a piece of scrap plywood at 22½°. Then clamp one of the pieces flush to the straight edge of a scrap, put the other piece against it to form a 45° angle, and draw a line (as shown in the photo at left). Use a square to check that the line is exactly 45° from the straight edge. If the angle is less than 45°, tilt your blade a tiny bit more. If it is more than 45°, tilt the blade less. (Remember, for every degree the 45° angle is off, the blade angle will be off by only ½°, so make very slight adjustments.) Cut scrap until the angle is correct.

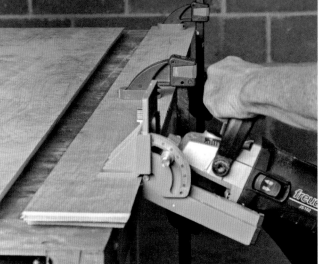

1 **LAY OUT THE BISCUIT SLOTS.** Align a side and its return edge to edge with dadoes down, then lay out for two biscuits between each pair of dadoes.

2 **CUT THE BISCUIT SLOTS.** With the cutting depth set at ½ in. and the fence flat against the back of the workpiece, cut the slots in the edges of the sides and returns.

Join the Returns to the Sides

The sides are joined to the returns with two biscuits evenly spaced between every two dadoes. Lay side A and return A with dadoes down on the bench and adjoining edges against each other and use a combination square to lay out the centers for the biscuits **(1)**.

Set your biscuit joiner for size #0 biscuits. Set the cutting depth to ½ in. rather than centered at ⅜ in. to ensure

that the cutter doesn't come through the back of the pieces when making the angled slots. Clamp a return to your bench with the angled edge overhanging **(2)**. With the joiner's fence flat on the return, set the angle to 22½°. Make the cuts on the "A" parts, then repeat the layout and cutting on the "B" parts.

Choosing the Right Biscuit

Joinery biscuits come in three standard sizes, all of which are ⁵⁄₃₂ in. thick to fit the slots made by biscuit joiners. The larger the biscuit, the stronger the joint, so in gen-

eral, use the largest biscuit you can without cutting through exposed surfaces of the stock.

Size #20, at left in the photo at left, is the largest. These biscuits are 1 in. wide by 2⅜ in. long—use them for edge-joining flat panels, joining members at right angles, and joining rails and stiles that are at least 2½ in. wide.

Size #0, at right, is the smallest biscuit, measuring ⅝ in. wide and 1¾ in. long. This size will be used to join the narrow rails and stiles of the door frame. It's also used to join the corner cabinet returns to the sides because deeper slots would come through the outside faces of the work pieces.

Size #10, not shown, are ¾ in. wide by 2⅛ in. long. These biscuits are not used for any of the projects in this book.

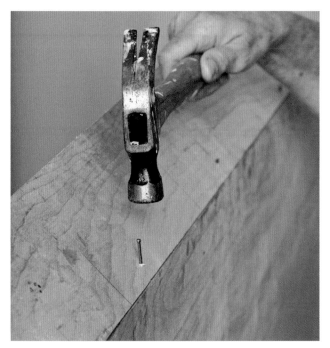

3 **ASSEMBLE EACH RETURN AND SIDE. Apply glue along the joint and in the biscuit slots, insert the biscuits, and assemble each return to its side piece. Secure the joints with 4d finishing nails.**

To assemble each return to its side, clamp a side piece to your bench with the 22½° angle facing up. Apply glue along the joint and in the slots on both pieces. Put the biscuits in place and assemble the pieces. Secure with 4d nails into the return, being careful to nail straight down **(3)**. Set the nails.

Make and Install the Shelves

With the two cabinet sides and returns assembled, the next step is to build the shelves. The five shelves and the top and bottom pieces are all the same size. You can get two of these pieces from each of the offcuts from the sides you cut earlier. For the remaining three pieces, start by cutting two pieces of plywood that measure at least 19 in. x 25½ in. Use the cardboard template (see the sidebar at top right) to lay out a shelf on the plywood, and then use the crosscutting jig to make the angled cut **(1)**.

Make a Shelf Template

In the course of cutting and assembling the case, you may have accumulated a slight variation from the dimensions in the drawing on p. 54. To check, measure each side assembly and make a cardboard template; test-fit the template into each side assembly to see if you need to adjust the size of the shelves.

1 **CUT THE SHELVES. Use a circular saw with the crosscutting jig to make the angled cuts for the shelves.**

2 **MAKE THE RETURN CUTS.** You can use the table-saw as shown to cut the shelves to fit the returns or you can use a power miter saw.

You can make the return cuts in the shelves on a table-saw **(2)**, or you can do it with a power miter saw. Use the first shelf as a template to cut six more. Lay out the shelves against the square edges of the template shelf and make the angled cut for each one.

Glue up the cabinet

Once the shelves are cut to size, you're ready to assemble the cabinet. Because of the angles involved, you'll need to use angled clamping cauls to hold everything together. Make three cauls by ripping a 45° face on a length of 4x4 and then crosscutting it into three pieces. Do a dry assembly to make sure everything fits and to get your clamps adjusted.

Put one side of the cabinet on the bench and glue the shelves in place. Slip three clamps underneath and position the cauls. Put glue on the shelf edges and install the other side. Add two clamps across the returns and then tighten all the clamps a little at a time to bring the sides together **(3)**. Make sure all the shelf fronts and the top and bottom are flush to the front of the returns.

3 **GLUE UP THE CABINET.** Use five long clamps and three angled clamping cauls to glue up the cabinet. Make sure the shelf fronts are flush to the front edge of the returns.

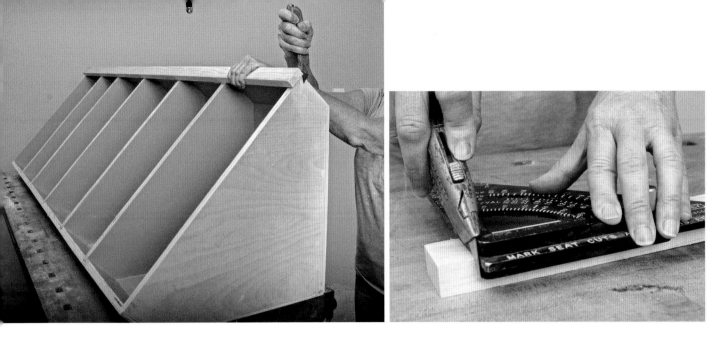

1 MARK THE STILES TO LENGTH. Use a utility knife against the cabinet to scribe cuts for the face-frame parts. It's more accurate than using a tape measure.

INSTALL THE TOP RAIL. After installing the stiles, glue and nail the top rail in place, then toenail it to the stiles.

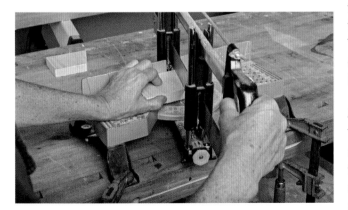

CUT PARTS FOR THE FEET. Use a hand miter saw to make the angled cuts for the feet.

Install the Face Frame, Feet, and Top Molding

Begin by preparing the pieces for the face frame. Rip stock to the widths listed in "What You'll Need" for the cabinet stiles, top rail, and shelf faces, leaving the pieces long so you can fit them to final lengths. Place a stile along one edge flush to the top, and notch the stile where it meets the bottom of the cabinet. On the bench, put the knife blade in the notch, set a square against the blade, and scribe the cutline **(1)**. Scribe and cut both stiles, then install them with glue and 4d finishing nails.

Next, scribe and cut the top rail to fit and install with glue and nails. Drive a toenail through the bottom of the top rail into each stile **(2)**. Scribe and cut the shelf faces to fit, then use glue and nails to attach them to the shelves. The shelf faces should be flush with the top of the shelves, except for the bottom one, which should be flush with the bottom of the cabinet.

Assemble and attach the feet

The feet raise the cabinet off the floor and add a touch of elegance to the design. Each foot is assembled from three pieces of 1x pine. Begin by ripping the pine to 4 in. and then crosscut into six 3-in.-long pieces. Rip one of the pieces down from 4 in. to 3¼ in.

FOOT LAYOUT

Front foot (make 2)

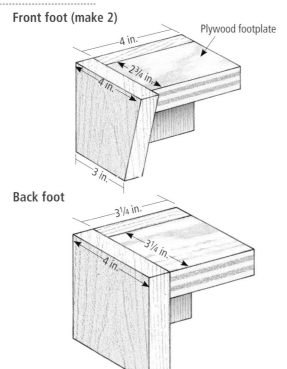

Plywood footplate

4 in.

2¾ in.

4 in.

3 in.

Back foot

3¼ in.

3¼ in.

4 in.

4 **GLUE UP THE FEET.** Glue and clamp one side piece to the footplate (left). Remove the clamp and glue and clamp the second side piece to the first side and the footplate (right). At rear is the assembled back foot.

Lay out the two front pieces as shown in "Foot Layout" above, and cut the angled sides with a hand miter saw **(3)** (p. 59). Cut the plywood footplates to the dimensions listed in "What You'll Need." (Be sure to use plywood for the plates—pine would probably split when screwed in place.)

Put down a piece of wax paper to protect your bench. Glue up each foot in two stages—glue and clamp one side piece to a plate, remove the clamp when the glue has set, then glue and clamp the other side piece to the plate and the edge of the first piece **(4)**. Be sure to orient the angled front pieces on opposite sides to create a left foot and a right foot.

Put glue on the top surface of the plates and attach each foot flush to the outside of the cabinet using two 1¼-in. all-purpose screws **(5)**.

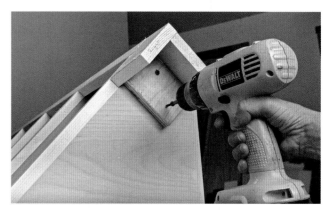

5 **ATTACH THE FEET.** Glue and screw the plates to the bottom of the cabinet.

Install the molding

The top molding is a simple door casing; various styles are available, but we chose one that's 1¾ in. wide, which seems about the right proportions for this cabinet. Set the molding in your miter saw with the back against the fence and the wider edge facing up. Cut a 45° angle **(6)**. Put the

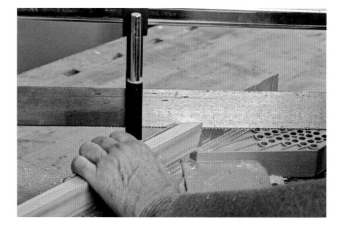

6 **CUT THE TOP MOLDING.** Hold the back of the molding against the fence with the wide part up to cut a 45° angle on the top molding.

 7 **CUT AND INSTALL THE SIDE TOP MOLDINGS.** Cut the side molding at 45° to make it flush to the back of the cabinet.

piece in place and scribe for the 45° angle on the other end. Make the cut, then tack-nail the molding in place.

Now cut and install the side moldings **(7)**. Cut a 45° angle on a piece of molding. Put it in place against the top molding and scribe and cut a 45° cut flush to the cabinet back. Do the same for the other side, then glue and nail the three pieces in place.

Make and Install the Doors

The cabinet doors are made from a pine frame around a plywood panel; prepare the frame first. Rip pine to 1½ in. wide for the stiles and rails. Cut the rails and stiles to the lengths listed in "What You'll Need," making any adjustments necessary to fit your cabinet. Rail lengths equal the width of the cabinet minus 6 in. (the combined width of the stiles) plus a ⅜-in. door overlap. Mark the pieces for biscuit joints **(1)**.

Join the rails to the stiles with glue and size #0 biscuits. Clamp across the joints **(2)**. Although these are the smallest biscuits available, they'll protrude slightly from both sides of the joints (as visible in the photo). Use a sharp chisel to cut the protruding biscuits flush.

Set a ⅜-in. piloted rabbeting router bit to a depth of ½ in. Raise the frame off the bench with plywood to make room for the nut at the bottom of the bit. Keep the plywood edge back on one side so the pilot bearing rides on the inside edges of the frame **(3)**. Rout one side, then adjust the plywood and pine as necessary to rout the remaining three sides.

The corners of the rabbets will be rounded after you've finished routing. Chop them square with a sharp chisel **(4)** (p. 62).

TIP When you sand the cabinet prior to painting, chamfer the bottom edges of the feet to prevent chipping when the cabinet is moved around.

1 **MARK THE DOOR FRAMES FOR BISCUIT JOINTS.** A combination square set to ¾ in. is a handy way to mark the rails and stiles for the center of the biscuit joints.

2 **GLUE UP THE DOOR FRAMES.** Use two clamps to glue up the biscuit joints between door rails and stiles.

3 **ROUT RABBETS FOR THE PANELS.** Moving in a clockwise direction, rout the rabbet on the inside of the door frames.

5 **GLUE THE DOOR PANELS.** Check that the panels will fit flush to the back of the frames, then glue and clamp them into the rabbets.

4 **SQUARE THE RABBET CORNERS.** Use a square to lay out where the corners of the rabbets will meet and then chop them square.

Cut and install the panels

The panels for the cabinet doors are cut from a 24-in. x 48-in. quarter sheet of ½-in. birch plywood available at home centers. (If you are starting with a full sheet of plywood for the door panels, see "Rough-Ripping Plywood" on p. 21). Rip the panels to width on the tablesaw and then cut them to length using the rip miter gauge. Alternatively, you can crosscut the panels to length as shown in "Making a Crosscutting Jig" on p. 22.

Put glue in the rabbets and clamp the panels in place **(5)**. Insert strips of pine at the edge of the panels to protect the door surface and to help distribute clamping pressure.

Trim one door and rout the overlaps

The doors come together at the center of the cabinet with a ³⁄₈-in. overlap. For the overlap to be in the center, and for the inner stiles of both doors to reveal the same width, it is necessary to rip ³⁄₈ in. off one stile of one door. You'll note in the drawing "Door Construction" on the facing page that the door on the left is 11⁷⁄₈ in. wide, whereas the door on the right is 12¼ in. wide. Make this rip by setting the tablesaw fence to 11⁷⁄₈ in.

Now set the ³⁄₈-in. piloted rabbeting bit to cut ³⁄₈ in. deep. Rout the back of the stile you just ripped and the front of one stile on the other door. Raise the door on pieces of plywood to allow room for the pilot-bearing

6 **ROUT THE OVERLAPS.** Rout a lip on the front of the wider door stile and a mating lip on the back of the other door's inside stile.

nut. Prevent the router from tipping by supporting it with a piece of pine clamped atop a piece of plywood on the bench **(6)**.

Install the doors

Tape one door in place on the cabinet and mark the door and cabinet for hinges positioned 2 in. from each end of the door **(7)**. Cut hinge mortises as described in "Cutting Hinge Mortises" on p. 26. Install the doors on their hinges. If the doors rub when you close them, give the mating edges of each door alternating strokes with a block plane until the doors close easily.

DOOR CONSTRUCTION

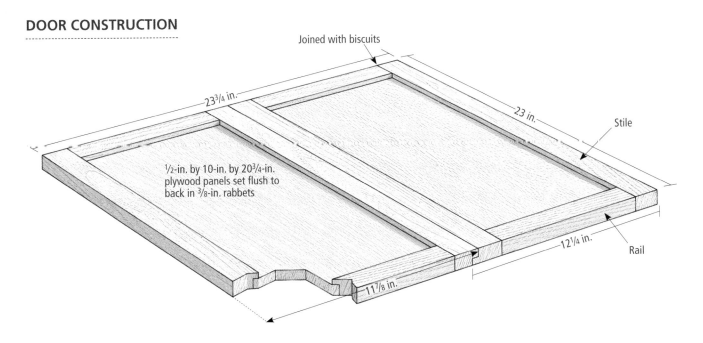

Joined with biscuits

23³/₄ in.

23 in.

Stile

¹/₂-in. by 10-in. by 20³/₄-in. plywood panels set flush to back in ³/₈-in. rabbets

12¹/₄ in.

Rail

11⁷/₈ in.

Remove the hinges, paint the cabinet, and reinstall the doors. Install magnetic stops under the second shelf from the bottom, positioned just inside the overlaps **(8)**. Predrill and install the catch plates on the doors using the two round-head screws provided. For each catch, place a plate on the magnet and close the door. The plate has little spikes that will mark the installation position on the door. Install each plate with the flat-head screws provided. Install knobs centered across the inside stiles, 3 in. from the top of the doors.

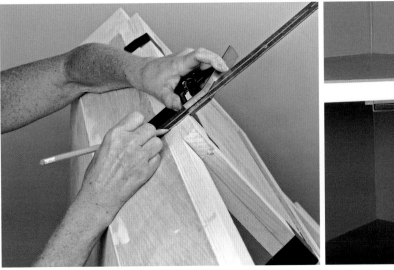

7 **MARK FOR HINGES.** Tape a door in place on the cabinet, making sure it is flush to the cabinet rail, then mark the hinge position on the door and cabinet rails.

8 **INSTALL THE DOOR CATCHES.** To locate the metal door catches, put the metal plate on the magnetic catch. Then close the door firmly so that the spikes on the plate mark its position on the inside of the door.

BUILT-IN SHELVES

Shelves built of 1x lumber are fine for short spans, but when they get longer than about 3 ft. they may sag under heavy loads. These built-in shelves use simplified torsion-box construction that allows them to span up to 8 ft. with no chance of sagging.

The shelves and their sides are rips of ¾-in. pine sandwiched between birch plywood—¾ in. thick on top, ½ in. thick on the bottom. Torsion boxes often have thinner skins and thicker cores than this, but that approach requires lots of small core pieces and lots of clamps. This design has fewer core pieces and allows you to assemble the components with glue and finishing nails, eliminating the need for clamps. You could use a hammer and nailset, but there are a lot of little nails to drive so a power finish nailer will greatly speed the work. If you don't own one, consider renting a nailer, at least to assemble the shelves and sides.

Like the core pieces, the cleats that attach the shelves to the walls and the shelf sides are hidden between the plywood skins. The result is a clean, handsome look that fits with any architectural style. The shelves shown here span a little short of 5 ft., providing a whopping 23 sq. ft. of storage surface. You can make yours shorter or longer. You can also vary the molding scheme to match the room—for example, if the room has crown molding, wrap the top of the unit with molding to match.

- 5 top skins — ¾ in. × 11¼ in. × 56 in., birch plywood
- 5 bottom skins — ½ in. × 11¼ in. × 56 in., birch plywood
- 2 inside vertical skins — ¾ in. × 11¼ in. × 88½ in., birch plywood
- 2 outside vertical skins — ½ in. × 11¼ in. × 88½ in., pine
- 10 shelf front and back core pieces — ¾ in. × 1 in. × 54⅜ in., pine
- 15 shelf short core pieces — ¾ in. × 1 in. × 8⁷⁄₁₆ in., pine
- 4 vertical support front and back core pieces — ¾ in. × 1 in. × 88½ in., pine
- 10 vertical support short core pieces — ¾ in. × 1 in. × 8⁷⁄₁₆ in., pine
- 2 vertical wall cleats — ¾ in. × ¾ in. × 82½ in., pine
- 10 side cleats — ¾ in. × ¾ in. × 11 in., pine
- 5 horizontal wall cleats — ¾ in. × ¾ in. × 54⅜ in., pine
- 2 face-frame stiles — ¾ in. × 2 in. × 88½ in., clear pine
- 5 face-frame rails — ¾ in. × 2 in. × 56 in., clear pine
- Shoe molding, as needed

FASTENERS

- Wood glue
- 1¼-in. finish nails
- 2¼-in. all-purpose screws

Make the Shelves and Sides

Ceilings and floors often aren't perfectly flat or level, so the first important step is to determine where each side piece will be located and then measure from the floor to the ceiling at those two points. If the two measurements are within ¼ in. of each other, subtract ⅛ in. from the longer measurement to get the length of the sides. If the measurements differ by more than ¼ in., make each side piece to fit. It won't matter if the sides are different lengths because the shelves will be attached to hidden

cleats that will be installed along level lines on the wall and on the side pieces.

Cut the plywood skins and core pieces

To make the plywood sheets easier to manage on the tablesaw, start by using the circular saw on the floor with a sacrificial piece underneath to rip them in half along their length (see "Rough-Ripping Plywood" on p. 21).

Now, because all the shelf skins will be the same length (56 in. for the shelves shown here), use a circular saw with a crosscutting jig to cut to final length the rough-rips that will be used for the shelves (see "Making a Crosscutting Jig" on p. 22). Crosscutting the shelf skin pieces to final length makes it even easier to move them through the tablesaw for final rips. (It doesn't pay to do this for the

> **TIP** Because all the plywood skins are 11¼ in. wide, you can save work by having all the plywood ripped at the lumberyard or home center. They may charge you a few dollars, but it's a good alternative if you don't have a vehicle that can transport full plywood sheets.

BUILT-IN SHELVES

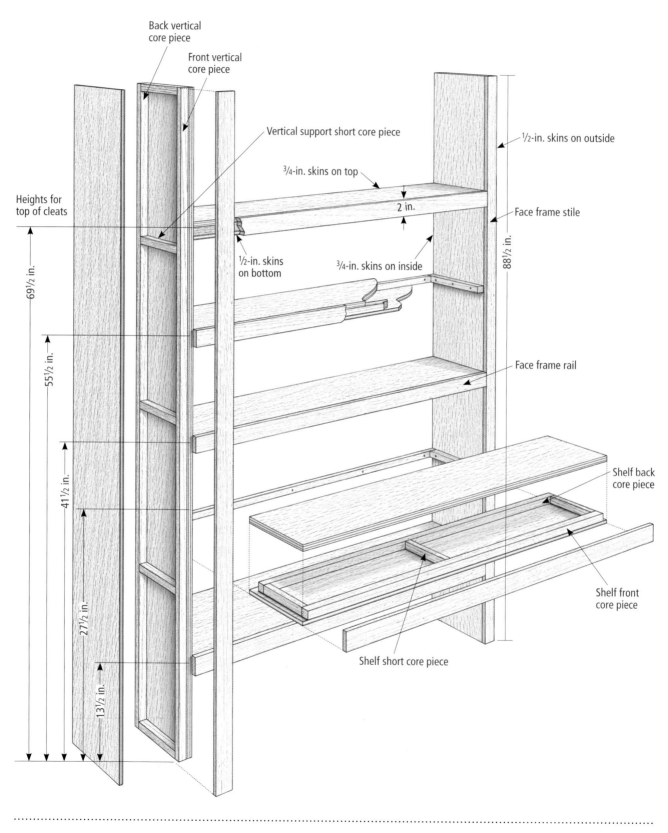

Back vertical core piece

Front vertical core piece

Vertical support short core piece

¾-in. skins on top

½-in. skins on outside

Heights for top of cleats

½-in. skins on bottom

¾-in. skins on inside

2 in.

88½ in.

Face frame stile

69½ in.

Face frame rail

55½ in.

Shelf back core piece

41½ in.

27½ in.

Shelf front core piece

13½ in.

Shelf short core piece

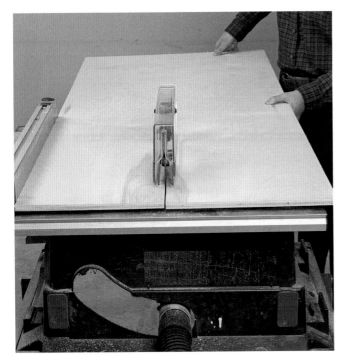

TIP Sawblade teeth enter the wood from the top when using a circular saw or power miter saw and from the bottom when using a tablesaw. The blade is much more likely to chip plywood face veneers when exiting than when entering. Since one face of every skin piece will be hidden, always cut with the good face up on the circular saw and miter saw and with the good face down on the tablesaw.

1 **CUT THE SKINS TO FINAL WIDTH.** Once the plywood panels are ripped in half and the shelf skins are cut to length, you can safely and easily rip them to final width on the tablesaw.

two side pieces, even if they will be the same length, because 8-ft.-long plywood sheets are only a few inches longer than the final side length.)

On the tablesaw, rip all the pieces to the final width of 11¼ in. **(1)**. Then cut the side pieces to their final lengths with the circular saw and crosscutting jig. Rip stock to 1 in. wide for the core pieces. Then crosscut the pieces to the lengths listed in "What You'll Need" using a hand or power miter saw (or with the miter gauge on a tablesaw) **(2)**.

Floating Shelves

Another way to create shelving with a sleek but chunky look is to use commercially available floating shelves (the ones shown here are from Merillat® cabinetry). The shelves typically come with a sturdy metal plate that you attach through the wall into studs or to drywall alone using "molly bolts" that expand behind the drywall. Brackets welded to the plate extend into the shelf. Screws driven up through the bottom prevent the shelves from slipping off the brackets.

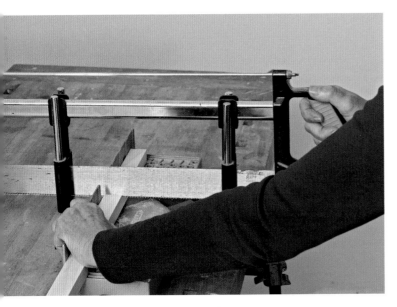

2 **CUT THE CORE PIECES.** After ripping the core pieces to width, cut them to final length. A few strokes with a hand miter box is one way to make each cut.

3 **LAY OUT THE PERIMETER CORE PIECES.** Use a combination square set to $^{13}/_{16}$ in. to lay out the positions of core pieces around the back and sides of the shelves and the back of the vertical supports. This space is for the hidden cleats that will support the shelves.

4 **ATTACH THE CORE PIECES.** Use glue and 1¼-in. finish nails to attach the core pieces to the top skins. Note that the front core piece is flush with the edge of the plywood, whereas the back core piece is recessed $^{13}/_{16}$ in. from the back edge of the plywood.

Lay out for the core pieces

Set a combination square to $^{13}/_{16}$ in. and use it to draw a line around three sides of the inside surface of all the ¾-in. shelf skins **(3)**. Then use the square to lay out a line $^{13}/_{16}$ in. from the back edge of each side support. The perimeter core pieces will be installed along the inside of these lines to leave room for the wall and side cleats. On the inside of all the ¾-in. skins, lay out the positions of the core pieces as shown in the "Core Layouts" drawing on the facing page. Draw Xs to indicate which side of the line the core pieces will be installed on.

Glue and nail the core pieces to a shelf top skin

Lay a ¾-in. shelf skin on your bench, with the layout facing up. Put glue on the 1-in.-wide side of a shelf back core piece and place it along the inside of its layout line, covering the X. Secure it with 1¼-in. finish nails. Secure a front core piece to the plywood in the same way, making sure the core piece is flush to the plywood edge. Finally, glue and nail the short core pieces in place **(4)**.

TIP Making the core pieces is a great chance to use up any pine scraps you may have. If you buy stock for the core, get 1x6s. You'll get 5 rips out of each of these 5½-in.-wide boards with no waste beside the kerfs.

CORE LAYOUTS

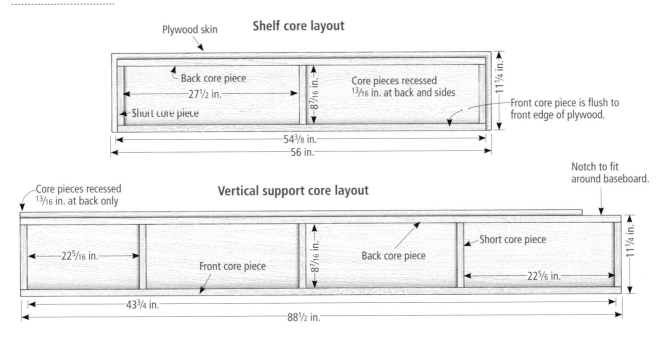

Shelf core layout

Plywood skin

Back core piece

—27½ in.—

Short core piece

8⁷⁄₁₆ in.

Core pieces recessed
¹³⁄₁₆ in. at back and sides

Front core piece is flush to
front edge of plywood.

11¼ in.

—54³⁄₈ in.—
—56 in.—

Notch to fit
around baseboard.

Core pieces recessed
¹³⁄₁₆ in. at back only

Vertical support core layout

—22⁵⁄₁₆ in.—

Front core piece

Back core piece

8⁷⁄₁₆ in.

Short core piece

—22⁵⁄₆ in.—

11¼ in.

—43³⁄₄ in.—
—88½ in.—

Attach the bottom skin

Set the squaring boxes (see the sidebar on p. 70) under
the ¾-in. top skin and put the ½-in. bottom skin in place,
layout lines up and ends flush **(5)**. Leave the core cross
pieces partially exposed so you can use them to mark the
outside of the ½-in. skin with approximate centerlines
for nailing.

Apply glue to the core pieces, then set the ½-in. skin in
place. Make sure the plywood pieces are flush at all edges
and that the front core piece is flush to both plywood
edges as you put 1¼-in. nails through the ½-in. piece
into the core pieces **(6)** (p. 70). Space the nails about 6 in.
apart. Repeat to assemble each shelf.

5 **TRANSFER THE LAYOUT LINES.** Mark the position
of the core pieces on the outside of the bottom
skin so you will know where to nail when the skin is
in place.

TIP You can use a glue brush or
even a roller that fits on the
end of your glue bottle to apply the
glue to the core pieces, but a digital
glue spreader like the one shown here
works perfectly well. Plus the price is
right and you'll never misplace it. Just
keep a bucket of water handy so you
won't be tempted to wipe your finger
on your jeans.

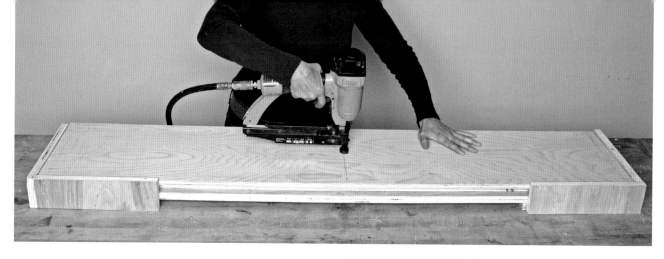

Assemble the side supports

The side support pieces are built in the same way as the shelves. Glue and nail the core pieces to each ¾-in. side support skin as you did for the shelves. In this installation, the room has a simple rectangular baseboard, so it was easier to notch the side supports to fit around the baseboard than to cut the baseboard to accept the supports. (If your baseboard has a more complex profile, see p. 47.)

To lay out the notch, measure the height and depth of the baseboard and add ¹⁄₁₆ in. to each dimension to make

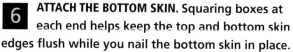

6 ATTACH THE BOTTOM SKIN. Squaring boxes at each end helps keep the top and bottom skin edges flush while you nail the bottom skin in place.

sure you have enough clearance. When you lay out the cuts, keep in mind that the ¾-in. inside skins will oppose each other—it's worth standing the pieces up against a wall in the right orientation to make sure you are notching the right corners. Then use a sabersaw to cut the notch in all four side-support skins **(7)**. Lay out the nailing, and glue and nail the ½-in. side support pieces in place as you did for the shelves.

Making Squaring Boxes

When gluing up the shelves and side supports, it's easier to get the edges flush if you take a few minutes to make a pair of squaring boxes from scrap plywood. The exact dimensions of the parts are not important—just be sure that the base is perfectly square and the sides are at least 3 in. high. Secure the boxes with glue and finish nails.

SQUARING BOX

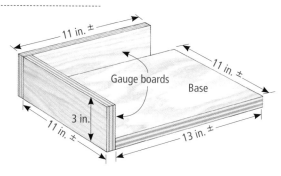

11 in. ±
11 in. ±
Gauge boards
Base
11 in. ±
3 in.
13 in. ±

NOTCH THE SIDE SUPPORTS.
Use a sabersaw to notch both side supports to fit around the baseboard, as necessary.

TIP To prevent splintering before cutting with a sabersaw, slice through the face veneer with a utility knife. Guide the knife with a combination square.

Assemble the Shelves to the Wall

The sides of the unit will be attached to vertical cleats that are in turn attached to the wall. In the same way, the back of each shelf will be supported by a level cleat that runs along the wall and level cleats attached to the inside of the sides of the unit.

Cut and attach the vertical wall cleats

Rip 1x stock (actual thickness ¾ in.) to ¾ in. wide for the cleats and then use a power or hand miter box or the miter gauge on the tablesaw to cut all the cleats to the lengths listed in "What You'll Need." The vertical cleats should fit between the ceiling and the top of the baseboard **(1)**.

In the installation shown here, one side of the shelving unit abuts the side of a door casing. Check that the casing is plumb. If it is, you can use a scrap of ½-in. plywood as shown in photo 2 on p. 72 to lay out the position of the first cleat (the ½-in. scrap is the same thickness as the

MEASURE FOR THE VERTICAL CLEATS. Measure between the ceiling and the top of the baseboard to determine the length of the vertical cleats.

2 LAY OUT THE POSITION OF THE VERTICAL CLEAT. If the shelving unit abuts a door casing or wall, use a scrap of ½-in. plywood to lay out the position of the first vertical cleat.

3 PREDRILL THE HOLES THROUGH THE VERTICAL CLEAT. You can also use the plywood scrap to position the wall cleat as you predrill and countersink for screws.

outside vertical skin) **(2)**. If the casing is not plumb, use a 4-ft. level to draw a ceiling-to-floor plumb line that is ½ in. from the casing at its closest point. Use the same procedure if one side of the unit will abut a wall. If both sides are freestanding, simply draw a plumb line.

Now you are ready to attach the first vertical cleat to the wall (you can use the ½-in. plywood scrap to help align the cleat). If the cleat is located along a door casing or a corner, there should be solid framing behind the wall to attach it to. If not, use construction adhesive in addition to 2¼-in. screws to attach the cleat. Predrill the holes with a countersink bit so you can make the screw heads flush without splitting the cleat **(3)**.

TIP It's a good idea to paint the shelves and side supports before you install them, as it's a lot easier to apply even coats of paint while the parts are laid out on a flat surface.

Countersink Bits

Countersink bits like the one shown here have a replaceable conventional drill bit that fits into a countersink and gets tightened in place with a setscrew. The bit predrills a hole for the screw body and then drills a slant-sided depression for the screw head.

Install the first vertical side support and side cleats

Fit the first side panel over the vertical cleat you just installed and secure it with 1¼-in. finish nails into the vertical cleat **(4)**.

Next, lay out the position of the shelves. In the installation shown here, there is 14 in. of space between the tops of the shelves. If that spacing works for you, measure from the floor to mark the shelf locations shown in the "Built-In Shelves" drawing on p. 66. Or, lay out spacing of your choosing. At each shelf location, use a square to draw a line across the vertical support **(5)**.

Attach side cleats to the side support with 2¼-in. screws in predrilled and countersunk holes **(6)**.

4 **ATTACH THE FIRST VERTICAL SUPPORT.** Set the vertical support over the wall cleat and attach with 1½-in. finish nails into the cleat.

5 **LAY OUT SHELF POSITIONS.** Use a square to lay out lines for the side cleats on the first vertical support.

6 **ATTACH THE SIDE CLEATS TO THE SUPPORT.** Screw the side cleats to the first vertical support.

Install the horizontal wall cleats

It's important to get the wall cleats level and flush to the top and bottom of the cleats already installed on the vertical supports. Hold a 4-ft. level against each cleat and draw a level line along the bottom of each one **(7)**. Use a stud finder to locate each stud along the level lines (see "Finding Wall Studs" on p. 28.) Attach the horizontal cleats to the wall with 2¼-in. screws in predrilled and countersunk holes **(8)**.

Install the second vertical side support

The next step is to transfer the location of the cleats to the other vertical support. Fit the shelves onto the cleats on the first vertical support and the wall. Put the second vertical support in place against the shelves. Make sure each shelf is level across its face and square to the vertical support as you use a knife to scribe a notch to locate the bottom of the top skin **(9)**.

Now set the second vertical support on a work surface. Put your knife blade in each notch, slide a square up against the blade, and scribe the position of each cleat **(10)**.

7 **LAY OUT THE HORIZONTAL WALL CLEATS.** Hold a level against the horizontal cleats while drawing layout lines to make sure the cleats will be perfectly level when installed.

8 **ATTACH THE HORIZONTAL WALL CLEATS.** Screw the horizontal cleats into each stud in the wall.

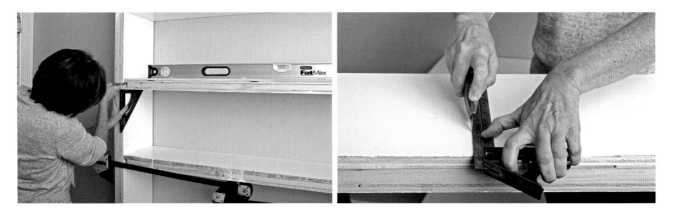

9 **SCRIBE THE POSITION OF THE CLEATS ON THE SECOND VERTICAL SUPPORT.** Put the second vertical support in place so you can precisely mark the positions of the side cleats that will be screwed to it.

10 **EXTEND THE LAYOUT NOTCHES.** Put the blade of a utility knife into the notch and scribe against a square to lay out the position of each side cleat.

Place each cleat along its line, about ⅛ in. from the back of the vertical support. (It will be equally short at the front, too.) Use a clamp and a square to keep the cleat in perfect alignment as you predrill and countersink for 2¼-in. screws **(11)**.

The process for locating the second vertical cleat is similar to how you located the first vertical cleat, but this time, use a ¾-in.-thick piece of scrap plywood because the ¾-in. skin of the vertical supports will meet the shelf ends **(12)**.

Put the second vertical support in place and secure it with 1¼-in. nails through its face into the vertical cleat, as you did for the first vertical support. Nail the shelves to their cleats **(13)**. Use two nails into each shelf end and three along each back edge. A 6-ft. clamp or a couple of 3-ft. clamps hooked together may be needed to pull the vertical supports tightly to the shelves.

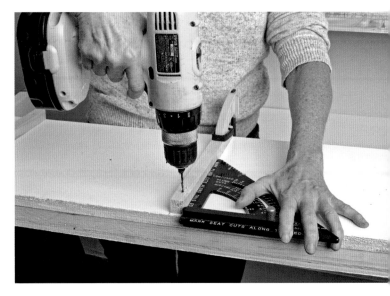

11 **SECURE THE CLEATS TO THE SECOND VERTICAL SUPPORT. Screw each side cleat to the second vertical support using a clamp and a square to keep it perfectly positioned.**

12 **LOCATE THE SECOND VERTICAL CLEAT. Use a scrap of ¾-in. plywood to lay out the position of the second vertical cleat.**

13 **NAIL THE SHELVES IN PLACE. After nailing the second vertical support to the vertical wall cleat, nail the shelves to the side cleats.**

Attach the Face Frame and Moldings

At this point, the rough plywood edges of the shelves and the vertical side supports are plainly visible. For a finished appearance, you need to cover these edges with a face frame. Depending on the installation, you may also need to run shoe molding around the vertical supports.

Begin by ripping ¾-in. pine to 2 in. wide for the stiles and rails. Cut the stiles to fit from floor to ceiling and then attach them with glue and 1¼-in. finish nails **(1)**.

Next, put a rail in place butted against one stile and scribe where it meets the other stile **(2)**. Cut it to length and install with glue and 1¼-in. finish nails. Install the remaining rails the same way.

In the installation shown here, the shoe molding used around the room is wrapped around the vertical supports. It's usually easiest to replace all of the shoe molding on the wall behind the shelves than it is to cut existing molding in place. To fit shoe molding around the vertical supports, scribe and cut pieces to fit both sides of a support with 45° miters. Install one of the pieces with 1¼-in. finish nails, then scribe and cut the short front piece before installing the second piece **(3)**. Once the shoe molding is in place, you are ready to caulk where the unit meets the walls and ceiling, fill nail holes, sand and paint the face frame, and do any final paint touch-up.

1 **ATTACH THE STILES. Glue and nail the stiles to the vertical side supports.**

2 **SCRIBE AND INSTALL THE RAILS. Scribe each rail for a snug fit between the stiles before cutting and installing with glue and nails.**

3 **INSTALL THE SHOE MOLDING. Scribe and cut shoe molding to fit against the baseboard and around the vertical supports and nail it in place.**

WINDOW SEAT

This handsome window seat features three generous drawers on full-extension slides, which greatly increases their usefulness. The seat has a custom-made cushion that is kept in place by a lip that runs around the top of the seat platform.

This window seat was built in a home with baseboard heating, which can present a challenge for built-in projects. The solution here was to create an insulated space with radiator screens to allow the heat to escape through the front. This strategy actually improves heating efficiency by forcing warmed air farther into the room. If you have baseboard heating, you can adapt the solution shown here for other built-in projects such as the Cabinet with Bookcase on p. 34.

Of course, you can also change the length or even the depth of the window seat to suit your space. If you do, make the drawer openings no wider than 24 in.—that's the maximum the drawer slides are designed to handle.

The window seat shown here was designed to span under the full width of a window in a den, but the design would also work nicely in a bedroom. The wood was stained and finished to match the trim in the home. Of course, you can choose to paint the window seat to match your décor.

FACE FRAME, SIDE PANELS, AND SEAT CLEATS

- 2 top and bottom front rails $3/4$ in. $\times$ $2\frac{1}{2}$ in. $\times$ $76\frac{1}{4}$ in., clear pine
- 3 front mid rails $3/4$ in. $\times$ $2\frac{1}{2}$ in. $\times$ $23\frac{3}{4}$ in., clear pine
- 3 rear seat cleats $3/4$ in. $\times$ $2\frac{1}{2}$ in. $\times$ $23\frac{3}{4}$ in., pine
- 3 front seat cleats $3/4$ in. $\times$ $1\frac{1}{2}$ in. $\times$ $23\frac{3}{4}$ in., pine
- 2 front end stiles $3/4$ in. $\times$ $2\frac{1}{2}$ in. $\times$ 18 in., clear pine
- 2 front mid stiles $3/4$ in. $\times$ $2\frac{1}{2}$ in. $\times$ 13 in., clear pine
- 4 top and bottom side rails $3/4$ in. $\times$ $2\frac{1}{2}$ in. $\times$ $15\frac{3}{4}$ in., clear pine
- 2 rear side stiles $3/4$ in. $\times$ $5\frac{1}{2}$ in. $\times$ 18 in., clear pine
- 2 front side stiles $3/4$ in. $\times$ $1\frac{3}{4}$ in. $\times$ 18 in., clear pine
- 2 side panels $1/2$ in. $\times$ $13\frac{11}{16}$ in. $\times$ $15\frac{11}{16}$ in., birch plywood
- 3 radiator screens   6 in. $\times$ $25\frac{3}{4}$ in.

BASE

- 4 front and back plates $1\frac{1}{2}$ in. $\times$ $3\frac{1}{2}$ in. $\times$ $79\frac{3}{4}$ in., lumber
- 8 side and mid plates $1\frac{1}{2}$ in. $\times$ $3\frac{1}{2}$ in. $\times$ 13 in., lumber
- 20 studs $1\frac{1}{2}$ in. $\times$ $3\frac{1}{2}$ in. $\times$ $5\frac{1}{4}$ in., lumber
- 1 sheet 1-in. $\times$ 4-ft. $\times$ 8-ft. foil-faced rigid foam insulation cut to fit
- Cold-weather foil tape

DRAWER SPACE

- 2 drawer space base and seat board $3/4$ in. $\times$ $23\frac{1}{4}$ in. $\times$ $81\frac{1}{4}$ in., AC plywood
- 6 slide-support panels $3/4$ in. $\times$ $8\frac{1}{4}$ in. $\times$ $22\frac{7}{8}$ in., AC or birch plywood
- 12 spacers $3/4$ in. $\times$ 1 in. $\times$ $22\frac{3}{8}$ in., plywood

DRAWERS

- 7 drawer sides $3/4$ in. $\times$ 6 in. $\times$ 22 in., pine
- 3 drawer fronts $3/4$ in. $\times$ 6 in. $\times$ $21\frac{3}{16}$ in., pine
- 3 drawer backs $3/4$ in. $\times$ $5\frac{1}{4}$ in. $\times$ $21\frac{3}{16}$ in., pine
- 3 drawer bottoms $1/2$ in. $\times$ $21\frac{7}{8}$ in. $\times$ $21\frac{9}{16}$ in., birch plywood
- 3 drawer false fronts $3/4$ in $\times$ 8 in. $\times$ $25\frac{1}{4}$ in., pine

TRIM

- 2 side lips $3/4$ in. $\times$ $1\frac{1}{2}$ in. $\times$ 24 in.
- 1 front lip $3/4$ in. $\times$ $1\frac{1}{2}$ in. $\times$ $82\frac{3}{4}$ in.
- 2 side shoe molding   24 in.
- 1 front shoe molding $82\frac{3}{4}$ in.

HARDWARE

- 3 sets 22-in. Accuride® 7434 full-extension plus 1-in. slides
- 2½-in. deck screws
- 1¼-in. all-purpose screws
- 4d finish nails
- 3d finish nails
- Construction adhesive
- Wood glue
- 3 drawer pulls

WINDOW SEAT

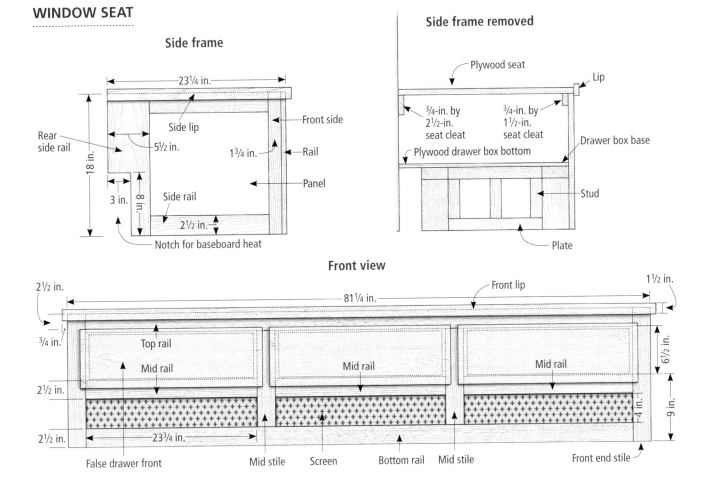

Side frame

23¼ in.

18 in.

Front side

Side lip

Rear side rail

5½ in.

1¾ in.

Rail

Panel

Side rail

3 in.

8 in.

2½ in.

Notch for baseboard heat

Side frame removed

Plywood seat

Lip

¾-in. by 2½-in. seat cleat

¾-in. by 1½-in. seat cleat

Drawer box base

Plywood drawer box bottom

Stud

Plate

Front view

2½ in.

81¼ in.

Front lip

1½ in.

¾ in.

Top rail

Mid rail

Mid rail

Mid rail

6½ in.

2½ in.

9 in.

4 in.

2½ in.

23¾ in.

False drawer front

Mid stile

Screen

Bottom rail

Mid stile

Front end stile

Make the Face Frame

The first step in building the window seat is to cut all the parts for the face frame. While you are at it, you'll cut stiles and rails that later will be used to make the side panels. These parts are all ¾ in. thick. Then you'll use pocket screws to assemble the face frame.

Cut the rails, stiles, and cleats

Cut the face frame and cleat pieces to the lengths listed in "What You'll Need." Use a hand or power miter saw with a stop block to cut pieces to the same length **(1)** (see "Making and Using a Stop Block" below). Cut the front and rear seat cleats at the same time as the mid rails as all these pieces are the same length.

Rip the front side stiles to 1¾ in. on the tablesaw. All the other stiles and rails are either 2½ in. wide or 5½ in. wide. If you are making these from nominal 1x3s and nominal 1x6s (see "How Big Is a 2x4?" on the facing page), there is no need to rip these pieces.

With the face-frame stiles and rails cut to length, place the end stiles side by side with the ends flush. Place the mid stiles alongside, and use a rail piece as a gauge to center the mid stiles along the end stiles. Clamp the pieces

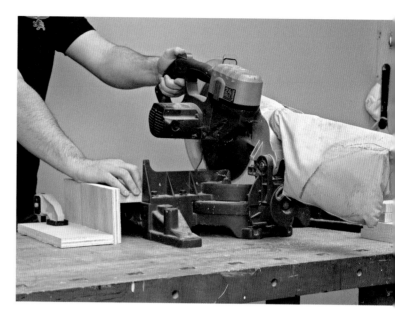

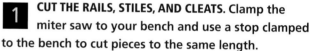

1 **CUT THE RAILS, STILES, AND CLEATS. Clamp the miter saw to your bench and use a stop clamped to the bench to cut pieces to the same length.**

together and draw a line 9 in. from one end of the end stiles **(2)**. Make an X on each piece to indicate which side of the line the mid rails will be positioned on.

Making and Using a Stop Block

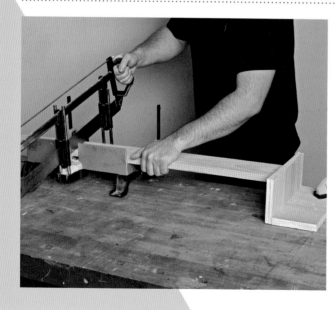

A stop block takes minutes to make, works equally well with a hand miter saw or power miter saw, and lets you quickly and accurately cut pieces to the same length. You need two scraps of ¾-in. plywood that are about 6 in. long. One piece will be the fence and needs to be wide enough so that when set upright, workpieces on the saw will butt into it. The other piece needs to be wide enough to clamp to the bench. Assemble the pieces with two or three 1¼-in. all-purpose screws through the face of the fence.

To use the stop, first clamp your saw to the bench so it can't shift position. To set the stop, measure and mark a cut on one workpiece and cut it to length. Place that piece against the saw, slide the stop fence up to other end of the piece, and clamp the stop to the bench. Now every piece of stock you butt into the fence will be cut to the same length as the first piece.

2 **LAY OUT MID-RAIL POSITIONS ON THE STILES.** The top of the mid rails will be centered along the stiles, 9 in. from the floor. Clamp all four face-frame stiles together to mark where the mid rails will meet them.

Assemble the face frames

The face frame and side frame members are joined with two 1¼-in. pocket screws at each joint. Use a pocket-hole jig to drill two holes in both ends of all the rails and the mid stiles **(3)**. Position the holes ½ in. from the sides of the members. This will keep the screws out of the path of the ⅜-in. rabbets you'll be making to receive the side panels.

3 **DRILL END POCKET HOLES.** Drill two pocket holes in each end of all the rails.

How Big Is a 2x4?

Lumber sizes are commonly described by their nominal width and thickness—this is the dimension the boards were before they were planed and dried to final dimensions. So, for example, a nominal 1x3 actually measures ¾ in. x 2½ in. The chart at right shows in inches the nominal dimensions and corresponding actual dimensions for the lumber and boards you'll find at a lumberyard or home center.

THICKNESS		WIDTH	
Nominal	**Actual**	**Nominal**	**Actual**
1	¾ in.	2	1½ in.
1¼	1 in.	3	2½ in.
1½	1¼ in.	4	3½ in.
2	1½ in.	5	4½ in.
2½	2 in.	6	5½ in.
3	2½ in.	7	6½ in.
3½	3 in.	8+	¾ in. less
4	4½ in.		
5+	½ in. less		

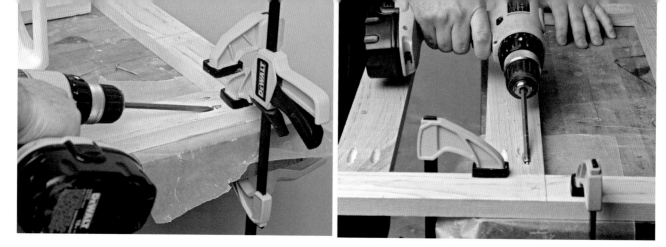

4 **ASSEMBLE THE TOP AND BOTTOM RAILS TO THE FRONT END STILES. Put glue on the end of a top or bottom rail, clamp it to the bench with its mating stile, and join the pieces with two pocket screws. Waxed paper keeps glue off the bench.**

5 **ATTACH THE MID STILES AND MID RAILS. Attach the mid stiles to the top and bottom rails, then attach the mid rails at the layout lines on the stiles as shown here.**

Clamp a face-frame end stile across the bench. Put glue on the end of a top or bottom rail and clamp it in place butted against the end stile. Make sure the end of the stile is flush with the outside of the rail. Drive a screw into each pocket hole **(4)**. Repeat this process to join the other rail to the stile and then both rails to the other end stile.

Use the three mid rails as spacers to position the two mid stiles between the top and bottom rail. Put glue on the ends of the mid stiles, set them in place, and insert pocket screws. Now move the mid rails into position along the layout lines you made previously. Then glue and screw them to the stiles **(5)**.

Assemble the side frames

The side-frame rails are 2½ in. wide. Their front frames are 1¾ in. wide because they will butt into the inside of the ¾-in.-thick front end stiles. The rear side stiles are 5½ in. wide to make room for the baseboard radiator; later, after the side frames are assembled, they will be notched to fit around the radiator.

Attach the side rails to the side stiles in the same way you attached the front top and bottom rails to the end stiles **(6)**.

Positioning the Pocket-Hole Jig

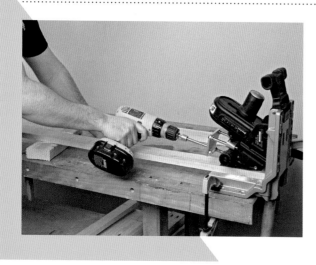

With the pocket-hole jig shown here, shorter rails and mid stiles can be drilled in the upright position, as shown in photo 3 on p. 81. For longer pieces such as the front top and bottom rails, the jig is designed to be used with the back screwed or clamped down as shown here. The positioning of the holes is the same as for the other rails. A 2x4 scrap is the right height to support the workpiece.

<table>
</table>

6 **ASSEMBLE THE SIDE FRAMES. Drive pocket screws through the rails into the stiles.**

1 **CUT THE SCREENS. Use aviation snips to cut the radiator screens. Protect your hands with leather gloves.**

Install Screens and Panels

The three bottom openings are covered with metal radiator screening to allow heat from the baseboard unit to escape under the seat and into the room. The screening comes in 3-ft.-square panels in several decorative patterns and is available at lumberyards and home centers.

Cut the screens to overlap the vent space openings by 1 in. all around. Use a pencil and metal straightedge to draw layout lines, and then use aviation shears to cut the screening to width and length **(1)**. Wear leather gloves; the cut edges are sharp.

Make a mark 1 in. from each back edge of the openings and use these marks to align the screens—you want the screens' hole pattern to be square to the opening. Attach the screens with staples spaced a couple of inches apart **(2)**. Tap down any protruding staples with a hammer.

2 **INSTALL THE SCREENS. Use a heavy-duty stapler to attach the screens to the back of the face frame.**

Make rabbets for the side panels

The next step is to prepare the side face frames to receive the side panels. Put a ⅜-in. rabbeting bit in a router and set the depth to ½ in. Raise a side frame on pieces of scrap to allow room for the router bit pilot bearing and clamp the frame to the bench. Rout the rabbets in a clockwise direction **(3)**. You'll need to stop the router and reposition the clamps to get around the narrow front stiles.

3 **RABBET THE SIDE FRAMES FOR THE PANELS. Rout a ⅜-in.-wide by ½-in.-deep rabbet inside each side frame to receive the side panels.**

TIP It's important to make the side panels flush to the back of their frames because the drawer-slide supports, which you will make later, will be attached across the panels and frames. To make sure they are flush, rout a test rabbet on a piece of scrap and then hold the scrap against the plywood you will use for the panels to make sure your router is set to precisely the right depth.

5 **CUT THE SIDE PANELS TO LENGTH.** After cutting the panels to width, use the rip fence to cut the panels to length. An outfeed roller stand is helpful for supporting the piece at the end of a cut.

4 **SQUARE THE RABBET CORNERS.** Chop along the rail first and then, as shown here, along the stile. Working in this sequence prevents the risk of splitting the stile.

Use a square and pencil to draw lines indicating where the top edges of the rabbets will meet at the corners. Then chop the rabbets out with a chisel **(4)**. For the first chop in each corner, put the back of the chisel along the rail rabbet. This way, you will be chopping across the grain of the stile so you won't split the stile when you chop along its grain.

Cut and install the side panels

Check the dimensions across the side-frame rabbets in case they vary a bit from those listed in "What You'll Need." Subtract about 1/16 in. from your measurements for an easy fit—the panels don't need to fit snugly since they won't be seen on the inside.

If you are starting with a full sheet of plywood, see "Rough-Ripping Plywood" on p. 21. In the case shown here, the panels are cut from a 24-in. x 48-in. quarter sheet of 1/2-in. birch plywood (available at home centers). Rip the panels to width on the tablesaw, then use the rip fence to cut them to length **(5)**. Alternatively, you can crosscut the panels to length as shown in "Making a Crosscutting Jig" on p. 22.

6 **CLAMP THE PANELS IN PLACE.** When gluing in the side panels, use four pieces of scrap to apply clamping pressure to the panel.

When gluing the panels in place, you want to put clamping pressure on the panels, not on the frames. Clamps won't span the frame, so cut two narrow pieces of scrap a little shorter than the panel length and have two wider pieces on hand that are long enough to span your bench. Put glue in the rabbets on the frame, insert the panel, and then set the two shorter scraps in place on the panel, positioned over the rabbets. Place the longer pieces across the two short scraps and clamp them to the bench **(6)**. You don't need a lot of pressure—don't tighten the clamps enough to bend the crosspieces.

Make the Base

The drawer box space and seat top sit on a base of nominal 2x4s that allows space for heated air to escape through the front screens. It's easiest to make the four sides of the frames and the two center supports in the shop and then assemble the components on site.

Cut the base pieces to length

The top of the base frame should be about ¼ in. above the top of the heating baseboard. In the case shown here, the baseboards are 8 in. high so the studs are 5¼ in. long, allowing 3 in. for the combined thickness of the top and bottom plates.

If you have a power miter saw, use it with a stop block to cut the shorter plates and studs to length as you did the face-frame pieces. The four front and back plates are too long to conveniently use a stop block. So measure and cut these pieces to a layout line. Clamping a piece of scrap in the bench end vise is one convenient way to support long work as you cut **(1)**. If you don't have a power miter saw, cut all the pieces to layout lines using a circular saw.

Lay out the stud positions

The four short frame sections get a stud on each end and one centered along the length of the plates. The front and rear frame sections get a stud on each end and one stud centered between each face frame mid stile. The drawing "Base Plan View" on p. 92 shows the stud locations for this window seat.

TIP A sawblade's teeth have an alternating offset—one tooth cuts slightly to the left, the next tooth slightly to the right. To align the blade for a precise cut to the right of a line, make sure a left-offset tooth is touching the line as shown in the photo. Conversely, when cutting to the left of the line, a right-offset tooth should touch the line.

1 **CUT THE PIECES FOR THE BASE TO LENGTH.** Clamping a block of wood into the bench end vise is a convenient way to support the long plates as you cut them to length. If you don't have an end vise, just rip a piece of scrap to width to match the height of your saw platform and clamp it across the bench.

2 **LAY OUT THE STUD POSITIONS.** Clamp the long plates together to mark where the studs will be located.

3 **ASSEMBLE THE BASE FRAME MEMBERS. Use 2½-in. deck screws to attach the plates to the studs.**

Clamp the eight short plates together to lay out the position of their center studs at the same time. Then use a square to transfer these lines to one face of each plate. Draw Xs to indicate the stud side of the line. Now clamp the four front and back plates together to lay out the positions of the mid studs in the same way **(2)** (p. 85). You can place the face frame on the bench as you do this to check that the front and rear studs will fall behind the face frame mid stiles.

Use 2½-in. deck screws to attach the studs to the plates. Use a clamp to help keep everything squarely aligned as you drive the screws **(3)**.

Cut the Drawer Box Base and Seat Board

At this point, the front face frame and side panels are assembled, as are the four sides of the base frame and the two center supports. The next step is to cut two pieces of ¾-in. plywood to the same size. One piece will be the drawer box base that will cover the base frame and center supports. The other piece will be the seat board that supports the seat.

The drawer box base and seat board are both cut from one sheet of ¾-in. plywood. Have your lumberyard or home center rip the sheet into two 2-ft. x 8 ft. pieces,

or make a rough-rip yourself as shown in "Rough-Ripping Plywood" on p. 21.

Shorter pieces are easier to maneuver through the tablesaw, so crosscut the plywood to length before ripping it to final width. Because the drawer box base and the seat board are the same size, you can cut them together using the circular saw with the crosscutting jig **(1)**. Set a piece of sacrificial plywood down on the bench, then place both pieces on top, good face down, and align the three factory edges. Clamp the three pieces to both sides of the bench. Use a square to draw the cutline, place the jig's base to the line, and clamp the jig to the plywood and the bench. Add the thickness of the jig base plus half the thickness of the sacrificial piece plus 1½ in. for combined thickness of the workpieces. Set your saw to this depth and make the cut.

Now rip the plywood to final width. Set the tablesaw rip fence 23¼ in. from the blade. Use roller stands or an out-feed table or have a helper on hand to support the plywood as it comes off the saw.

Make Installation Gauges Now

During on-site installation, you'll need to use several gauge pieces. Now is a good time to make them. Label each piece with its purpose as you cut it. The first three listed here should be about 20 in. long.

- To gauge the height of the drawer slides, ¾-in. x 1½-in. pine or plywood
- To gauge the space at the drawer bottoms, two pieces ³⁄₁₆-in. x ¾-in. pine
- To gauge the heights of slide support spacers, ¾-in. x 3-in. plywood (this gauge will also be used to assemble the spacers to the slide support panels)

Additionally, from a piece of ¾-in. pine or plywood about 17 in. long, make one each at the following widths to position false draw fronts on the face frame: 1¾ in., 1¼ in., and 1 in.

1 **CUT THE DRAWER BOX BASE AND SEAT BOARD TO LENGTH.** Use the crosscutting jig to cut both pieces at the same time.

Make the Drawer Slide Supports and Spacers

The drawer-slide supports provide a mounting surface for the slides that is flush to the inside of the face-frame drawer openings. They also bear on the frame below to support the seat. They are cut ⅛ in. shorter than the side panels to allow for any irregularities in the wall. Rip the slide-support parts to the dimensions listed in "What You'll Need." Use the miter gauge on the tablesaw to crosscut the support panels to length **(1)** (below).

1 **CUT THE SLIDE-SUPPORT PANELS TO LENGTH.** The panels are a bit too wide to cut with most miter saws, but you can easily cut them to width using the miter gauge on the tablesaw.

2 **CHECK FOR FLUSH. Sandwich a test rip between two scraps of the plywood you used for the slide-support panels to make sure your spacers will bring the panels flush to both sides of the mid rails.**

3 **NAIL SPACERS TO THE SLIDE-SUPPORT PANELS. Use a 3-in.-wide installation gauge to quickly and easily position the spacers on two of the slide-support panels.**

Next cut the spacers. These pieces bring the slide-support panels flush with the face-frame drawer openings. Theoretically, the spacers should be 1 in. wide, but they may need to be slightly wider because the support panel plywood might be slightly less than ¾ in. thick. To get exactly the right width, rip a 1-in.-wide scrap piece on the tablesaw and clamp it between two scraps of the plywood you used to make the slide supports **(2)**. Place this assembly on the inside of the face frame to check if it is flush to both sides of a mid stile. If it is not, adjust the tablesaw fence until you rip a scrap of the perfect width.

Use the tablesaw with miter gauge or a power miter saw to crosscut plywood to length for the spacers. Then rip the spacers to width on the tablesaw.

Assemble the spacers to two slide-support panels

The two outer slide supports have only one panel each and will be assembled on site: For these, spacers will be nailed to the inside of the side panels and then the slide support panels will be nailed to the spacers. The two mid slide-supports have a panel on each side—for those, it's easiest to attach spacers to one panel now. Then, on site, you'll nail through the bottom spacer into the drawer space base and then attach the other drawer-slide panel to the spacers.

Use the 3-in.-wide slide-support spacer gauge described in "Make Installation Gauges Now" on p. 86 to gauge the positions of the spacers on the support panels. (It's quicker and easier to use the gauge rather than measuring each

one.) Use glue and 4d finishing nails to attach three spacers each to two support panels **(3)**. Remember to bring the 3-in. gauge piece on site to position the side spacers. Write "spacer" on the guide piece so you will know what it is for.

Make the Drawer Parts

The drawer boxes need to be exactly 1 in. narrower than the drawer openings to properly fit the slides. In theory, this means the drawer fronts and backs should be 2½ in. shorter than the opening, allowing 1½ in. for the combined thickness of the drawer sides. However, before you cut the back and front pieces, check the thickness of the drawer-side stock. The stock used here was actually ²⁵/₃₂ in. thick, so we subtracted an extra ¹/₁₆ in. from the length of the fronts and backs, making these pieces 21³/₁₆ in. long to compensate for the combined extra thickness of the sides. This resulted in drawer boxes that are exactly 22¾ in. wide.

Make the drawer bottoms

Use the tablesaw to rip the drawer bottoms to ¹³/₁₆ in. narrower than the drawers. Then use the rip fence to crosscut the pieces to ⅜ in. shorter than the drawer length.

Cut the dadoes for the drawer bottom

The drawer sides and fronts get a ½-in.-wide x ⅜-in.-deep dado to hold the bottom in place. The quickest way

1 SET THE BLADE HEIGHT FOR THE DADOES. Use a combination square set to ³⁄₈ in. to set the height of the tablesaw blade for the dado that will hold the drawer bottom.

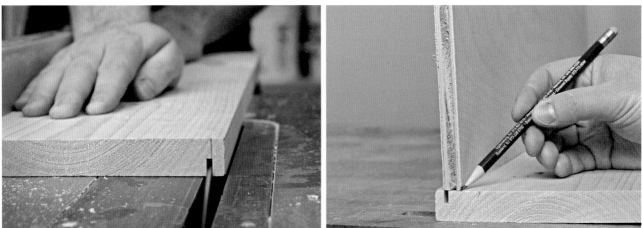

2 MAKE THE FIRST DADO PASS. Be sure to cut to the fence side of your layout line when you make the cut that will define the bottom of the dadoes that will receive the drawer bottoms.

3 LAY OUT THE DADO WIDTH. Use a drawer bottom to locate the top of the dado on a drawer side.

TIP Check the length of the openings on the face frame—if they vary slightly from those listed in "What You'll Need," you'll have to adjust the length of the drawer backs and fronts to fit.

to make these dadoes is with several passes on the tablesaw. Start by using a combination square to set the blade height to ³⁄₈ in. **(1)**.

The dadoes will be ¼ in. from the bottom of the drawer side and front. Before making the first dado pass, mark a line ¼ in. from the bottom edge of one drawer side and set the fence so that the blade will cut to the fence side of this line **(2)**. Make this cut on a piece of scrap and use a combination square to check its depth. Readjust the blade as necessary. When the depth is right, make this cut on all the sides and all three fronts.

To lay out the dado width, place a drawer side on the bench. Align a piece of the drawer bottom plywood to the first cut and use it to scribe the dado width **(3)**.

Now set the fence so that the blade will cut inside the dado as shown in photo 5 on p. 90, and make another pass on all the sides and both fronts. Move the fence to make a cut that slightly overlaps the one you just made and run the pieces through again. Do this two or three more times until the dadoes are complete. If necessary, clean out the bottom of the dadoes with a chisel.

5 **COMPLETE THE DADOES.** After making passes that define both sides of the dadoes, reset the fence for overlapping cuts until you have removed all the waste.

6 **ASSEMBLE THE DRAWER BOXES.** Glue and clamp the drawer front and back between the sides, then drive in the pocket screws.

Assemble the drawer boxes

The boxes are assembled with glue and pocket screws driven through the outside of the front and back where they won't be seen. Drill four pocket holes for each joint. On the front pieces, space the pockets approximately evenly between the dado and the top edge. Space them evenly on the back pieces.

Put glue on the ends of the drawer back and front and clamp them between the sides with the dadoes up. Make sure the parts are flush on the bottom and sides as you drive the pocket screws **(6)**.

Slide the drawer bottoms into the dadoes and secure each with three 1¼-in. screws into the back **(7)**. Sand the boxes, rounding over the top edges of the sides.

DRAWER CONSTRUCTION

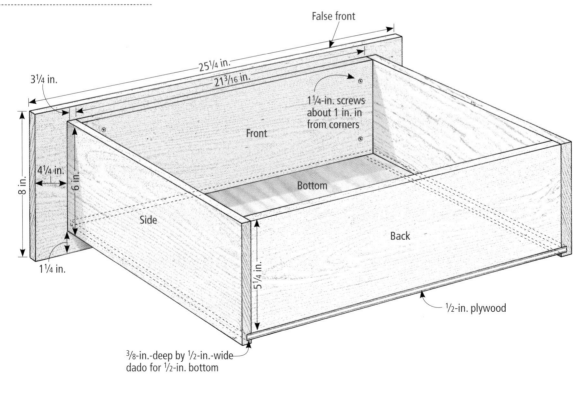

False front

25¼ in.

21³⁄₁₆ in.

3¼ in.

1¼-in. screws about 1 in. in from corners

Front

8 in.

4¼ in.

6 in.

Side

Bottom

Back

1¼ in.

5¼ in.

½-in. plywood

⅜-in.-deep by ½-in.-wide dado for ½-in. bottom

7 **INSTALL THE BOTTOMS.** Slide the drawer bottoms into place and secure each with three 1¼-in. screws driven into the back.

Assemble the Base on Site

With the drawer boxes and other components assembled, it's time to start building the window seat on site. For our installation, the first step was to scribe and cut the notches on the side frames to accommodate the baseboard heater.

Set the rear base frame section into place centered under the window. Now put a side frame atop the baseboard heater and use a square to mark the baseboard's depth on the frame **(1)**. Then place the side frame on the floor to mark the heater's height. Use the marks to draw a square notch, then cut the notch with a sabersaw.

Place the rear base frame section against the baseboard heater. Check it for level and shim if necessary. Then secure the frame to the floor with 2½-in. deck screws staggered across the width every 12 in. or so. Level and, if necessary, shim the short base frames and secure each to the rear base frame with two screws **(2)**. Position them as shown in the drawing "Base Plan View "on p. 92.

TIP Framing lumber is not always perfectly straight. Clamping a joint before driving screws can help pull joints tightly together.

1 **SCRIBE AND CUT THE NOTCHES ON THE SIDE FRAME.** Place the side frame against the baseboard heater to scribe the depth of the notch as shown here. Then put the panel on the floor to scribe the notch height.

2 **INSTALL THE BASE FRAME.** Assemble the base frame sections with screws into the floor and adjoining studs. Shim as necessary to level the assembly.

BASE PLAN VIEW

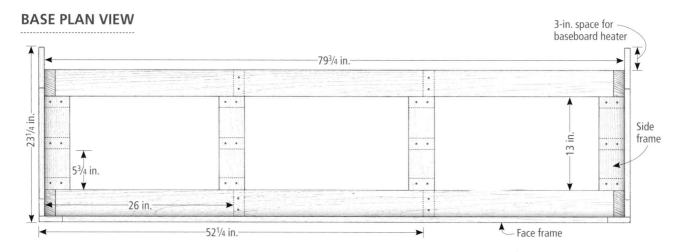

3-in. space for baseboard heater

79¾ in.

23¼ in.

5¾ in.

26 in.

13 in.

Side frame

52¼ in.

Face frame

DRAWER BOX PLAN VIEW WITHOUT SEAT

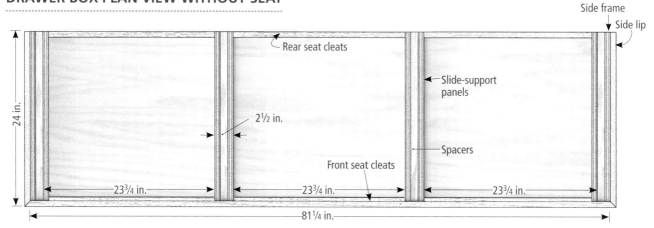

Side frame

Side lip

Rear seat cleats

Slide-support panels

24 in.

2½ in.

Spacers

Front seat cleats

23¾ in.

23¾ in.

23¾ in.

81¼ in.

3 **INSULATE THE BASE FRAME.** Cut three pieces of rigid-foam insulation to fit the base frame and seal them with foil tape.

4 **ATTACH THE DRAWER BOX BASE.** Secure the base with 1¼-in. screws into the framing every 6 in. or so.

The space between the floor and the drawer space base needs to be insulated so that all the warm air from the baseboard heater will be forced out into the room and not up into the drawers. Use a utility knife to scribe and cut pieces of 1-in. foil-faced rigid foam to friction-fit in the three base frame sections **(3)**. Seal them in place with cold-weather foil tape. Be sure to place the shinier side of the insulation down to better reflect the heat away from the drawer space.

Put the drawer box base in place and use a framing square to lay out the approximate centers of the rear base frame and short base frames. Then secure the plywood with 1¼-in. screws about every 6 in **(4)**.

Assemble the Drawer Box

With a solid platform installed, the window seat is finally beginning to take shape. Next, we need to assemble the side frames and face frames in preparation for installing the drawer boxes.

Install the side panels and face frame

Level the side frames and attach them to the base with 4d nails spaced about 6 in. apart. For stronger connections, drive the nails through the stiles and bottom rails, which are thicker than the side panels. Then tack-nail the face frame in place in case you need to pull a nail to make an adjustment **(1)**. Start by attaching the face frame to the edges of the side frames. Then tack-nail the face frame mid rails, keeping the mid rails flush with the top of the plywood drawer box base. Once you've checked that everything aligns correctly, install and set nails about every 12 in. along the bottom and mid rail and all the stiles.

1 **TEST-FIT THE FACE FRAME.** Tack-nail the face frame to the side frames and flush to the top of the drawer box base to make sure everything is properly positioned before you install and set all the nails.

2 **INSTALL A SLIDE-SUPPORT BOTTOM SPACER.** Glue and nail a spacer to the side frame and then down into the drawer box base.

Install the spacers and slide-support panels

Begin installing the slide-support spacers inside either of the side panels. Apply glue to one of the bottom spacers, place it down on the drawer box base, and nail it into the side stiles and then the drawer box base with 4d nails **(2)** (p. 93).

Use the 3-in.-wide spacer gauge you prepared in the shop to position the middle spacer, then glue and nail it to the side panel **(3)**. Now place the spacer gauge on the middle spacer to position the top spacer before gluing and nailing it into place. Repeat this process for the spacers on the side panel at the other end.

3 **INSTALL THE REMAINING SPACERS. Use the 3-in. spacer gauge to position the remaining two spacers as you glue and nail them to the side frame.**

4 **PREPARE TO INSTALL THE SLIDE SUPPORT. Put glue on the spacers before nailing the slide-support panel in place.**

5 **INSTALL THE MID-SLIDE SUPPORTS. Attach the mid-slide support assembly to the drawer box base, then glue and nail the panel to the spacers before nailing the face frame to the assembly.**

6 **INSTALL THE REAR SEAT CLEATS. After attaching a rear seat cleat with construction adhesive, drive in a couple of screws to keep the cleat from slipping while the adhesive sets.**

Put glue on the edges of the three spacers, then nail the side slide panels in place **(4)**. Assemble the slide support on the other end in the same way.

Now you're ready to install the mid-slide support assemblies that you made earlier. Apply glue to the bottom of one of the assemblies and put it in place flush to one side of the face-frame drawer opening. Put the rear seat cleat against the wall as a spacer to help keep the assembly square to the face frame as you nail it to the plywood base **(5)**. Glue and nail the panel in place at the other side of the slide support, then nail the face frame to the support.

Install the rear seat cleats

The rear seat cleats provide attachment for the back of the seat board. Use construction adhesive to install a cleat flush to the top of the slide-support panels **(6)**. Drive two 1¼-in. screws into the drywall just to keep the cleats from sliding down until the adhesive sets. Install the other mid-slide support and the remaining two seat cleats.

Dealing with Electrical Outlets

If there is an electrical outlet on the wall where your window seat will be, you can leave it there as long as it is accessible by removing a drawer. Simply use a sabersaw to notch a rear seat cleat around the outlet.

Install the Drawers

Next up, it's time to install the three drawer boxes. Here, we'll use the gauges we cut earlier to simplify the installation.

Attach the drawer slides

Set a combination square to ⁷⁄₁₆ in. and use it to draw vertical lines on the stiles inside the drawer openings (for aligning the front screw hole). Place the 1½-in.-wide slide height gauge (see "Make Installation Gauges Now" on p. 86) against a slide support and put a slide on top **(1)**. Pull the slide open until you can see the front-most oval hole through the small square opening. Center that hole over the vertical line you drew on the stile and trace its position. Trace the position of the rear-most oval hole. Predrill those holes with a ³⁄₃₂-in. bit, then attach the slide with two of the screws provided.

1 **PREPARE TO ATTACH THE DRAWER SLIDES TO THE SLIDE SUPPORTS. With the slide on the height gauge, mark the position of the first two attachment screws.**

ATTACH THE SLIDES TO THE DRAWERS. With the drawer raised on the scrap-wood gauges, align the slide to the line ⅛ in. from the front of the drawer and drive a screw into the cam adjuster.

FINISH DRAWER ATTACHMENT. With the rear of the drawer still supported by the scrap-wood gauges, install screws in the oval hole on each side of the drawer.

Now prepare to attach the slides at the front of the drawers. Use a combination square to draw vertical lines on the sides of the drawers, ⅛ in. from the front. Put a drawer in its opening with one of the ³⁄₁₆-in.-thick gauges under each side and extend the drawer out about halfway. Pull the slide out until it reaches the vertical line, and press down on the back of the drawer to make sure it is flat against the gauges. Then drive one of the provided screws through the slide's cam adjuster located at the front of the slide **(2)**. Do this for the other side of the drawer as well.

To finish attaching the drawers, pull the slide most of the way out with the sides still resting on the gauges and install screws in the oval holes at the back of the slide **(3)**. Remove the gauges and close the drawers. Adjust the cams if necessary to create an even gap between the drawers and mid rails. When completely closed, the drawer fronts will be about ⅛ in. proud of the face frame. Now open the drawers and install the screws provided into all the small round holes in the slides.

Install the front seat cleats

The front seat cleats provide attachment for the front of the seat board. Put glue on the front cleats and use 1¼-in. screws to attach them to the inside of the face frame flush to the tops of the slide supports **(4)**.

4 **ATTACH THE FRONT SEAT CLEATS.** Glue and screw the front seat cleats to the face frame flush to the tops of the slide-support panels.

Install the Seat Lips

The 1½-in.-wide lip wraps around the top of the window seat and protrudes ¾ in. above the seat board to hold the cushion in place. Begin by installing one of the two side lips.

Hold stock for the side lip against one side of the window seat and make a notch with a utility knife to locate a 45° miter cut **(1)**. Make the cut with a miter saw. Set a combination square to ¾ in. and use it to scribe a line down the length of the stock. Apply glue to one side of the line and put the piece in place with the line at the top edge of the side frame. Attach the side lip with 3d finish nails.

Cut a 45° angle on one end of the front-lip stock and clamp it in place flush to the top of the face frame and meeting the installed side lip. Notch and cut the 45° angle on the other end **(2)**. Remove the front lip and use the combination square set to ¾ in. to draw a line along the length of the piece. Fit, cut, and install a piece for the other side lip. Then glue and nail the front lip in place.

Sand the lip, rounding all edges. Then apply finish to the window seat and the false drawer fronts. It's also a good idea to prefinish the shoe molding.

1 **MARK THE SIDE LIP TO LENGTH.** Use a utility knife to mark where the side lip will meet the face frame.

2 **MARK THE FRONT LIP TO LENGTH.** Clamp the front lip in place against the first side lip to mark the miter cut on the other end.

Install the False Drawer Fronts, Seat, and Shoe Molding

False drawer fronts are the only part of the drawers that are visible when the drawers are closed. They hide the actual fronts of the drawer boxes. The first step is to attach the drawer pulls to the false drawer fronts. Next, with the drawer boxes installed on their slides, it will be easy to use spacers against the face frame to align the false fronts as you attach them to the front of the drawer boxes. Then you'll install the seat board and finally the shoe molding that wraps around the bottom of the window seat, covering any gaps and providing a finished look.

Attach the drawer pulls

Working from the back of the false drawer fronts, lay out and drill holes to center the drawer pulls. Then use a ⅜-in. bit to drill a counterbore so the screws for the pulls will be flush or a little below the back surface of the false fronts **(1)**.

Install the false drawer fronts

You'll use the gauge blocks you prepared in the shop to position the drawer fronts on the face frames. First, clamp the 1¼-in. guide block under the seat lip of the left drawer. Have a helper hold the 1¾-in. gauge block against the left stile, flush to the corner, while holding the false drawer front in place against the two blocks and the face frame **(2)**. While the helper holds the false front in position, counterbore holes for four 1¼-in. screws, one into each inside corner of the drawer front (see the "Drawer Construction" drawing on p. 90). Repeat this process to attach the right false front.

1 **LAY OUT AND DRILL HOLES FOR THE DRAWER PULLS.** Use a ⅜-in.-dia. bit to slightly counterbore the holes for the drawer pulls so that the false fronts will be flat against the drawer fronts.

2 **INSTALL THE LEFT AND RIGHT FALSE DRAWER FRONTS.** Have a helper hold spacer blocks along the outside and top of the false front while you drill attachment holes.

To install the center false drawer front, first clamp the 1¼-in. spacer above the front. Put the 1-in. spacer against the left false front, set the center false front against it, and attach the center false front to the drawer with four screws in counterbored holes through the inside of the drawer **(3)**.

Install the seat board and shoe molding

Draw lines on the seat board to indicate the approximate centers of the two inside drawer slide supports. Put the board in place and secure it to the supports and perimeter cleats with 1¼-in. screws in counterbored holes **(4)**.

Use the same approach for fitting the shoe molding as you used for the seat lip. Notch, cut, and install shoe molding for one side and install it with 4d finish nails **(5)**. Then cut a 45° angle on the front shoe molding and notch and cut it to fit on the other end. Cut and fit the other side, then nail the front and side pieces into place.

3 **INSTALL THE CENTER FALSE DRAWER FRONT. Use the 1-in. block to gauge the space between the** center false front and the outside false fronts.

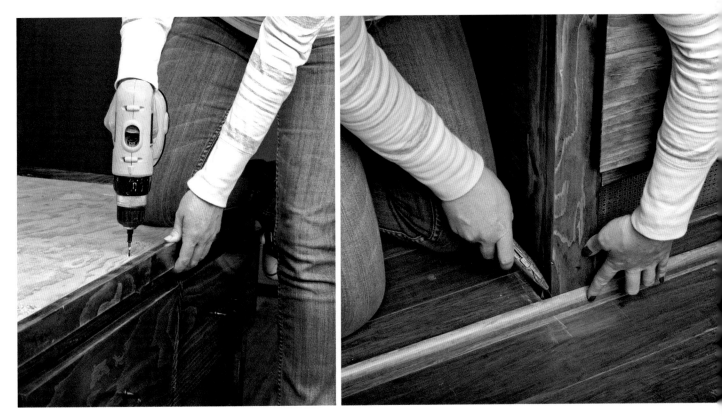

4 **INSTALL THE SEAT BOARD. Counterbore holes for the 1¼-in. screws that will attach the seat board.**

5 **INSTALL THE SHOE MOLDING. Scribe and cut shoe molding to fit around the bottom of the** window seat.

CHAPTER FOUR

THE KITCHEN

PERHAPS YOU CRAVE MORE STORAGE
for your little galley kitchen in an apartment.
Or maybe you have a big country kitchen
with runways for countertops and plenty
of cabinets but you don't have the *right*
storage. For most of us, it's a combination—
our kitchens need more of the right kinds
of storage.

The good news is that you can add convenient and efficient storage to
virtually any kitchen without adding a single cabinet. If counter space is
at a premium, take a look at the Toaster Caddy/Breadbox project that lets
you store your toaster and bread in one small footprint. Or free up counter
space by building the simple wall-mounted Spice Rack that fits neatly on
the backsplash. Need more counter space, drawers, and shelves? Consider
building the Rolling Kitchen Cart. This versatile cart is big enough to serve
as a central island. Or, thanks to locking wheels, you can tuck it into a corner
and roll it out to a convenient spot when you need more counter space.

And, of course, there is an entire industry devoted to increasing the
efficiency of kitchen storage. Drawer dividers of every imaginable size and
configuration, lazy Susans, appliance garages, door shelves—if you can
think of it, somebody is manufacturing it. Some of the major companies are
listed in Resources on p. 230.

ROLLING KITCHEN CART

With two drawers, two shelves, and a solid maple top, this rolling kitchen cart is a versatile way to add storage and work surface to your kitchen. You can even roll it into the dining room when you need an extra serving surface. The cart shown here was given a black paint job to highlight the solid maple top and drawer fronts that complement it.

There are lots of steps involved in building this project, but there's no complicated joinery or advanced skills required. The legs are connected to the aprons and face frame with simple biscuit joints. The drawers are quickly assembled with pocket screws and are easy to fit, thanks to forgivingly adjustable drawer slides and false fronts that overlap the face frame. To make the project even more home-shop friendly, the maple top comes precut to size and prefinished so you need only attach it to the cart. Take your time and enjoy the process. You'll be rewarded with a handsome, high-quality piece of furniture you'll be proud to say you made yourself.

WHAT YOU'LL NEED

CART

• 4 legs	2½ in. × 2½ in. × 30½ in., poplar
• 1 apron	¾ in. × 8 in. × 29 in., clear pine
• 2 aprons	¾ in. × 8 in. × 18 in., clear pine
• 2 stiles	¾ in. × 1½ in. × 8 in., clear pine
• 1 stile	¾ in. × 1½ in. × 5 in., clear pine
• 2 rails	¾ in. × 1½ in. × 26 in., clear pine
• 1 slide cleat	¾ in. × 1½ in. × 29 in., pine
• 2 shelves	¾ in. × 20 in. × 31 in., birch plywood
• 8 shelf cleats	¾ in. × ¾ in. × 1¾ in., pine

- 8 shelf cleats   ¾ in. × ¾ in. × 1 in., pine
- 4 shelf faces   ¾ in. × 1⅝ in. × 18 in., clear pine
- 4 shelf faces   ¾ in. × 1⅝ in. × 29 in., clear pine

DRAWERS AND COUNTERTOP

- 4 drawer sides   ¾ in. × 4¾ in. × 18 in., pine
- 2 drawer fronts   ¾ in. × 4¾ in. × 10½ in., pine
- 2 drawer backs   ¾ in. × 4 in. × 10½ in., pine
- 2 drawer false fronts   ¾ in. × 6½ in. × 13¼ in., maple
- 2 drawer bottoms   ½ in. × 11¼ in. × 18⁵⁄₁₆ in., birch plywood
- 1 tabletop   1½ in. × 25 in. × 36 in., prefinished, precut solid maple (such as Grizzly® H9687)

HARDWARE AND FASTENERS

- Wood glue
- #20 joinery biscuits
- 1¼-in. pocket-hole screws
- 4 #8 wood screws, ⅜ in.
- 10 all-purpose screws, 1¼ in.
- 2 Accuride model 1029 19-in. center-mount slides
- 2 drawer knobs
- 12 tabletop fasteners
- 4 locking wheels with ⅜-in.-dia. threaded stem and total height of 4 in. (such as item #350-75-BEBL-BL-TS-NB from CoolCasters.com)

Cut the Cart Parts

Begin by ripping stock for the two rails and three stiles on a tablesaw to the dimensions listed in "What You'll Need." Then cut these parts to length with a power or hand miter saw using a stop to quickly and accurately cut pieces of the same length (see "Making and Using a Stop Block" on p. 80). The legs are made of poplar. Sold as 3x3s, this stock is actually 2½ in. x 2½ in., so you need only cut it to the lengths listed using a miter saw with a stop **(1)**.

TIP With its greenish cast, poplar isn't the prettiest wood, but it's very stable and takes paint well. At home centers, you may find poplar 3x3s made of glued-up pieces. These are less likely to warp than lumber cut from one piece, so they make excellent legs for this cart.

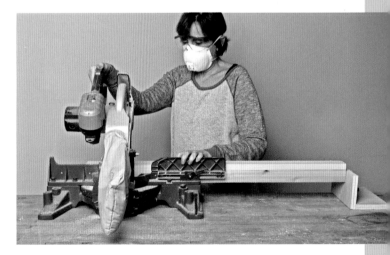

1 **CUT THE LEGS TO LENGTH.** Clamp the miter saw and a stop to the bench to ensure that the legs are all exactly the same length.

ROLLING KITCHEN CART

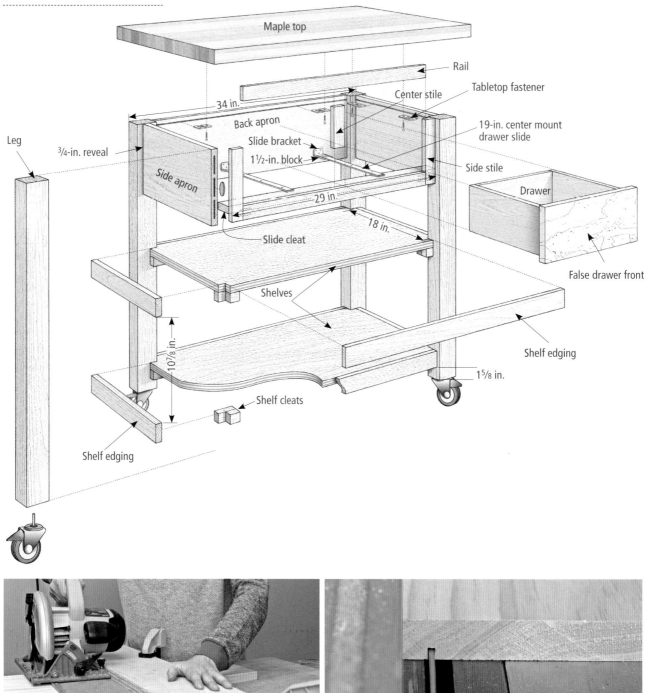

Maple top

Rail

Tabletop fastener

Center stile

34 in.

Back apron

19-in. center mount
drawer slide

Leg

Slide bracket

1½-in. block

¾-in. reveal

Side stile

Side apron

Drawer

29 in.

18 in.

Slide cleat

False drawer front

Shelves

Shelf edging

10⅞ in.

1⅝ in.

Shelf edging

Shelf cleats

2 CUT THE APRONS. Use a circular saw with the crosscutting jig to cut the side and back aprons to length.

3 CUT GROOVES FOR THE TABLETOP FASTENERS. Make one pass over the tablesaw to cut grooves in the aprons and top rails for the tabletop fasteners.

On the tablesaw, rip stock for the three aprons. The 8-in. aprons are too wide to cut on a miter saw unless you have a sliding model. Instead, use a circular saw with the crosscutting jig (see "Making a Crosscutting Jig" on p. 22) to cut them to length **(2)**. Lay out the cuts: The two side aprons are 18 in. long; the back apron is 29 in. long. Place a sacrificial piece of plywood on your bench and set the saw to cut through the stock and into the sacrificial piece but not your bench. Align the jig to the layout line, make sure it is square, and clamp the jig and workpiece to the bench before making the cut.

Cut grooves for the tabletop fasteners

The tabletop is attached to the cart with S-shaped clips that fit into one-saw-kerf-wide grooves in the top rail and aprons and then get screwed to the bottom of the tabletop. Not only is this an easy method of attachment, but it also protects the tabletop from cracking by allowing it to expand and contract with humidity changes independently of the base.

To make the grooves, raise the blade on the tablesaw to $5/16$ in. and set the fence $7/16$ in. from the blade. With the top edges against the fence, cut a groove on the inside face of the aprons and face frame top rail **(3)**.

Assemble the Face Frame

The face frame for the drawer (made from the two rails and the three stiles you just cut) will be assembled with glue and pocket-hole screws. Set up a pocket-hole jig to make two holes in both ends of each rail and both ends of the center stile **(1)**.

Now attach the rails to the stiles **(2)**. Secure one of the end stiles in a bench vise. Put glue on the end of a rail and clamp it to the stile as shown in the photo below. Make sure the side of the rail is flush with the end of the stile. Secure with two 1¼-in. pocket-hole screws. Attach the other rail the same way, then put the other end stile in the vise and glue and screw the rails to it.

1 **DRILL POCKET HOLES.** Use a jig to make two pocket holes for each face-frame joint.

2 **ATTACH THE RAILS TO THE STILES.** Assemble the face-frame rails to the end stiles with glue and two 1¼-in. pocket screws at each joint.

3 **INSTALL THE CENTER STILE.** Drive pocket screws through the center stile into the rails to complete the face-frame assembly. Note the groove in the top rail to receive the tabletop fasteners.

To install the center stile, first measure across the top and bottom of the face frame and mark the exact center on the inside of both rails. Put the center stile in position

and adjust until both sides are equidistant from the inside of the other stiles. When they are, extend the centerline mark onto the top and bottom of the center stile. Apply glue to the ends of the center stile, put it in position, align the marks, and clamp. Then install the pocket-hole screws on both ends **(3)**.

Make the Leg Joints

You'll use three #20 biscuits for each joint between the three aprons and the legs. The face frame will be joined to the front legs with two #20 biscuits at each joint. Lay out the biscuit lines on the legs as shown in "Biscuit Slot and Shelf Cleat Layouts" below. Use letters to label the legs and to indicate which ends of the aprons or face frame will join them **(1)**.

BISCUIT SLOT AND SHELF CLEAT LAYOUTS

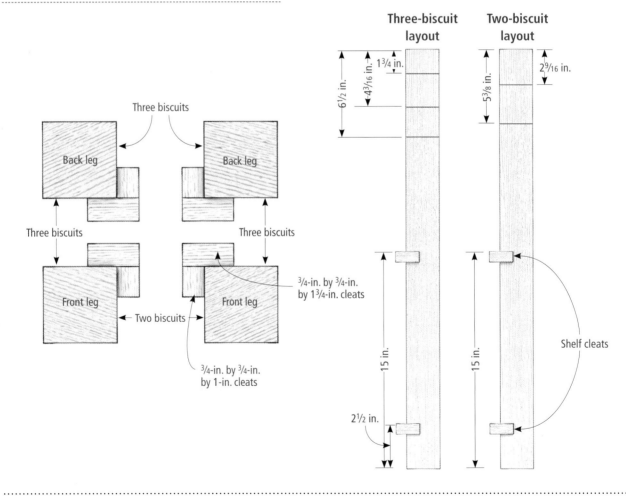

1 **LAY OUT THE SLOT LOCATIONS.** Label the parts to ensure you make the right number of slots in the proper sides of the legs and to avoid confusion during glue-up.

2 **MAKE A DRY RUN.** Orient the parts to double-check that everything lines up before cutting the biscuit slots.

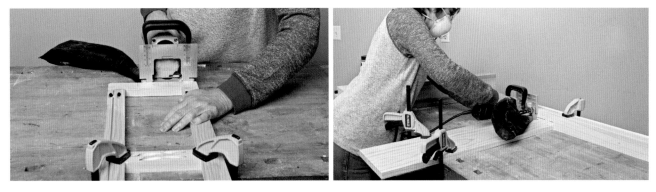

3 **CUT BISCUIT SLOTS IN THE APRONS AND FACE FRAME.** Hold the workpiece flat on the bench as you cut the slots.

4 **CUT BISCUIT SLOTS IN THE LEGS.** Raise the biscuit joiner on a ¾-in. board as you cut the slots in the legs. This will create the ¾-in. reveal between the legs and the aprons and face frame.

Getting the right number of biscuit slots on the correct faces of all the legs can be a little tricky. So once you have all joints labeled, orient the parts to double-check before you cut the slots **(2)**. To do this, place the back apron and the back legs on the bench in their proper orientation. Then put the side aprons in place standing up on the back legs. Now note how the front legs and the face frame will be oriented.

Cut the biscuit slots

Cut the slots in the aprons and face frame first. Remove the fence on the biscuit joiner and set the cutting depth for #20 biscuits. Clamp the workpiece across the bench inside face up **(3)**. As you cut the slots, press down on the work-piece to make sure it is flat on the table.

Now clamp a leg to the bench, making sure that an outside face of the leg is down on the bench. The aprons and face frame are recessed ¾ in. from the outside of the legs. To position the slots in the legs, raise the joiner on a ¾-in.-thick piece of stock clamped to the bench. Press down on the joiner to make sure the piece stays flat on the bench as you cut **(4)**.

1 **CUT THE SHELF CLEATS.** Use a stop to cut the shelf cleats to length on a miter saw. To prevent the little pieces from flying off the saw, be sure to let the blade come to a full stop before raising it after each cut.

2 **LAY OUT THE CLEAT LOCATIONS.** Clamp the legs together to lay out the location of the shelf cleats. Mark a small X at each layout line to make sure you glue the cleats to the correct side of the lines.

Install Shelf Cleats and Glue Up the Base

The two shelves are supported on the cart by shelf cleats attached to the cart legs. Rip stock for the shelf cleats to ¾ in.; you'll need eight cleats that are 1 in. long and another eight that are 1¾ in. long. Clamp a stop to your miter saw to cut 1-in.-long cleats, then reset the stop to cut the 1¾-in.-long cleats **(1)**. If you are using a power miter saw, allow the sawblade to come to a complete stop after each cut before raising the blade. This will prevent the small pieces from flying off the saw.

Lay out cleat locations

Each leg gets two sets of cleats on its inside faces to support the shelves (see "Biscuit Slot and Shelf Cleat Layouts" on p.106). To ensure that the cleats are all at the right heights on the legs, clamp the legs together with an inside face up, making sure they are all flush at top and bottom **(2)**. Then lay out the shelf heights shown in the drawing. Unclamp the legs and transfer the locations to the adjacent inside faces.

At each location, glue and clamp a 1-in.-long cleat in place **(3)**. Use a square to check that it is square to the leg. When the glue sets, remove the clamps and glue the

1¾-in. cleats in place. Clamping the leg overhanging the bench as shown in photo 3 will make it easier to clamp the mid-leg cleats.

Assemble the base

Do a dry test assembly with clamps to make sure everything fits properly. Then put glue in the biscuit slots of the two back legs and in the slots of the back apron. Also put glue on the apron ends. Assemble these pieces upside down with their tops on the bench—the assembly will stand on its own. Assemble the side aprons to the back legs and then to the front legs. Finally, assemble the face frame to the front legs. Squeeze the joints together with clamps as necessary, then remove the clamps.

Tip the base over so the outsides of the back legs are flat on the bench with the apron aligned to one edge of the bench. Apply two clamps—one from each top leg to the bottom of the bench as shown in photo 4 on the facing page. Then add two more clamps from front leg to front leg and from back leg to back leg. Use a framing square to check the top corners for square. Push on the top as necessary to square the base.

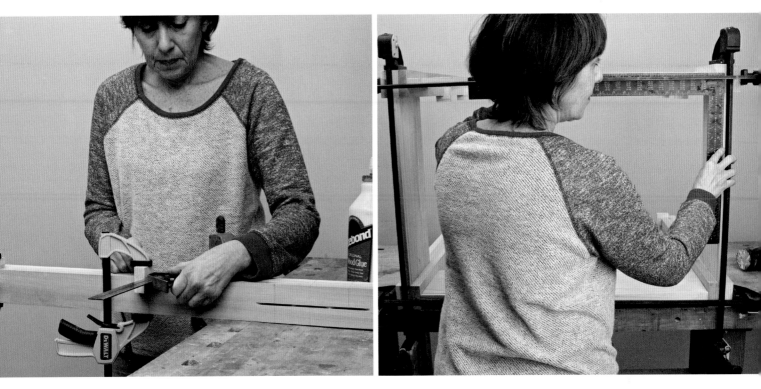

3 **ATTACH THE CLEATS.** Attach each shelf cleat with glue on the X side of the line. Clamp, then check for square.

4 **ASSEMBLE THE BASE.** Clamp from under the bench to ensure the front legs are parallel and to make it easier to square the base during glue-up.

Get Ready for Glue-Up

The key to a successful, panic-free glue-up is to get everything organized in advance. Always do a dry test assembly so you'll know which clamps to use where and exactly how many you will need. Then lay out all the parts with mating joints near each other. And make sure you have everything you need within easy reach. Here's a pre-glue-up checklist for the kitchen cart base:

- Four long clamps
- #20 biscuits
- Tape measure for checking diagonals
- Rubber mallet for tapping joints together
- Framing square for checking that corners are square
- Bucket with water and sponge for cleaning up glue
- Wood glue

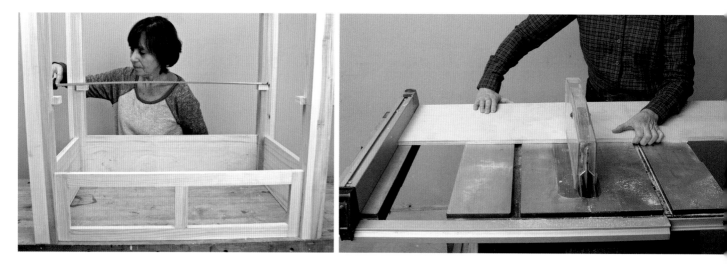

1 MEASURE FOR THE SHELVES. Measure the distance from the outside of opposing cleats to determine the exact dimensions for the shelves.

2 CUT THE SHELVES. Mark the length of the shelves, then cut the plywood with the waste side against the fence. Be sure the offcut workpiece is supported through the whole cut.

Cut and Install the Shelves

The dimensions for the two shelves are given in the "What You'll Need" list, but variations in material dimensions sometimes result in actual dimensions that are slightly different from those listed. Measure across the cleats from side to side and from front to back to get the actual dimensions for the shelves **(1)**.

Each shelf can be made from a 24-in. x 48-in. quarter sheet of plywood, available at home centers. If you are starting from a full sheet of plywood, see "Rough-Ripping Plywood" on p. 21.

Cut the shelves

Rip the shelves to your measured width. On some table-saws, you can extend the fence more than 24 in. from the blade. If your saw can do this, you still won't be able to extend the fence far enough from the blade to make the 31-in.-or-so-wide cut for the shelf length, but you can make this cut by running the waste side of the piece against the fence **(2)**. To do this, mark the length on the edge of the plywood and adjust the fence until the blade meets the waste side of the mark. If you don't have rollers (as shown in photo 2) or a table, have a helper on hand to support the workpiece at the end of the cut. If your table-saw is too small to make this cut, do it with the circular-saw crosscutting jig as you did the aprons.

The shelves are notched at the corners to fit around the inside of the legs. Set a combination square to 1 1/32 in. to lay out corner notches in the shelves (the extra 1/32 in. will ease installation). Cut through the top veneer with a utility knife to prevent splintering **(3)**, then cut the notches with a sabersaw.

Install the shelves

Start with the bottom shelf. Put glue on the top surface of the cleats and the sides of the legs that will meet the shelves. Attach the shelf to the cleats with one clamp across each corner **(4)**. When the glue is set, remove the clamps and glue up the top shelf in the same way.

Install the shelf facing

Rip stock for the shelf facing to 1 5/8 in. wide. For each side of each shelf, cut one end of a facing piece square and scribe it in place for a perfect fit between the legs **(5)**. You'll need two long facings for the front and back edges and two shorter lengths for the sides. Cut the pieces to length with a hand or power miter saw.

One at a time, glue and clamp each shelf facing flush to the top of the shelves **(6)**. If you want to avoid waiting for glue to set, you can install the facing with glue and 4d finish nails.

3 **SCORE AND NOTCH THE SHELVES.** Cut through the veneer with a utility knife before notching the shelves with a sabersaw.

4 **ATTACH THE SHELVES.** Use glue and one clamp at each corner to attach the shelves to the cleats.

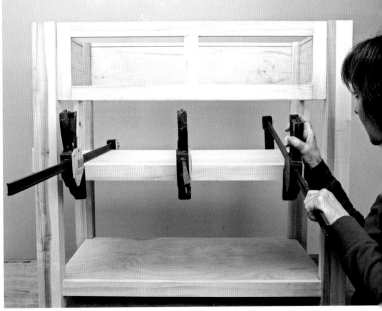

 5 **LAY OUT THE SHELF FACING.** Scribe the shelf facing pieces to fit by butting one end into a leg and notching the other end with a utility knife. Then use a square to extend the notch into a line scribed across the face of the piece.

6 **INSTALL THE SHELF FACING.** Glue and clamp the facing flush to the top of the shelves.

Make the Drawer Parts

In preparation for building and installing the drawers, the first thing you need to do is install the drawer-slide cleat. This cleat provides an attachment surface for the center-mount drawer slides. Cut the cleat to fit between the face frame and the front legs. Put glue on a ¾-in.-thick side and clamp the cleat to the inside of the face frame flush with the bottom of the drawer opening **(1)**.

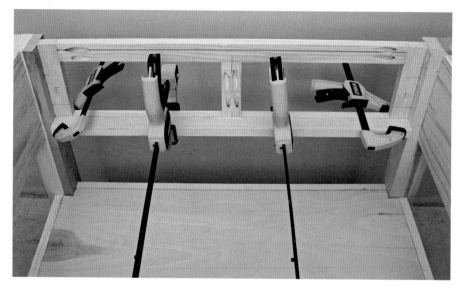

 INSTALL THE DRAWER-SLIDE CLEAT. Glue and clamp the cleat flush to the inside of the face-frame openings.

DRAWER CONSTRUCTION

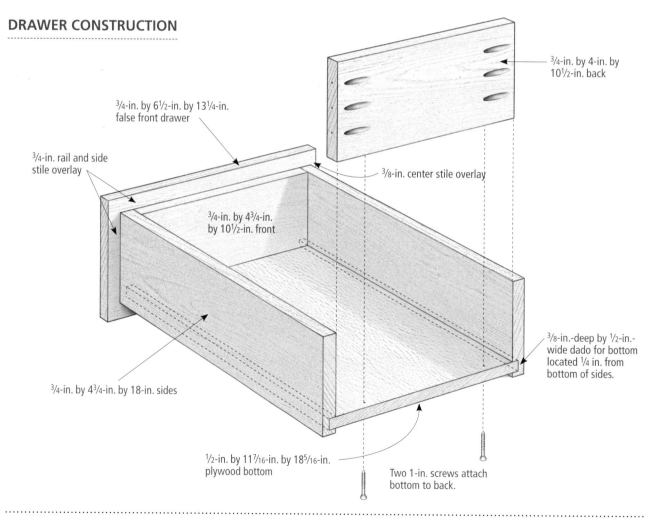

¾-in. by 4-in. by 10½-in. back

¾-in. by 6½-in. by 13¼-in. false front drawer

¾-in. rail and side stile overlay

⅜-in. center stile overlay

¾-in. by 4¾-in. by 10½-in. front

¾-in. by 4¾-in. by 18-in. sides

⅜-in.-deep by ½-in.-wide dado for bottom located ¼ in. from bottom of sides.

½-in. by 11⁷⁄₁₆-in. by 18⁵⁄₁₆-in. plywood bottom

Two 1-in. screws attach bottom to back.

Blade guard removed for clarity.

2 CUT THE DRAWER BOTTOMS. After ripping the bottoms to width, use the rip fence to cut them to length.

3 SET THE BLADE HEIGHT FOR THE DRAWER BOTTOM DADOES. Use a combination square set to $^3/_8$ in. to set the tablesaw blade height for dadoes in the drawer sides and fronts.

Cut the drawer parts

Rip stock to width for the drawer sides and fronts, and then reset the fence to rip the backs to width. Cut these parts to length using a stop on a hand or power miter saw. Rip plywood for the drawer bottoms to length. Then cut them to width using the rip fence on the tablesaw **(2)**.

Cut the dadoes

The drawer sides and fronts get a $^1/_2$-in.-wide x $^3/_8$-in.-deep dado to hold the drawer bottom in place. The quickest way to make these dadoes is with several passes on the tablesaw. Start by using a combination square to set the blade height to $^3/_8$ in. **(3)**.

The slides specified in "What You'll Need" will be mounted under the drawer bottoms—a nice touch because unlike side-mounted slides, you can't see them when you open the drawers. To allow the proper space for the slides, the drawer bottoms must be $^1/_4$ in. up from the bottom of the drawer sides and fronts. Mark a line $^1/_4$ in. from the bottom edge of one drawer side and set the fence so that the blade will cut to the fence side of this line **(4)**. Make this cut on a piece of scrap and use a combination square to check its depth. Readjust the blade if necessary. When the depth is right, make this first dado cut on all the sides and both fronts.

Now lay out the dado width. Clamp a drawer side to the bench, align a drawer bottom to the first cut, and use it to scribe the dado width **(5)** (p. 114). To complete the dadoes, set the fence so that the blade will cut inside the dado and make another pass on all the sides and both

4 MAKE THE FIRST DADO PASS. Make the first pass for the drawer dadoes $^1/_4$ in. from the bottom of the drawer sides and fronts.

fronts **(6)** (p. 114). Move the fence to make a cut that slightly overlaps the one you just made and run the pieces through again. Do this two or three more times until the dadoes are complete.

Assemble the drawer boxes

The boxes are assembled with glue and pocket screws driven through the outside of the front and back where they won't be seen. Drill three pocket holes for each joint. On the front pieces, space the pockets evenly between the dado and the top edge. Space them evenly across the width of the back pieces.

5 **LAY OUT THE DADO WIDTH.** Use a drawer bottom to scribe the width of the dadoes on one drawer side.

6 **COMPLETE THE DADOES.** Set the tablesaw fence to cut the width of the dado before adjusting it three more times to remove the waste.

Put glue on the ends of the drawer back and front and clamp them between the sides with the dadoes up. Make sure the parts are flush on the bottom and sides as you drive the pocket screws **(7)**. Slide the drawer bottom into the dadoes and secure it with two 1¼-in. screws into the back. Sand the boxes, rounding over the top edges of the sides.

Install the Slides

Each slide has three parts: a member that attaches to the drawer, a member that attaches to the case, and a bracket that attaches to the inside of the back apron.

Attach the drawer member

Pull the drawer member out of the cabinet member. Center the drawer member along the length of the underside of the drawer. When you find the exact center, set a combination square so you can use it to make sure the slide stays aligned as you drive a screw at an angle into the front and one down into the back piece **(1)**. Use the screws provided. Although they are not provided, it's a good idea to drive ⅜-in.-long #8 screws into the bottom through the two additional round holes in the drawer slide. Now is the time to sand and paint the frame of the cart.

Locate the case member and attach the bracket

Refer to the drawing "Locating the Drawer Slide Case Member and Bracket" on the facing page. Use the dimensions given in parentheses below as an example; take your

7 **ASSEMBLE THE DRAWER BOXES.** Glue and clamp the drawer front, back, and sides and secure with three pocket screws at each joint.

own measurements in case the dimensions of your base vary slightly. Here is the procedure:
A. Mark the center of the drawer opening (6⅛ in.) across the slide cleat. This line will be used to locate the slide case member.

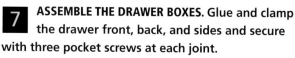

TIP If you are left with a thin sliver after cutting the dadoes, you can quickly zip it out with a chisel.

1 **ATTACH THE DRAWER MEMBER. After screwing the drawer member under the front of the drawer, use a combination square to make sure it is parallel to the sides before screwing it down at the back.**

2 **ATTACH THE BRACKET. Attach the bracket to the back apron with a screw through the slot. Leave the bracket loose enough so you can slide it in the slot to adjust its position if necessary.**

B. Measure from the inside of the nearest front leg to the center of the drawer opening (7⅝ in.) and transfer this measurement to the back apron.

C. Measure from the top of the face frame to the bottom of the drawer opening (6½ in.).

D. Subtract ¹³⁄₁₆ in. from measurement C and mark this distance (5¹¹⁄₁₆ in.) down from the top of the back apron. Locate the bracket-positioning screw where B and D meet. Attach the bracket through its horizontal slot using the screw provided **(2)**. Don't tighten the screw all the way.

3 **ATTACH THE CASE MEMBER. Screw the front of the case member to the slide cleat and make sure it is square before tightening the bracket-positioning screw.**

LOCATING THE DRAWER SLIDE CASE MEMBER AND BRACKET

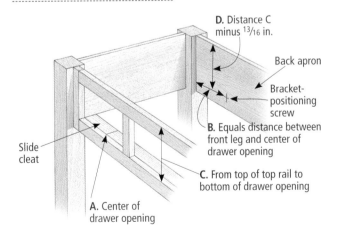

D. Distance C minus ¹³⁄₁₆ in.

Back apron

Bracket-positioning screw

B. Equals distance between front leg and center of drawer opening

C. From top of top rail to bottom of drawer opening

Slide cleat

A. Center of drawer opening

Shellac the Drawers

Oftentimes drawer boxes receive no finish at all. Because this cart will be used in the kitchen, it's a good idea to seal the boxes so they can be cleaned occasionally (there's no need to finish the underside of the bottom).

Don't use polyurethane or other oil-based finish on the drawer boxes. Because drawers are enclosed, the smell of these finishes could linger for a year or more. Shellac, a nontoxic finish that dries quickly without odor, is an excellent choice, either brushed or sprayed from a can.

4 MARK FOR THE SHIMS. Mark the positions of the shims that will support the drawers and keep them from wobbling.

5 INSTALL THE DRAWER SHIMS. Press the drawer shim spikes into the slide cleat.

Attach the case member

Assemble the case member to the rear bracket and extend it flush with the joint between the slide cleat and the face frame. Center it across the opening and drive the screw provided into the slide cleat. Square the slide across the face frame **(3)** (p. 115), then tighten the bracket-positioning screw.

Now install the drawers to check that you have an even gap on both sides. If necessary, remove the drawers and adjust the position of the case member by loosening the screws and moving it in the slotted holes. When the drawer slides are properly positioned, drive one provided screw into one of the round holes in each bracket to fix its position. Then mark the approximate center of each drawer side on the face frame **(4)**.

Each drawer slide comes with two plastic shims for the bottom of the drawer sides to slide along. The shims look like thumb tacks with a short spike and a flat rectangular head. Using the marks you just made as a guide, use your thumb to press the shim spikes into the slide cleat **(5)**.

Make and Install the False Drawer Fronts

The solid maple false drawer fronts are attached to the front of the drawers, overlapping the face frame. You'll attach the false fronts with the drawers installed, which makes it easy to get the false fronts perfectly aligned to the face frame and to each other.

1 PREPARE THE FALSE DRAWER FRONTS FOR INSTALLATION. Clamp ¾-in.-wide scraps against the legs and flush to the bottom of the face frame to position the false fronts. Clamp the false fronts and drawer fronts, and extend the knob holes through the fronts.

2 **ATTACH THE DRAWER FRONTS TO THE FALSE FRONTS. Predrill and countersink four holes through the inside of each drawer front for screws to attach the front to the false front.**

On the tablesaw, rip stock to 6½ in. wide for the false drawer fronts. Use a circular saw with the crosscutting jig to cut two pieces to 13¼ in. wide. Sand the drawer fronts with 80, 120, and then 220 grit, and finish both sides with three coats of wipe-on polyurethane.

With a straightedge positioned across diagonal corners, pencil a light X where the diagonals meet at the center. Drill holes for the knob screws at these locations.

Install the drawers

Clamp ¾-in.-wide pieces of scrap to the face frame against each leg and flush to the bottom of the bottom rail **(1)** (facing page). Set the false fronts in position against the scrap pieces and clamp them to the front of the drawers. This will fix them in position against the face frame. Now extend the holes in the false fronts through the front of the drawers and install the drawer knobs.

Inside the drawers, mark for four screws located about 1 in. from the sides and 1 in. from the top or bottom. Predrill these holes with a countersink bit set to predrill 1⅛ in. deep. Secure each drawer with four 1¼-in. all-purpose screws **(2)** (above).

> **TIP** When installing the false fronts, orient them in the same way they were cut from the board. This way, the grain will flow attractively across the fronts.

Attach the Top and Wheels

The tabletop specified comes cut to size and prefinished. Place the tabletop upside down with a pad beneath to protect the finished top surface. Predrill holes and secure the top with 12 fasteners. Center fasteners across the front, the back, and the sides and place two at each corner **(1)** (below).

The final step is to install the wheels. Use a straightedge to draw diagonal lines across corners to find the center point on the bottom of each leg. Drill a ⅜-in.-dia. hole about 1 in. deep, and tap in the sleeve nut that came with the wheel **(2)** (below). Hand-screw the wheels into the sleeve nuts. If it becomes difficult to screw a wheel all the way down, put a smaller-diameter bit in the drill, insert it through the sleeve nut, and ream out any wood that is obstructing the opening. Have a helper lift the cart onto the wheels. Don't tip the cart up onto the wheels—the sideways pressure might enlarge the holes and loosen the wheels.

1 **INSTALL THE TABLETOP FASTENERS. Put the fasteners into the grooves and screw them into predrilled holes in the bottom of the tabletop.**

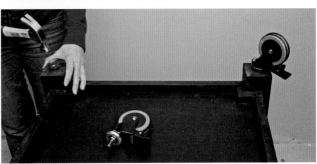

2 **INSTALL THE WHEELS. Tap a sleeve nut into the hole drilled into the bottom of each leg before screwing the wheels in place.**

TOASTER CADDY/ BREADBOX

This simple and handy project saves valuable kitchen counter space by storing bread below the toaster. The one shown here was made for a kitchen with red cabinets and natural-finish butcher-block countertops. The caddy/breadbox is made of birch plywood with a natural wipe-on polyurethane finish—except for the door, which is painted the same red as the cabinets. You can customize your breadbox to fit the décor of your own kitchen—perhaps using oak or cherry plywood to match your cabinets. You can paint the door to match your cabinets or wall color, or you can give it the same finish as the rest of the box.

The top edges of the box are rounded to add a little flair—you can leave them square if you prefer. The project uses birch veneer edging that's easy to apply; the edging comes precoated with an adhesive that you activate with a clothes iron.

WHAT YOU'LL NEED

- All wood parts are ½-in. birch plywood.
- 1 top   7½ in. × 14½ in.
- 1 bottom   7½ in. × 14½ in.
- 2 sides   8 in. × 10 in.
- 1 back   6¾ in. × 14¾ in.
- 1 door   7 in. × 13¹³⁄₁₆ in.
- Veneer edging   1 roll, ¾ in. × 25 ft.
- Wood glue
- 1-in. × 1-in. butt hinges
- 1 magnetic catch
- 1 Pull

Front View

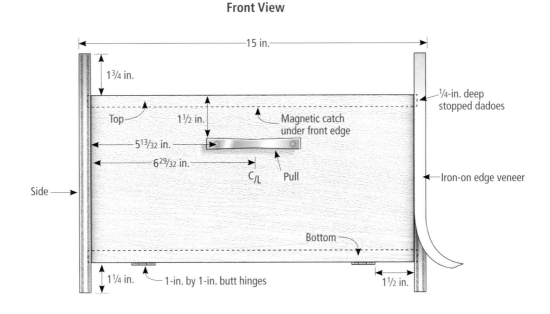

Cut the Parts and Dadoes

As shown in the "Cutting Diagram" on p. 120, you can cut all the parts from one 2-ft. x 4-ft. quarter sheet of ½-in. plywood, available at home centers. Start by ripping a 15-in.-wide piece from the quarter sheet on the table-saw, then make a rough crosscut at 22½ in. This will yield two pieces short enough to safely and easily use the table-

saw fence as shown in the photo to rip the top, bottom, and side pieces to final width **(1)**. You'll cut the door and the back to fit after gluing up the box.

Now lay out cutlines and use the miter gauge on the tablesaw to cut the sides, top, and bottom to final lengths **(2)**. You can also make these cuts with a power miter saw.

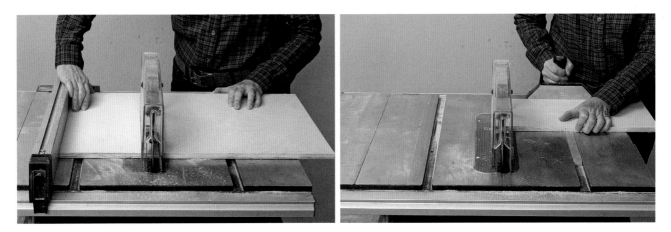

1 **CUT THE TOP, BOTTOM, AND SIDES.** After ripping the quarter sheet of plywood to 15 in. wide, use the rip fence on the tablesaw to cut the parts to final width.

2 **CUT THE PARTS TO FINAL LENGTH.** Mark the boards to length and make the cuts guided by the miter gauge on the tablesaw. These cuts can also be made with a power miter saw.

CUTTING DIAGRAM

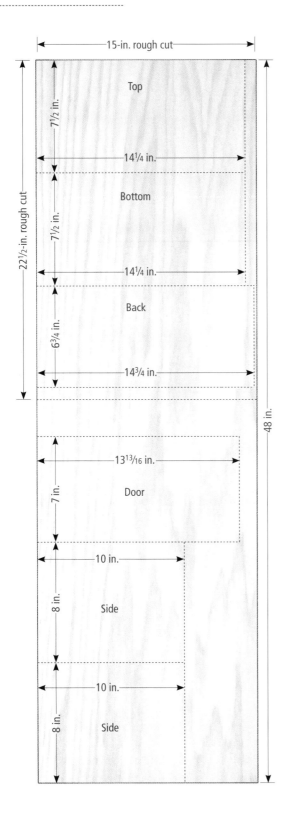

←———15-in. rough cut———→

Top

7½ in.

←——14¼ in.——→

Bottom

7½ in.

←——14¼ in.——→

22½-in. rough cut

Back

6¾ in.

←——14¾ in.——→

Door

7 in.

←—13¹³/₁₆ in.—→

←——10 in.——→

Side

8 in.

←——10 in.——→

Side

8 in.

48 in.

3 **LAY OUT THE DADO CUTS.** After placing the side pieces edge to edge to lay out the dadoes simultaneously, separate the pieces and use a combination square set at ½ in. to lay out stop lines.

Lay out the dadoes

Place the side pieces edge to edge on the bench, flush at the top and bottom so you can lay out the dadoes on both at the same time. Lay out the dadoes as shown in the drawing "Dado and Curve Layouts" below. Set a combination square to ½ in. to lay out the stop lines at the end of the dadoes **(3)**.

TIP Whether you are cutting a piece to length or making dadoes, get in the habit of making an X on the side of the line you will cut or rout.

DADO AND CURVE LAYOUTS

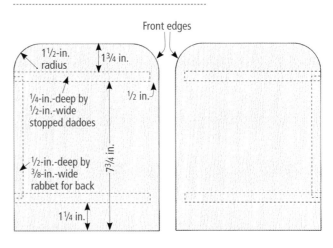

Front edges

1½-in. radius

1¾ in.

¼-in.-deep by ½-in.-wide stopped dadoes

½ in.

½-in.-deep by ⅜-in.-wide rabbet for back

7¾ in.

1¼ in.

4 CUT THE DADOES. Make two passes with the router using the small-parts dado jig to cut snug dadoes.

Cut the dadoes

Most nominally ½-in.-thick plywood is actually slightly thinner, so your dadoes would be loose if you cut them with a ½-in.-dia. router bit. Instead, use the small parts dado jig (see the sidebar on pp. 122–123) with a ¼-in.-dia. straight bit to cut the stopped dadoes in each side piece. Set the bit to cut ¼ in. deep. Slide one side piece in place, aligning a dado layout on the side piece to the positioning dado on the jig. Screw a cleat into place at both sides of the workpiece, then rout the dado in two passes, moving in a clockwise direction and carefully cutting just short of the stop line.

Remove one of the cleats and the first side piece, then put the other side piece in place against the remaining cleat. Replace the second cleat and rout the opposing dado **(4)**. Repeat this procedure to rout the other pair of opposing dadoes.

Clamp each side piece to the bench and use a chisel to square the stopped ends of the dadoes **(5)**.

Lay out the top curves

The top edges of the sides have a 1½-in.-radius curve, which adds a bit of pizzazz to the design. Use a combination square set to 1½ in. to find and mark the points 1½ in. from the top and side of each side piece **(6)**. Set a compass to 1½ in., place it on the point, and draw the curve on each corner.

(Continued on p. 124)

5 CHOP THE DADOES SQUARE. Square the dado stops by striking a chisel with a mallet to chop straight down.

6 LAY OUT THE TOP CURVES. Use a combination square to mark the pivot point, then draw 1½-in.-radius curves at the top of each side.

DADO JIG FOR SMALL PARTS

This jig is designed specifically to cut dadoes in small pieces such as the sides of the Toaster Caddy/Breadbox. The widths and lengths of the base, positioning boards, and fences can vary according to the scrap you have on hand. You'll need the following pieces:

- 1 base   ¾ in. × 16 in. × 24 in., plywood
- 2 positioning boards   ½ in. × 2 in. × 16 in.
- 2 fences   ½ in. × 2 in. × 20 in.
- 2 cleats   ½ in. × 1½ in. × 6 in.

1. To make the jig, first clamp the base to your workbench so it can't shift around. Then use 1-in. all-purpose screws to secure one positioning board across the base, square to the long edges of the base and about 6 in. from one short edge of the base. Set a workpiece—in this case a side piece—against the positioning board with the dado layouts parallel to the long edges of the base. Put the other positioning board against the workpiece and screw it in place as shown in photo **1.** Remove the workpiece.

1. ATTACH THE POSITIONING BOARDS TO THE BASE.

2. ATTACH ONE FENCE.

3. ROUT A DADO IN ONE OF THE POSITIONING BOARDS.

4. MARK THE FINAL DADO WIDTH ON A POSITIONING BOARD.

5. MARK THE POSITION OF THE SECOND FENCE.

SMALL-PARTS DADO JIG

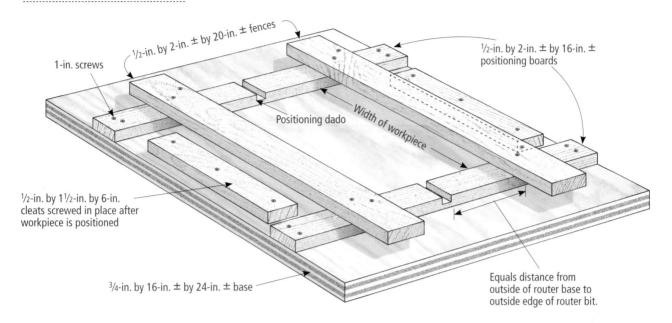

1-in. screws

½-in. by 2-in. ± by 20-in. ± fences

Positioning dado

Width of workpiece

½-in. by 2-in. ± by 16-in. ± positioning boards

½-in. by 1½-in. by 6-in. cleats screwed in place after workpiece is positioned

¾-in. by 16-in. ± by 24-in. ± base

Equals distance from outside of router base to outside edge of router bit.

2. Place one of the fences across the positioning boards, near one edge of the base as shown in photo **2**. Use a square to make sure the fence is perpendicular to both positioning boards, then screw it in place.

3. When you use the jig, you will align the dado layout lines on the workpiece with the positioning dadoes on the jig. This will ensure that you are locating dadoes accurately on the workpiece. Place a ¼-in.-dia. bit in the router and set the depth to ¼ in. With the router base against the fence, rout from left to right to make a dado in one positioning board.

6. WIDEN THE FIRST POSITIONING DADO.

4. To mark the final dado width on the positioning board, you'll need a piece of the nominally ½-in.-thick plywood you used to make the parts. Place this piece on edge, with one face resting against the fence side of the dado you just routed in the positioning board. Use a utility knife to scribe a notch indicating the actual thickness of the piece. Then use a pencil and square to extend the notch across the face of the positioning board.

5. To mark the position of the second fence, first place the router on the marked positioning board as shown in photo **5**. Align the outside of the router bit with the layout line, then use a utility knife to notch where the outer edge of the router base meets the positioning board. Again, use a pencil and square to extend a line from the notch across the face of the positioning board. Now align the inside edge of the second fence to this line. Use a square to make sure this fence is perpendicular to both positioning boards, then screw the fence in place.

6. Run the router from left to right against the second fence to widen the dado in the positioning board. Place a piece of the nominally ½-in. plywood in the dado to make sure it fits snugly. If it is too loose, you can remove the second fence and mark again to reposition it. If it is too wide, you'll need to disassemble the jig and replace the positioning board. If the fit is right, rout a dado in the other positioning board, guiding the router from left to right against one fence and then back against the other. You'll install the cleats when the workpiece is in position.

7 **CUT AND SMOOTH THE TOP CURVES. After cutting the top curves, sand them fair and smooth with a power sander or, as shown, with a piece of sandpaper wrapped around a scrap of wood or plywood.**

Clamp each side to the bench. Use a thin, fine-cutting blade in the sabersaw to cut the top curves on each side piece. Now sand the curves smooth. You can do this most quickly with a power palm sander or orbital sander, but a piece of sandpaper wrapped around a scrap of plywood will do the job, too **(7)**.

Assemble the Box

Now that the sides have been routed and rounded, you are ready to glue up the box and rabbet it to accept the back.

Using two clamps across the top and two across the bottom, test-assemble the box to get your clamps pre-adjusted and to make sure the parts fit together properly. Then put glue in the dadoes and clamp the box together. Check that the sides are square to the top and bottom **(1)**.

Rabbet for the back

The back of the box (which you haven't cut yet) fits into rabbets in the sides, top, and bottom. Put a ³⁄₈-in. piloted rabbeting bit in the router and set the cutting depth to the thickness of the plywood you are using (nominally ½ in.). You'll be leaving an edge that's only ⅛ in. as you cut the rabbet, so you'll need a wider surface to keep the router from tipping. To provide this surface, cut two scraps of 2x4 to fit between the sides of the box and two to fit along the height of the box. Clamp the scraps to the box, making sure they are all flush to the back edges of the box. Secure one front edge in a bench vise and rout the rabbet, moving in a clockwise direction along the inside edges **(2)**.

Use a chisel and mallet to square the corners of the rabbet. Leave the 2x4s in place while you do this; they will prevent the thin walls of the rabbets from breaking as you chop the corners **(3)**.

1 **GLUE UP THE BOX. Assemble the box with glue and four clamps, then check for square.**

2 **RABBET FOR THE BACK. Pieces of 2x4 clamped to the box provide a stable base as you rout the rabbet for the back.**

3 **SQUARE THE RABBETS.** Leave the 2x4s clamped in place as you use a chisel to square the corners of the back rabbet.

4 **INSTALL THE BACK.** Put glue in the rabbets, then secure the back to the box with glue and four clamps.

Install the back

Measure between the rabbets in case you need to adjust the back dimensions from those listed in "What You'll Need." Don't cut the back for a tight fit—you don't want to break the walls of the rabbets. The joint between the back and sides will be covered with birch edge veneer, so slight gaps are not a problem. Install the back with glue and four clamps **(4)**.

Cut the door

Likewise, check the measurements for the door, which fully overlays the top and bottom and fits between the sides. Cut the door $3/16$ in. shorter than the distance between the two sides. The edge veneer is about $1/32$ in. thick, so allowing for veneer on both edges of the door will leave you with a gap of $1/16$ in. on each side.

Freeing Up Counter Space

Manufacturers offer lots of options for freeing up valuable counter real estate in your kitchen. One popular accessory is a shelf for standing mixers. The shelf stows the mixer in a cabinet and is pulled up to counter height for use. The model shown at far left has a spring-loaded counterweight mechanism that makes it easy to pull the shelf and heavy mixer up and down. There's room for a shallow drawer below the mixer, saving even more counter space.

Appliance garages are another way to keep counters clear. Most of these don't use conventional swing-out doors that would obstruct the counter, compromising the space-saving purpose. Some appliance garages have tambour doors that roll up like a roll-top on a desk. The one shown at left has a door that matches the other cabinetry and pulls conveniently up and out of the way.

1 SQUARE THE END OF THE VENEER. Use a sharp utility knife and a combination square to cut the end of the edge veneer square.

2 CUT THE VENEER TO LENGTH FOR THE TOP AND BOTTOM PIECES. Put the veneer in place along the front edge of the top or bottom and mark it for length.

3 INSTALL THE VENEER. Use a piece of aluminum foil or kraft paper under the iron as you press the veneer into place.

4 ROLL OVER THE VENEER. Use a roller to make sure the veneer is adhered along its entire length.

Apply the Edge Veneer

Now you are ready to apply veneer to the exposed plywood edges. The veneer comes in rolls that you can purchase at a hardware store or home center. All you need to apply it are a household iron, a rubber or wooden roller, some aluminum foil or kraft paper, and a utility knife with a fresh blade.

Cut the veneer

First square the end of the edge veneer. Place the end of the veneer along the edge of a straight piece of scrap and use a combination square and utility knife to cut a square edge **(1)**.

Next, cut the veneer to length for the top and bottom pieces. Butt the square edge of the veneer into the side, lay it over a front edge of the top piece, fold it at the other side, and use a utility knife to mark it for length **(2)**. Cut the second end square as you did the first. Now repeat

this process to install a piece of veneer across the front edge of the bottom piece.

Install the veneer

To activate the edge-veneer glue, use a clothes iron on the cotton setting. Put the veneer in place then place a piece of aluminum foil or kraft paper to protect the iron from glue and the veneer from scorching. Press down with the iron. It takes only a few seconds for the glue to activate **(3)**. If you misalign the veneer, just reheat it, then reposition and iron it again.

While the edge veneer is still hot and the foil or paper is still in place, run over the veneer with a roller **(4)**. You can use a rubber roller or a wooden wallpaper-seam roller like the one shown in the photo. Use a scrap of wood to press the veneer into the corners where the roller can't fit.

5 **TRIM THE EDGES.** Trim the veneer with a utility knife, then sand it perfectly flush to the faces of the plywood.

Use a sharp utility knife to trim the edge veneer flush to the top and bottom surfaces **(5)**. Sand perfectly flush with a sanding block or an orbital sander.

Now apply veneer to the bottom edges **(6)**. Cut two pieces of edge veneer to about 9 in. long. Iron it onto the bottom edges of the box with about ½ in. overhanging as shown. Cut the veneer flush to the front and back of the box, then trim and sand the edges.

The next step is to apply veneer to the edges of the sides. Set a combination square to ½ in. and use it to scribe lines around the perimeter of the back. Without cutting it off the roll, run veneer along the layout line at one side with about ½ in. overhanging the bottom, as shown in photo 7. Apply heat to the veneer

6 **VENEER THE BOTTOM EDGES.** Apply veneer to the bottom of the sides, then cut it flush at front and back before trimming it flush to the faces of the sides.

7 **VENEER THE SIDE EDGES.** Activate the glue at the bottom edge of the veneer so it will stay in place as you align the veneer to the layout line and wrap it all the way around the side.

8 **VENEER THE BACK EDGES.** Scribe and cut veneer to fit across the back, then iron it in place along the layout line. Trim off the overhanging edges at the top and bottom of the box.

just at the bottom of the box to hold it in place while you wrap it over the top and round the front of the side piece. Then cut it off about ½ in. long. Iron the veneer in place, then trim it flush to the faces and bottom edges of the side. Apply veneer to the other side in the same way.

Now add veneer across the back of the box **(8)**. Cut the end of the veneer square and put it in place along the line at the top of the back. Scribe and cut it to fit, then iron it in place. When you have done this for both horizontal pieces, use the utility knife to slice them flush to the top and bottom. Sand flush the edges of the veneer.

The final veneering step is to veneer each edge of the door. Cut a piece of veneer to overlap an edge by about ½ in. on each side. Iron the veneer and trim it in place just as you did for the edges of the bottom pieces. Slice flush with a utility knife. When all four edges are veneered, sand flush the edges of the veneer.

Install the Door

The final steps in this project are to install the door, the door pull, and the catch.

Scribe for the hinge mortises

The hinges will be attached to the front edge of the bottom and the inside face of the door as shown in photo 1 on the facing page. These hinges are too small to safely hold in place while you scribe the hinge mortises, so screw them into place before scribing their perimeter. To position the hinges, mark the front edge of the bottom 1½ in.

from the inside of the box on both sides. Predrill and screw the hinges to the box.

Place the door on a piece of ½-in. plywood, and shim the plywood until you can put the hinge leaves flat on the inside face of the door. Position the door equidistant from both sides (you can eyeball this) and clamp the door to the bench. Screw the hinges to the door and the box, then deeply scribe their perimeters **(1)**.

Before you cut the hinge mortises, you need to remove the edge veneer from the mortises in the box. To do this, heat the area with a heat gun or a hair dryer set on high and lift the sections of veneer away with a utility knife **(2)**. Then cut the hinge mortises as described in "Cutting Hinge Mortises" p. 26.

Install the pull and catch

The pull is centered across the width of the door. Start by measuring the distance between the screw holes on your pull—for the pull shown here, that distance is 3 in. To calculate the screw-hole locations, divide the width of the door (here, $13^{13}/_{16}$ in.) by 2 to find the center point across the width ($6^{29}/_{32}$ in.). Subtract 1½ in. (half the distance between screw holes) to find the screw-hole locations ($5^{13}/_{32}$ in.). For this pull, mark for screw holes $5^{13}/_{32}$ in. from each side and 1½ in. down from the top, as shown in the drawing on p. 119.

TIP Choose a pull that extends ¾ in. from the outside face of the door. That way, when the pull is resting on the counter, the inside of the door will be level with the box.

1 **SCRIBE FOR THE HINGE MORTISES. To protect your fingers, screw the hinges in place before scribing for the hinge mortises.**

2 **NOTCH OUT THE VENEER. Before cutting the hinge mortise to final depth, heat the area and lift off the veneer.**

Finally, add a magnetic catch centered under the top, attaching the catch with two of the screws provided. Once the catch is in place, center the metal strike plate on the catch and measure from the center of the hole to the top edge of the box **(3)**. Use this measurement to locate the plate screw hole on the inside of the door. Screw the hinges to the box and the doors and the strike plate to the inside of the door.

> **TIP** Most tape measures don't show increments of $\frac{1}{32}$ in. That's no problem when installing door pulls, which need not be centered so precisely. If your calculations tell you to locate a screw hole $5\frac{13}{32}$ in. from one side of the door, just make your mark between the $5\frac{3}{8}$-in. and $5\frac{7}{16}$-in. marks on your tape.

3 **LOCATE THE STRIKE PLATE. Measure to determine how far the strike plate screw hole will be from the top edge of the door.**

Painting and Finishing

On this breadbox, the sides and face of the door are painted, while the inside of the door has a natural polyurethane finish. Paint and apply finish to the door before installing it. To keep paint off the inside face of the door, apply painter's tape along the perimeter, as shown in the photo at left. Rather than trying to align the tape perfectly, let it overlap the edges and trim the tape flush with a utility knife.

The other surfaces are finished with wipe-on polyurethane, which is also most convenient to apply before you attach the door. (For more, see "Painting and Finishing" on p. 28.)

SPICE RACK

This space-saving spice rack is a snap to build and a great way to keep your spices organized and easily accessible. It consists of 10 pieces of strategically spaced dowels between two boards. The one shown here is sized to be mounted on the backsplash between kitchen cabinets and counter. It has two racks that will hold a total of 16 spice jars that are about 1¾ in. wide.

The beauty of this design is its adaptability. You can make a single-tier rack with 6-in. sides or add another tier with 16-in. sides. You can shorten the dowels or make them as long as 20 in. or so (longer dowels would make assembly unwieldy, however).

The two-tier rack shown here is made with maple sides and poplar dowels. Both components can be of any hardwood you like. There are keyhole slots on the back edges of the sides for hanging the rack on the wall. You'll need a plunge router and keyhole bit to make these slots. Skip the slots if you want your rack to be freestanding.

WHAT YOU'LL NEED

- 2 sides   ¾ in. × 3 in. × 10 in., maple
- 10 dowels   ⅜ in. dia.× 14½ in., poplar
- Wood glue

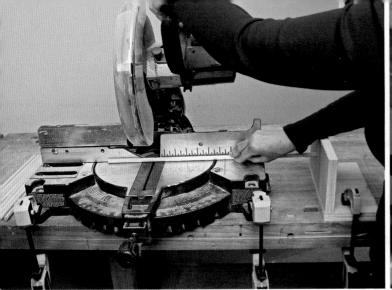

1 CUT THE DOWELS. Use a stop clamped to the bench to quickly cut all the dowels to exactly the same length.

2 LAY OUT AND DRILL THE TEMPLATE. Drill holes in the template with a ³⁄₈-in.-dia. bit.

Cut the Parts

There is very little to cut for this project: just the two sides, a template to mark the dowel-hole locations, and the dowels themselves.

Rip stock for the sides to 3 in. wide on the tablesaw. You'll use a template of ¼-in. plywood to locate the holes for the dowels. Rip this plywood to width while you have the fence set for the sides. Then cut the sides and template to 10 in. long using a power miter saw or the miter gauge on the tablesaw.

For speed and accuracy, use a stop on a hand or power miter saw to cut the dowels to length (14½ in.) **(1)**. Clamp the saw to the bench. Measure and cut the first piece, then use that piece as a gauge to set the stop the proper distance from the sawblade. Clamp the stop, then cut all the dowels. (See "Making and Using a Stop Block" on p. 80.)

Lay out the holes in the template as shown in "Dowel Hole Layout" on p. 132. Drill the holes with a ³⁄₈-in. bit, and label the bottom and back edge of the template to avoid layout confusion **(2)**.

Hidden Spices

If you want to stash your spices out of sight but still have them handy and organized, you have a few options. You can purchase a spice rack that is designed to mount on the inside of a cabinet or pantry door. If you are redoing your kitchen, you can include a drawer that includes a spice organizer like the one shown at left, or for an existing kitchen, you can buy a similar spice organizer as an insert sized to fit standard-width drawers. These inserts are available in wood or plastic.

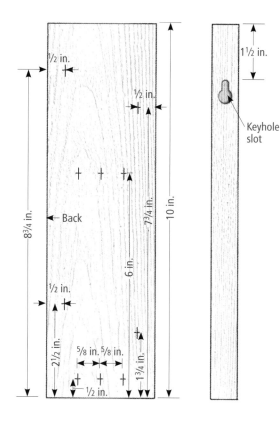

Drill the Holes and Rout the Keyhole Slots

Align the bottom and back of the template flush with the inside face of one side piece, and clamp the template and side piece to the bench. Use the drill stop to make the holes **(1)**. Flip the template over, as if you were turning the page of a book, to repeat the process for the inside face of the other side piece.

Lay out the keyhole slots

The optional keyhole slots in the back edges of the sides provide a hidden way to attach the spice rack to the wall. Clamp the inside faces of the sides together with the back and top edges flush **(2)**. Lay out the start and stop marks as shown in "Keyhole Slot Layout" on p. 134.

Rout the keyholes

To rout the keyholes, you'll first need to make a simple, two-piece guide, as explained in the sidebar on the facing page. Put both side pieces together in your bench end vise. (One side is there to add stability while routing the other.) Set the base of the slot guide against the piece to be routed and clamp it to the bench, as shown in photo 3 on p. 134.

Make a Drill Stop

The dowel holes are $3/8$ in. dia. The precise depth of the holes is not important as long as the depth is exactly the same for all the holes. Making a simple drill stop will ensure consistent depth.

First, measure how far a $3/8$-in.-dia. bit protrudes from the chuck. Cut a $1\frac{1}{2}$-in. x $1\frac{1}{2}$-in. scrap block to this length minus $7/8$ in. to allow for the thickness of the template and the depth of the holes. The bit shown here protruded $4\frac{1}{4}$ in. from the chuck, so the stop is $3\frac{3}{8}$ in. long. Draw diagonal lines across one end of the stop to mark the center, and put the stop in a vise.

Drill through the length of the stop with the $3/8$-in. bit. To help you drill straight down into the block, use a level to make sure the block is plumb in the vise. Some drills have a built-in plumb bubble that will also help you drill straight down.

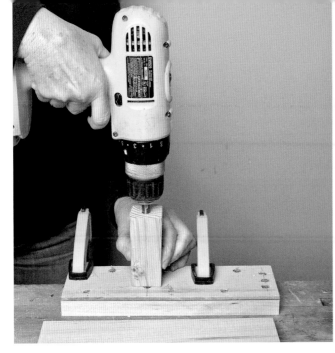

1 **DRILL THE HOLES IN THE SIDES.** Use the drill stop and template to drill matching holes in the inside faces of both side pieces.

2 **LAY OUT THE KEYHOLE SLOTS.** Clamp the sides together to lay out the keyhole stop and start lines.

Make a Keyhole Slot Guide

Keyhole slots allow you to hang objects right against the wall instead of standing off from the wall by the thickness of hardware. Because the slots are narrow, they are ideal for hidden attachment of the spice rack's ¾-in.-wide sides.

Put a keyhole bit in your plunge router and measure from the center of the bit to the guiding edge of the router base as shown in the photo below. For the router used here, the measurement was 2½ in. Sub-tract ⅜ in. to allow for half the thickness of the sides you'll be routing. Rip a scrap of plywood to this width for the base of the guide—2⅛ in. for the router used here. Make the piece long enough to clamp to both sides of your bench. Rip a guide board to about 2 in. wide and cut it to about the same length as the base. Screw the guide to the side of the base, making sure the two pieces are flush at bottom.

KEYHOLE SLOT GUIDE

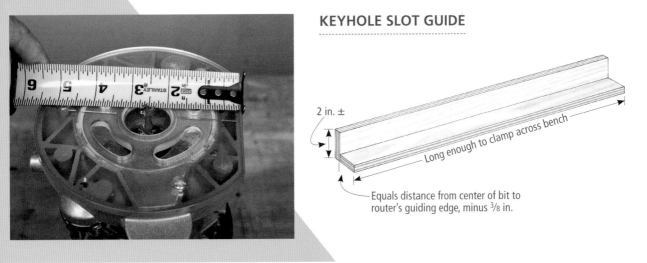

2 in. ±

Long enough to clamp across bench

Equals distance from center of bit to router's guiding edge, minus ⅜ in.

1½ in.

⅝ in.

Stop line

Start line

3 ROUT THE KEYHOLE SLOTS. Align the bit to the start line, raise it, turn the router on, and plunge. Lock the plunge mechanism, then carefully rout up to the stop line. Let the router come to a complete stop before you remove it.

Now set a keyhole bit in a plunge router to cut $\frac{7}{16}$ in. deep. Routing keyholes isn't hard, but you have to get the sequence right—it's a good idea to try it on a piece of scrap if you have never routed keyholes before. Pull a chair up to the bench so you can keep a close eye on the bit as you rout the slot **(3)**.

1. Plunge. Place the guiding edge of the router against the fence and align the outside of the bit to the start line. Plunge the cut.

2. Lock before you move. Once you have plunged to the bottom of the cut, lock the plunge mechanism. Then rout to the stop line.

3. Turn off and remove. When you reach the stop line, shut off the router. Wait for the bit to come to a complete stop. Then slide the router back so you can remove the bit from the hole.

Apply Finish before Assembly

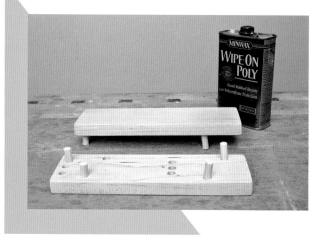

The spice rack is finished with two coats of wipe-on polyurethane varnish. It's much easier to get an even coat of varnish if you finish the side pieces before assembly so you don't have to work around the dowels. Just be careful not to get finish in the dowel holes.

You can take advantage of the dowel holes to speed the job by applying finish to both sides and all the edges at the same time. Just cut eight 1-in. lengths of scrap dowel. Apply finish to the hole side of each piece (the inside face), then stick four dowel pieces into each one to hold the workpieces up while you apply finish to the outside surfaces and edges.

Assemble the Spice Rack

Place one side piece on a pad to protect the finished surface and clamp it to the bench. Put a small dab of glue in the holes and insert the dowels. Tap them home with a rubber mallet **(1)**. Unclamp the assembly. Clamp the other side piece to the bench, and put glue in the holes. Starting at one end, place a few dowels in their holes and tap lightly on the other side piece to just set them but don't tap them all the way in. When all the dowels are in place, tap more firmly to set them to the bottom of their holes.

To prepare for clamping, place the rack on its back on a flat surface. You may have to twist it a little to get both back surfaces to lie flat. Use two clamps across the rack **(2)**. Don't use a lot of pressure—the clamps are there mostly to make sure all the dowels are completely seated. You don't want to bend the dowels. When the glue sets, apply finish to the dowels.

1 **ASSEMBLE THE SPICE RACK.** Work from one end to the other, getting the dowels slightly set into their holes. When all the dowels are in position, tap them all home.

> **TIP** If you don't have a rubber mallet, you can protect the ends of the dowels and the side pieces with a scrap of wood and tap the scrap with a regular hammer.

> **TIP** Pour a little wood glue into a disposable container, and use a small watercolor brush to dab glue into the holes.

2 **CLAMP THE RACK.** Use just enough clamping pressure to ensure that all the dowels are seated to the bottom of their holes.

HANGING WINE RACK

There are plenty of wine racks available for you to buy—some designed to hang on the wall, others freestanding or designed to fit in a cabinet. But here's a design that probably won't take much longer to build than the time you'll spend shopping for a commercial model. And you might save enough money to buy a good bottle of wine!

That's because this rack is an extremely simple, inexpensive, and clever way to store bottles of wine. Two boards. Six holes. Five screws. A little sanding, a couple of coats of wipe-on polyurethane, and you're done. (Of course, you can stain or paint your wine rack if you are so inclined.) It's so simple to build, why not make a few to give as presents while you are at it?

The secret to why the bottles are held securely is that the holes are drilled at an angle that alternates up and down from one hole to the next. The bottles are inserted against the slope of the holes. You'll need a drilling guide or a drill press to drill the holes at the proper angle.

WHAT YOU'LL NEED

- 1 backer   ³/₄ in. × 2³/₈ in. × 20 in., pine
- 1 hanger   ³/₄ in. × 2³/₈ in. × 17 in., pine

HARDWARE
- 3 all-purpose screws, 1¹/₄ in.
- 2 brass wood screws, #8 × 2 in.

Cut and Drill the Parts

You'll start by cutting two pieces of wood to size. Then you'll drill small holes for assembly and hanging, and bigger holes to hold the bottles.

Cut the boards and lay out the holes

Rip the backer and hanging boards to width on the tablesaw, then cut them to length with a power miter saw or the miter gauge on the tablesaw. Set a combination square to 1³/₁₆ in.—half the width of the pieces—and use it to draw a centerline along one face of the hanger **(1)**. Clamp the hanger to your bench so it won't slide around while you draw the line. Then mark the centers for the six holes as shown in the drawing on the facing page.

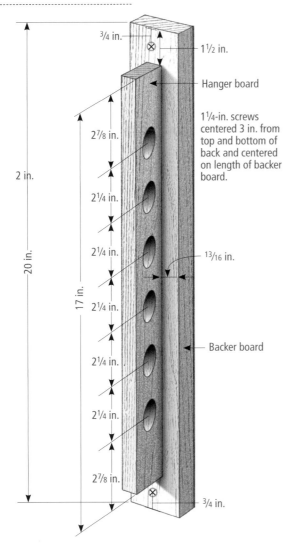

- ¾ in.
- 1½ in.
- Hanger board
- 1¼-in. screws centered 3 in. from top and bottom of back and centered on length of backer board.
- 2⅞ in.
- 2 in.
- 2¼ in.
- 20 in.
- 2¼ in.
- 17 in.
- ¹³/₁₆ in.
- 2¼ in.
- 2¼ in.
- Backer board
- 2¼ in.
- 2⅞ in.
- ¾ in.

1 **LAY OUT THE HOLES.** Use a combination square to draw a line centered down the length of the hanger board, then lay out the hole positions along the line.

Drill the hanger holes

The holes in the hanger board are 1¼ in. in diameter. Put a 1¼-in. Forstner bit into a drill guide (see the sidebar on p. 138) or drill press and set the angle at about 5° off square. Clamp a sacrificial scrap of ¾-in. wood or plywood to the bench, and set the stop on the guide or press so that the bit will just pass completely through the board **(2)**.

Make sure the base of your drill guide is square to the board so the holes will be parallel to the sides of the hanger board. The back and the holder are 2⅜ in. wide because the drill guide used here happens to have a 2⅜-in. recess. As a result, the guide fits snugly over the boards, ensuring that the holes will be drilled parallel to the sides of the hanging board.

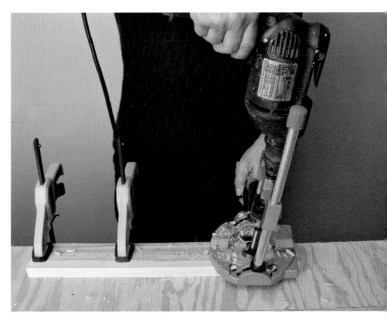

2 **DRILL THE FIRST HANGER HOLE.** Set the drill guide to an angle of about 5°. Clamp the hanger board over a sacrificial piece of plywood, then drill the first hole.

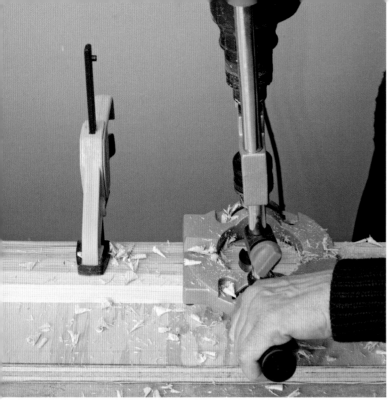

Turn the guide around to drill the second hole **(3)**. Then continue alternating the direction of the slope for each of the remaining four holes.

Predrill the backer

Predrill and countersink two holes through the front of the backer centered across the width and ¾ in. from each end **(4)**. These are for securing the rack to the wall. Then flip the board over and predrill holes 3 in. from each end, again centered across the width. Add a third hole centered across the width and approximately centered along the length.

3 **DRILL THE REMAINING HOLES.** Turn the guide around to drill the second hole at the opposing angle.

4 **PREDRILL THE BACKER.** Predrill and countersink hanging holes on each end of the face of the backer board. Turn the board over and predrill three holes for attaching the hanger board.

Drill Guides: A Versatile Addition to Your Shop

A drill press is, of course, the easiest and quickest way to drill accurate holes at any angle. But a good drill press is expensive, and even a tabletop model will eat up valuable real estate in a small shop. A portable drill guide like the one used in this project is an inexpensive and surprisingly versatile alternative.

Like a drill press, a drill guide will make accurate holes that are square to the work or at any angle, and both tools can be set to stop holes at the depth of your choosing. Both tools can accurately drill through round stock or pipe, and both can be fitted with a spindle sander for sanding edges.

The drill guide even has a couple of tricks up its sleeve that you can't perform with a drill press. The most obvious is drilling in place—for example, making a hole for a doorknob in a door that's already hung. Also, you can quickly center holes in a narrow board or the narrow edge of a board, simply by rotating the base plate until it engages both sides of the piece.

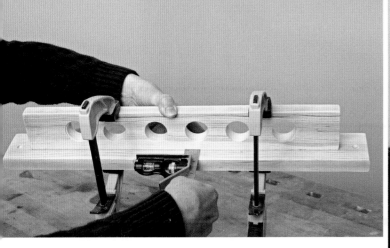

1 **CENTER THE HANGER.** Use a combination square to help position the hanger board along the backer board.

TIP It's much easier to sand the two pieces before assembly. Round the edges except for the edges of the backer board that will be against the wall and the edges of the hanger board that will be against the backer board.

2 **HANG THE RACK.** After driving the top screw into a stud, plumb the wine rack and drive the bottom screw into the stud.

Assemble and Hang the Rack

Make a light pencil mark $1\frac{1}{2}$ in. from each end of the face of the backer board. Set a combination square to $^{13}/_{16}$ in. Clamp the boards together, aligning the hanger board to the marks on the backer board and using the combination square to center the hanger along the length of the backer **(1)**. Drive $1\frac{1}{4}$-in. all-purpose screws into the holes in the back.

Six bottles of wine add up to significant weight, so be sure to attach the wine rack to a stud—don't rely on mollies or other drywall anchoring systems. (See "Finding Wall Studs" p. 28.) Use 2-in.-long #8 screws (brass screws look nice). Drive in the top screw, then check the rack for plumb before inserting the second screw **(2)**.

Use a Forstner Bit for a Smooth Hole

A Forstner bit is a better choice than a holesaw for drilling holes in the hanger board. As the name implies, a holesaw uses teeth to cut the hole, which can leave a jagged hole when the saw exits the wood. But the rim of a Forstner bit comprises two sharp blades that are designed to pull the bit through the work, resulting in an extremely smooth and accurate hole with little or no tearout. That's important because both sides of the holes in the hanger board will be visible.

CHAPTER FIVE

THE BEDROOM

YOU WANT YOUR BEDROOM to be a peaceful oasis of relaxation. That means no clutter. The closet is the first line of attack when it comes to stowing stuff you don't want to look at, and whatever size closet or closets you have, you want to maximize every inch of space.

The challenge is that just like the clothing it stores, there is no such thing as a one-size-fits-all closet. We all have different amounts of different types of clothing and other stuff we want to stash. And beyond that, our needs change over time. That's why you can't beat a modular storage system like the one shown in the Closet Tower project that lets you change the height of poles and shelves and add and subtract baskets, drawers, and other accessories. If you don't want to start from scratch, you can get a closet kit or have a system professionally installed.

Most of the projects in the Living Room chapter will work just as well in a bedroom. The Built-in Shelves (p. 64) are strong enough to span a wall behind the widest bed, and, of course, the Window Seat (p. 77) would be a great addition to a bedroom, where the two deep and wide drawers would add welcome storage.

Kids' rooms have one special storage need—where do you keep all those toys? The Toy Chest project is a personalized solution for your tyke or grandchild.

CLOSET TOWER

This easy-to-build tower organizer employs a standardized system of peg holes that are 32mm apart and 5mm in diameter. This makes the tower extremely versatile because you can purchase accessories that will fit the holes and spacing (see "Other Closet Accessories" on p. 144). Accessories shown in the photo at left include sliding baskets, adjustable closet pole supports, a tie/scarf rack, and a valet rod. You'll be able to quickly add or remove accessories or adjust their heights any time your needs change thanks to this standardized system of peg holes.

While the three towers shown provide maximum flexibility, you can build just one or two and place fixed closet poles on one or both sides. The dimensions provided in the "What You'll Need" list are for the center tower shown here. The side towers are constructed in exactly the same way, but you'll need to adjust their dimensions to fit your closet.

The tower can easily be adapted to your closet space—not only in the size and number of towers you build but also in the installation method you use. If, for example, you are lucky enough to be working with a closet that has a level floor along with walls that are plumb and square to each other, you can set the tower(s) on the floor and just screw the top and bottom cleats to studs in the wall. For this installation method, you may need to "pack out" with a board behind the top cleat that's equal in thickness to the baseboard in the closet. Or you can simply remove the baseboard. (See "Mounting Options" on p. 146.)

The three towers shown here were installed in a closet in an old house that has a severely sloped floor. To get around this problem, the towers are hung on a level ledger running across the back wall. In addition, the back wall of this closet leans away from the front, and the right wall leans in and is not square to the back wall. You'll learn simple solutions to these problems, should you face them.

WHAT YOU'LL NEED

Note: The parts listed here are just for the central tower. All parts are plywood.

- 2 sides   ¾ in. × 16 in. × 66¾ in.
- 1 top   ¾ in. × 17¼ in. × 24 in.
- 1 bottom   ¾ in. × 16 in. × 24 in.
- 2 adjustable shelves   ¾ in. × 16 in. × 23⅞ in.
- 2 cleats   ¾ in. × 3½ in. × 24 in.
- 1 back   ¼ in. × 25½ in. × 66 in.

HARDWARE

- Birch veneer edgebanding, 22 ft.
- 8 shelf pins, 5mm
- 20 joinery biscuits, #20
- 1 lag screw per stud, ¼ in. dia. x 1¾ in.
- 4 brass wood screws, #10 x 1¾ in.
- 3 all-purpose screws, 2¼ in.
- 1¼-in. all-purpose screws as needed

CLOSET TOWER

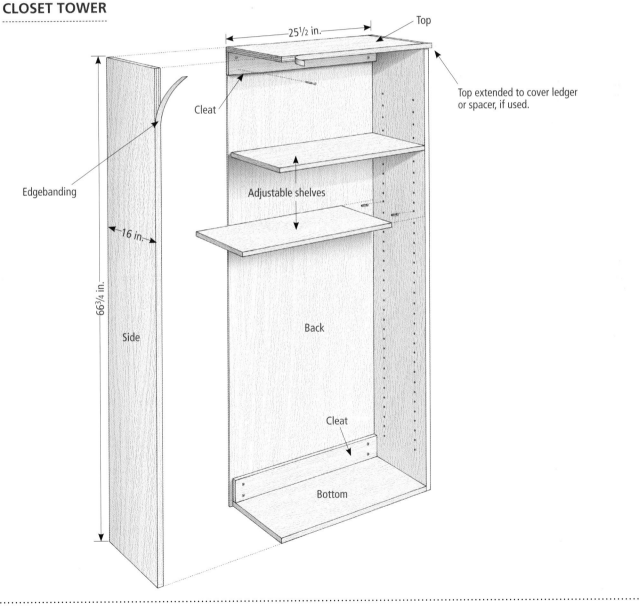

25½ in.

Top

Top extended to cover ledger or spacer, if used.

Cleat

Edgebanding

Adjustable shelves

16 in.

66¾ in.

Side

Back

Cleat

Bottom

Design Considerations

When planning your closet, the three critical considerations are the width, height, and depth.

Decide on the width

"What You'll Need" provides dimensions for a tower that has an interior width of 24 in., which is a standard width for the sliding baskets used. These baskets also are available 18 in. and 30 in. wide. For a reach-in closet such as the one featured here, you don't want to install baskets or drawers in side towers that would be obstructed by the closet's front return walls—the walls that frame the door(s). So, in the closet shown here, only the center tower is sized for sliding baskets. The side towers are sized to split the remaining width equally and are reserved for adjustable clothes poles and shelves. Making the side towers the same width allows poles and shelves to be used interchangeably.

Decide on the height

There's no standard height for top shelves or clothes poles. The Association of Closet and Storage Professionals (ACSP; www.closets.org) suggests that as a rule of thumb the highest clothes pole should be about 2 in. or 3 in. above the forehead of the person who will use the closet. You'll need at least 1½ in. between a closet pole and the top shelf—in this case the top of the towers—to hook hangers over the pole. The towers shown here were sized to fit between the top of the baseboard and the bottom of a ceiling that slopes on one side to accommodate a staircase above.

Decide on the depth

The most common depth for reach-in closets is 24 in. If this is the depth of your closet, make your tower(s) 14 in. deep—ACSP recommends at least 10 in. of space at front for easy access. The closet shown here is about 30 in. deep. The towers shown are 16 in. deep to make efficient use of 48-in.-wide plywood. The baskets used are available in depths of 12 in., 14 in., 16 in., and 20 in.

Size Up the Closet

As mentioned, the closet walls may not be plumb or perfectly square to each other (especially if you live in an old house). So you have two goals when measuring the closet: You want the three towers to be plumb when you install them so that the shelves will be level. And, if the side walls are not parallel to each other, you want to find the point where the distance between the side walls is shortest so you'll know your tower(s) will fit between them. For example, in the closet featured here, the left wall is square to the back wall but the right wall is not. Also, the right wall slopes in a bit. As a result, the two side walls are not parallel.

Check for plumb

Place a level against the back wall to check for plumb. If the back wall is more than slightly out of plumb, you'll

Other Closet Accessories

A number of manufacturers provide accessories that fit the peg-hole system used for this project. Shown here are a pants rack that pulls out and an ironing board that folds down behind a drawer front. At right is a rotating shoe rack that doesn't use the peg holes but easily screws into the top and bottom of the tower.

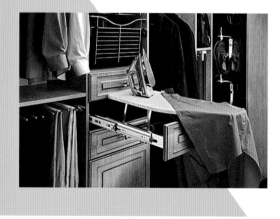

> **TIP** It's a good idea to make your towers just a little narrower than the available space to ease installation and allow for any irregularities in the wall surfaces. Be sure to measure the thickness of the nominal ¾-in. plywood you are using. You may find it's actually about 1/16 in. thinner than ¾ in. If it is, that's your wiggle room. If the plywood is a full ¾ in. thick, make the side towers ⅛ in. narrower than the closet's inside width.

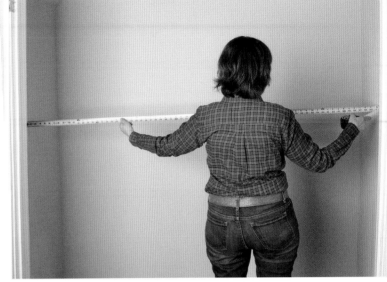

1 **DRAW PLUMB LINES ON THE SIDE WALLS.** After checking the back wall for plumb, draw plumb lines on both side walls to indicate the front of the towers.

2 **FIND THE SHORTEST WIDTH.** To make sure your towers will fit inside, measure the width of the closet along the back and along plumb lines on the side walls.

They Grow So Fast

The closet organization needs in a nursery are a lot different than in other bedrooms, but those needs are so short in duration that it's not practical to design a closet for an infant. Instead, you can temporarily install an inexpensive nursery storage set. The one shown at left includes hangers, a hanging organizer with six shelves, and storage bins.

need to make adjustments as explained in "Mounting Options" on p. 146. Make a plumb line on each side wall to designate the front of the tower—the sides of the towers shown are 16 in. wide and the back is ¼ in. thick, so the plumb line is 16¼ in. from the back wall **(1)**.

Find the shortest width

Measure the distance between side walls at the back wall, sliding the tape measure from the top to the bottom of the wall. If you are lucky, the measurement will be the same from top to bottom. If the distance varies, note the shortest measurement; here, the shortest measurement on the back wall was 69⅜ in. Now do the same thing to get the shortest distance between the two plumb lines you made on the side walls **(2)**; here, this measurement was 69⅛ in. Use the shortest measurement to determine the combined total width of all of your towers.

MOUNTING OPTIONS

There are three options for mounting the closet tower:
resting on the floor, hanging from a ledger with a plumb
wall, or hanging from a ledger with a sloped wall.

1. MEASURE THE GAP.

ON THE FLOOR

If your floor is level and the back wall is plumb, you can
rest the tower(s) on the closet floor. The advantage to this
approach is that all the weight of the tower(s) and their
contents will bear on the floor, requiring a less robust connection to the wall than you'll need if you hang the towers
from a wall ledger. If there is a baseboard along the back
wall, you can either remove it or install a spacer that will
be overlapped by the top of the tower. If you use a spacer,
keep it about ¼ in. below the tower top so no weight bears
on it. Secure the tower to the wall with two 2¼-in. all-
purpose screws into the studs. Use two screws into the top
cleat and two into the bottom.

HANGING FROM A LEDGER
WITH A PLUMB WALL

If the floor is sloped either from back to front or side to
side, the best approach is to hang the tower(s) on a ledger.
If the back wall is plumb, you can make a ledger that is the
same thickness as the baseboard and allow the bottom of
the cabinet to rest against the baseboard above the floor.
Use a 4-ft. level to draw a level line across the back wall at
the height you want for the top of your tower(s). Measure
between this line and the floor at both sides of the closet to
make sure your towers will fit under the line.

HANGING FROM A LEDGER
WITH A SLOPED WALL

If the back wall is out of plumb, you need to determine
by how much. Mark the tower height on the wall. Hold a
4-ft. level against a straight board. Place the board against
the wall and tilt the top or bottom out until the board is
plumb. Measure the gap at the bottom or the line that des-
ignates the top of the tower as shown in the photo at left.

If the wall slopes back, make a ledger that is equal in thickness to the gap. If the wall slopes forward, use a ¾-in. ledger and make a spacer for the bottom that's equal in thickness to the gap plus ¾ in. Make your ledger from stock that is slightly less than 3 in. wide so you can rip it to thickness with a tablesaw blade set to maximum height. The closet shown had a gap at the top of 1¼ in. The ledger is made of a 2x4 that was first ripped to 2⅞ in. wide and then ripped to 1¼ in. thick.

MOUNTING OPTIONS

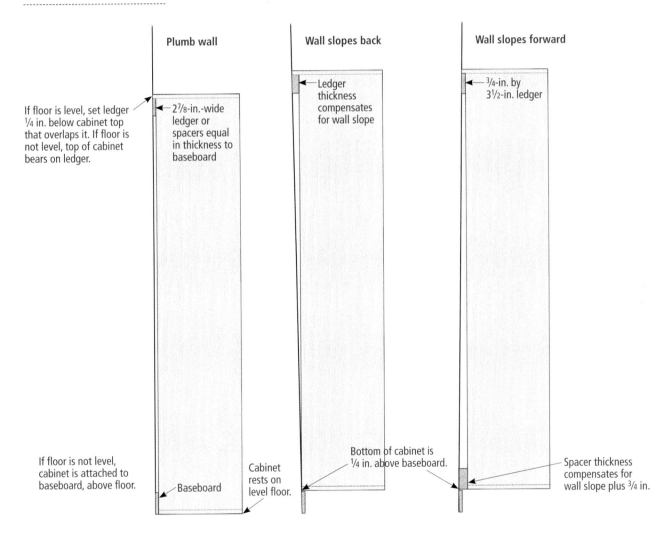

Plumb wall

If floor is level, set ledger ¼ in. below cabinet top that overlaps it. If floor is not level, top of cabinet bears on ledger.

2⅞-in.-wide ledger or spacers equal in thickness to baseboard

If floor is not level, cabinet is attached to baseboard, above floor.

Baseboard

Cabinet rests on level floor.

Wall slopes back

Ledger thickness compensates for wall slope

Bottom of cabinet is ¼ in. above baseboard.

Wall slopes forward

¾-in. by 3½-in. ledger

Spacer thickness compensates for wall slope plus ¾ in.

Cut the Parts

Because all of the ¾-in.-thick parts, with the possible exception of the top, will be the same width—16 in. for the towers shown—it's easiest to have your plywood ripped to width on a panel saw at the lumberyard or home center. Sheets of cabinet-grade plywood such as birch are about 48½ in. wide to allow three 16-in. rips with kerf waste. Have the ¼-in. backs ripped to width as well.

Cut the sides to length

As mentioned, to avoid the problem of a severely sloped floor, the towers shown here were designed to fit between the baseboard and a ceiling that is sloped at one side to accommodate a stair above. In this case, the floor slopes downhill from the side with the sloped ceiling. To determine the length of the sides in a case like this, draw a level line across the entire back wall starting at the point where the sloped ceiling meets the wall. Then, in the uphill corner, measure the distance from the top of the baseboard to the level line—67 in. in this case. Subtract ¼ in. for wiggle room to arrive at sides that are 66¾ in. long.

Use the crosscutting jig with the circular saw to cut the sides to length (see "Making a Crosscutting Jig" on p. 22). Because the sides are the same length, you can save time by cutting them together **(1)**. This will also ensure that they are exactly the same length.

1 **CUT THE SIDES TO LENGTH. Use a circular saw with the crosscutting jig to cut both sides to length at the same time.**

First, place a piece of sacrificial plywood on the bench, then set both workpieces on top, good face down, and align the edges. Then clamp the three pieces to the bench. Use a square to draw the cutline, align the jig to the line, and clamp the jig to the plywood on the side where you will start the cut. Stack two pieces of ¾-in. plywood scrap to support the jig where it overhangs the workpieces, and clamp the jig and scrap pieces to the bench, as shown in the photo above.

Add the thickness of the jig base plus half the thickness of the sacrificial piece plus 1½ in. for the combined thick-

Consider a Kit

If you don't have the confidence to build your own closet tower from scratch (and you want to avoid the expense of having your closet organization professionally designed and built), another option is to buy a closet kit. The one shown at left uses vertical panels that hang from metal ledgers. The panels can be sized and positioned to suit your closet and your needs, and they have peg holes that let you adjust the positions of the shelves, drawers, poles, and baskets. Other accessories are available.

The drawer sides, front, and back come folded but preattached. You unfold them, insert the bottom in a groove, and glue the assembly together.

2 **RIP THE CLEATS.** After using the circular saw with the crosscutting jig to cut plywood to length for the cleats, rip them to width on the tablesaw.

ness of the workpieces. Set your saw to this depth and make the cut.

Make the horizontal parts

You want the top piece to butt into the back wall, so its width will be determined by your mounting method (see "Mounting Options" p. 146). For our closet, the back wall slopes back enough to require a 1¼-in.-thick ledger. This measurement was added to the 16-in. width of the sides to arrive at the 17¼-in. width of the tower's top piece, which will cover the top of the ledger. If you won't be using a ledger, the top will be the same width as the sides and bottom. If necessary, rip plywood for the top to width on the tablesaw.

In any case, the top and bottom pieces and the cleats are all the same length (here, 24 in.). While your circular saw is set to cut through two thicknesses of plywood, stack two offcuts from the sides and guide the cut with the crosscutting jig as you did the sides. One of these pieces will be the bottom or top, while the other will be ripped for cleats. (Note that a circular saw with a standard 7¼-in. blade won't cut deeply enough to go through three layers of ¾-in. plywood.)

Now reset the circular saw blade to cut through one layer of ¾-in. plywood and use the crosscutting jig to make the other top or bottom. If the top and bottom pieces will both be the same width as the sides, you can make this piece from the third offcut from the sides. If you made the top or bottom piece wider because the back wall is out of plumb, you'll need to make it from a

TIP When you cut with a circular saw, the teeth come up through the bottom of the workpiece and out the top, so any splintering of plywood veneer will happen on top. That's why, if only one side of a cut will show, as is the case with the tower sides, you always want to cut with the good side down when using a circular saw. The opposite is true when using a tablesaw or power miter saw.

rip of the appropriate width. For the towers shown here, a second sheet of plywood was ripped to 17¼ in. at the lumberyard to make the top pieces for the three towers.

Use the circular saw with the crosscutting jig to cut the adjustable shelves to a length that is ⅛ in. less than the length of the top and bottom. This allows room for the shelf pegs and makes the shelves easy to install and remove.

Set the tablesaw fence 3½ in. from the blade, and rip the two cleats **(2)**. You can rip four cleats from this piece if you are planning to make another tower of equal or lesser width.

Assemble the Tower

The top and bottom pieces will be joined to the sides with five #20 biscuits at each joint. Lay out centers for the slots on the ends of the sides at 1⅝ in., 4¹³⁄₁₆ in., 8 in., 11⅜ in., and 14⅜ in. Because the inside of the tower will be visible and the outside will not, do the layouts on the better face of each side piece.

For each joint, butt the end of the top or bottom against the mating edge of a side. Make sure the front edges are flush, then transfer the biscuit slot layout marks to the top and bottom pieces **(1)**.

1 **LAY OUT THE BISCUIT SLOTS.** Lay out centers for five biscuit slots on the ends of both side pieces, then transfer the locations to the ends of the top and bottom pieces.

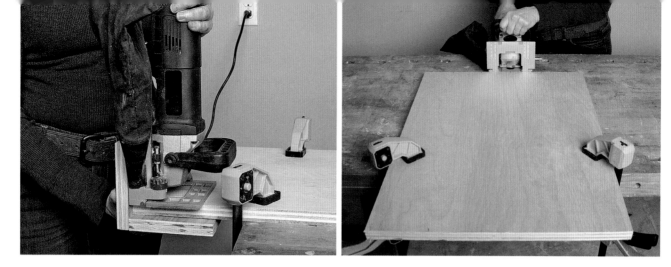

2 **CUT THE SLOTS IN THE SIDES. A simple L-shaped fence accurately positions slots the proper distance from the edges of the side pieces.**

3 **CUT THE SLOTS IN THE TOP AND BOTTOM PIECES. Clamp the top and bottom flat across the bench to cut slots in the ends.**

Cut the slots

To prepare to cut the slots in the sides, first remove the fence from the biscuit joiner. To help make the slots in the inside face of the side pieces, make an L-shaped fence from two 5-in.-square scraps of ¾-in. plywood. Screw the pieces together to make a square corner. Clamp one of the side pieces to the work surface with the face to be slotted facing up and overhanging about 6 in. Extend your layout marks into lines to make them easier to see. Hold the L-fence firmly against the bottom and edge of the workpiece, put the base of the joiner against the L-fence, and plunge down to make slots **(2)**.

Now cut slots in the top and bottom pieces. Clamp the top to the bench. Hold the joiner firmly down on the bench as you cut the slots in the edges **(3)**. Repeat for the tower bottom.

Glue up the tower

Do a test assembly to make sure everything fits and to get your clamps preadjusted to save time during glue-up. Place one side on the bench and put glue and biscuits in

TIP As you lay out the biscuit slots, write the same number at the mating edge of each piece. Also note which is the front of each piece. This will save time when you prepare for glue-up.

A Helping Hand

If you don't have a helper on hand during test assembly and glue-up, it can be tricky to keep the bottom piece from tumbling over while you assemble the second side to the top piece. For an easy solution, grab a scrap that's about 1½ in. wide and 12 in. to 20 in. or so long. Clamp the scrap edge down to the bench and then clamp the bottom piece to the scrap. In addition to easing assembly, this will help keep the tower square during glue-up.

Test assembly is shown here. During actual glue-up, wrap the scrap in waxed paper so glue squeeze-out doesn't bond the scrap to the tower. Also during glue-up, clamp the tower only snugly to the scrap—you don't want to impede the clamps you'll place across the bottom piece.

4 **GLUE UP THE TOWER. Tack a scrap diagonally across the top and one side to ensure that the tower remains square while the glue sets.**

the slots. Put glue in the mating slots, and put the top and bottom pieces in place, making sure the parts are flush at the front. Assemble the other side to the top and bottom pieces in the same way.

Clamp the assembly to the bench with two long clamps at each end as shown in the photo above. Here, a 2x4 is used across one end because the bench is too wide for the clamps to reach. Check for square and tack-nail or screw a scrap diagonally across a corner to keep the assembly square until the glue sets **(4)**.

Apply Edgebanding

The front edges of the tower and the shelves and the exposed edge of each cleat will be covered with birch veneer edgebanding. Available at a lumberyard, hardware store, or home center, edgebanding has an adhesive that is activated by the heat of a household iron. The banding is easy to use because if you get it misaligned you can just reheat the glue and reposition the banding.

Band the long edges

Set a household iron for cotton. Cut a piece of banding about 1 in. longer than your tower height. Put the banding in place along one long front edge of the tower, overhanging a bit on both ends. Place a piece of aluminum foil or kraft paper on the banding to protect the iron from glue and the banding from burning, and press the iron along the banding, keeping the banding flush to the inside face of the tower side **(1)**. Stop every few inches to press the banding with a wooden or rubber roller while the glue is still hot. Band both long edges.

Band the top and bottom

Use a combination square and a utility knife to cut a square edge on the roll of edgebanding, then cut off a piece that's about ½ in. longer than the inside width of the tower **(2)**.

1 **BAND THE LONG EDGES. Cut strips of edgebanding a little longer than the sides, and iron them in place flush to the inside edges. Use a piece of aluminum foil or kraft paper to protect the iron from glue squeeze-out.**

2 **CUT BANDING FOR THE TOP AND BOTTOM. Guide a utility knife against a combination square to make a square cut on one end of the edgebanding.**

3 BAND THE TOP AND BOTTOM. After ironing the top and bottom edging into place, cut it to fit against the side banding. Guide the cut with a combination square.

4 TRIM THE BANDING. Put a new blade in the utility knife and trim the edgebanding flush to the outside of the tower.

5 BAND THE SHELVES AND CLEATS. Band the exposed edge of each shelf and the two cleats, then trim the banding flush.

Place the banding on the top or bottom edge of the tower with the square edge butted against the edging you applied to one long side and iron it into place, flush to the inside. Now use a utility knife guided by a square to cut the banding to fit against the banding on the long side **(3)**.

Use a utility knife with a sharp blade to trim the banding flush to the outside of the tower **(4)**. Sand it perfectly flush to the outside with 80 grit. Then sand the inside of the tower with 80, 120, and 220 grit.

Band the shelves and cleats

Apply banding to the front edge of each shelf and one long edge of each cleat. Trim the edging flush **(5)**. Then sand both sides of each shelf and the exposed face of each cleat. It's a good idea to apply finish to the inside of the towers now, so that finish won't clog the peg holes you'll drill in the next step.

Install Cleats and Drill Support Holes

To prepare to glue the cleats in place, set the tower face down on your bench. Put glue on three edges of one of the cleats, and clamp it in place using one long clamp across the sides and three short clamps against the top **(1)**. Do the same for the cleat at the other end of the tower. (Note that if you will be mounting the tower to a ledger, the top cleat will be flush to the back of the sides but not flush to the back of the top.)

Drill holes for pegs and accessories

The keys to the flexibility of this tower system are the two columns of holes drilled into the inside of each side—one column near the front edge and one near the back edge. These holes are 5mm in diameter to fit 5mm shelf pegs and also 5mm "Euro screws" used to fasten accessories such as the slides for the baskets used here.

Certain accessories, such as the closet rod supports used, have two prongs that fit into the holes that must be spaced at 32mm (see "Installing Accessories," p. 155). To drill 5mm holes that are 32mm apart, you'll need a commercially available shelf pin template or jig. The one shown in photo 2 on the facing page, from Kreg®, has a removable fence that lets you set the holes either 1½ in.

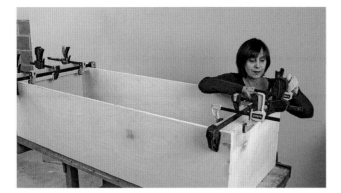

1 GLUE THE CLEATS IN PLACE. Use one long clamp across the tower and three short clamps across the cleats when gluing the cleats in place flush to the back.

2 DRILL THE SUPPORT HOLES. A plywood spacer ensures that the first holes in both columns are aligned. A locator pin (shown to the right of the jig) will keep the holes aligned as you move the jig along the front and back of the sides.

or 2½ in. from the front and back edges of the sides. The 2½-in. spacing aligns with the holes on the basket slides used here. The jig comes with a 5mm bit with a stop collar to drill to the proper depth.

Make a plywood spacer that's 6 in. wide and at least as long as your tower is deep. Put the spacer against the inside of the top, hook the jig over the front or rear, and drill holes, working down the length of each side **(2)**. Place the jig's locator pin in the last hole, place the jig over the hole, and keep drilling, repeating the process until you get to about 6 in. from the bottom of the tower. Then drill the other column of holes.

If you're using a closet pole at the top of your tower, add holes at the front until you get to within about 1½ in. of the top.

Install the Back

The width of the back equals the width of the tower—which, for the tower shown here, is 25½ in. If you didn't have the ¼-in. plywood ripped to width at the store, do it now on the tablesaw. Be sure the pieces will be supported on the outfeed side of the saw by rollers, an outfeed table, or a helper.

Cut the back to length

If your tower top overhangs at the back (as ours does), cut the back to fit between the overhang and the bottom of the tower. Otherwise, cut the back to lap the back edge of the top. Place ¼-in. plywood on a sacrificial piece of plywood on the workbench and lay out the cutline. Set the saw to cut through the workpiece and into the sacrificial piece and cut along the line **(1)** (below). Here, there's no need for the crosscutting jig, as the cut won't be seen and need not be perfectly straight.

1 CUT THE BACK TO LENGTH. Place the back piece on a sacrificial piece of plywood and crosscut to length along a layout line.

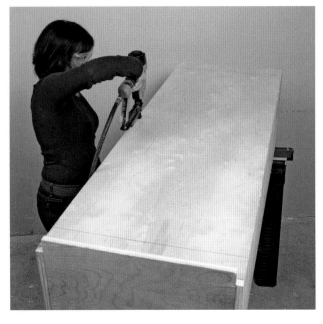

2 **GLUE AND NAIL THE BACK INTO PLACE. Lines drawn across the back ensure that brads won't miss the cleats.**

Test-fit the back and draw lines across the top and bottom to indicate the inside edges of the cleats below. Put glue on the back edges of the sides and on the back of the cleats. Secure the back with 1-in. brads every few inches using a hammer or a finish nailer **(2)**.

Install the Tower

If you haven't already done so, use a 4-ft. level to draw a level line across the back wall to indicate the top of the tower or the top of the spacer or ledger if you will be using one of those mounting options. (Remember, the ledger will be ¾ in. below the top of the tower[s]). Use a stud finder to locate the studs along this line **(1)** (see "Finding Wall Studs" on p. 28).

Also find the stud locations at the bottom and measure their distance from the wall—you'll need these measurements either to install a spacer at the bottom or, if you are not using a spacer, to know where to drive screws through the bottom cleat.

1 **MARK THE LOCATION OF THE STUDS ALONG THE LEVEL LINE. Then find the locations of the studs at the bottom of the wall.**

Dealing with Bow

Because the plywood sides are long (66¾ in. for the tower shown here), they may be bowed a bit. Measure across the inside at the middle. If the measurement is slightly more than the width of the tower at top and bottom (meaning that the sides are bowing out), just push the sides flush to the back while nailing the back into place. If the measurement at the middle is less than at the ends (meaning that the sides are bowing in), cut a piece of scrap to the same length as the cleats and wedge it in place at the middle, a few inches below the back edges as shown. Remove this piece after you attach the back piece.

Installing Accessories

Now that your tower has two columns of regularly spaced holes, installing accessories designed to work with those holes is a snap.

To install a closet pole, you'll need a pair of supports that each have two 5mm-dia. prongs spaced 32mm apart—Hafele is one manufacturer you'll find online. As shown in photo **1** at far left, you just insert the prongs of one support into holes on one side of the tower at any height you choose and then install the other support in opposing holes at the same height. Drive the wood screws supplied into the center hole in the supports to secure them as shown in photo **1** at near left. Cut a piece of 1¼-in.-dia. closet pole to ¼ in. less than the inside width of the tower. Slip the pole into the supports, and you are ready to hang clothes.

Other accessories are installed with special short, blunt 5mm Euro screws (see p. 16). The tie/scarf rack and the valet rod shown in the photo of the finished towers, for example, both employ hardware that is mounted with Euro screws in holes at front and back that allow the rack or rod to slide in and out. In the case of the valet rod, the rod slides in and out of a tube that slips through holes in the front and rear fittings as shown in photo **2**. Setscrews in the fittings hold the tube in place.

The pull-out baskets installed in the central tower shown here are made by Rev-A-Shelf®. They come with slides that have predrilled holes that align with holes at the front and back of the sides. You simply align the holes at whatever height you choose and drive in the Euro screws as shown in photo **3** at far left. (Each slide comes with a conventional wood screw, for applications where a back hole in the side doesn't align with the hole in the back of the slide.) The baskets just clip in at the back and have tabs that slip into slots at the front as shown in photo **3** at near left.

1. INSTALLING CLOSET POLE SUPPORTS

2. INSTALLING A VALET ROD

3. INSTALLING PULL-OUT BASKETS

Install spacers and the ledger

If you will be using spacers and/or a ledger, rip them to size as described in "Mounting Options" on p. 146. Then cut them to length to fit across the back wall.

No weight will bear on the spacers, so attach them with two screws into each stud, placing one screw above the other. Use screws that are at least 1½ in. longer than the thickness of the spacer.

If you are using a ledger, attach it to the wall with one ¼-in.-dia. lag screw into each stud. Use lag screws that are at least 1½ in. longer than the thickness of the ledger. But first, place the ledger along the level line and drive an all-purpose screw into a stud near the middle of the wall **(2)**. Level the ledger and drive screws into studs near each side of the wall to fix the ledger's position. Now use a ¾-in. spade bit to counterbore a hole at each stud so the lag-screw heads will be below the surface. Predrill the holes with a ³⁄₁₆-in. bit, put a washer in place, then drive the screws in with a socket wrench or box wrench.

Install side towers

If you're installing three towers in a closet with return walls (as in the project here), most likely you'll find you need to get the side towers in position first and then slide the center tower straight in between them. Once you have your towers in place on the ledger or on the floor, align the front edges and attach them together with three or four 1¼-in. screws in countersunk and predrilled holes near the front edge **(3)**.

If there is a spacer or ledger behind a cleat, counterbore and predrill for four 1¾-in. #10 brass wood screws located about 1 in. down and 2 in. over from each corner **(4)**. If there is no spacer or ledger behind, use the measurements you took earlier to locate studs and put two screws through the cleats wherever a stud is located. Now you are ready to insert shelf pins for adjustable shelves and install baskets and/or other accessories (see "Installing Accessories" on p. 155).

> **TIP** Remember, the two side towers (if you're building them) are built in the same way as the central tower, but you'll need to adjust the dimensions to fit your closet.

2 **INSTALL THE LEDGER.** First, use three all-purpose screws to position the ledger on the wall. Next, counterbore with a spade bit as shown in the top photo above. Then predrill holes before driving the lag screws with a socket wrench or box wrench.

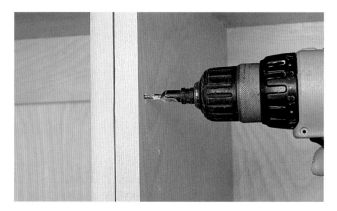

3 **JOIN THE TOWERS.** Once the towers are in position with front edges flush, pull them together with screws in countersunk holes.

4 **DRIVE SCREWS THROUGH THE TOP AND BOTTOM CLEATS.** Drive brass wood screws into countersunk and predrilled holes in the cleats.

TOY CHEST

This colorful toy chest is sturdy enough to become a family heirloom, yet it's surprisingly easy to build: Essentially, you'll make four pine frames, rabbet the inside of the frames, and set in plywood panels. Joining the four sides is simplified by the use of biscuit joints.

The most critical thing to do when building this chest, or any toy chest, is to use the right lid supports. The supports must offer enough resistance to prevent the lid from slamming shut but not so much resistance that the lid won't stay closed. Manufacturers use a simple formula to determine which support to use and whether you need one or two of them: Lid weight multiplied by front-to-back size divided by two. The lid on this chest weighs about 7½ lb. and is 18¾ in. wide. So 7.5 x 18.75 equals 140.6 divided by 2 equals 70.3 inch pounds (in. lb.). In this case, two supports rated for 35–40 in. lb. each will do the job.

WHAT YOU'LL NEED

CLEAR PINE

• 4 front and back rails	¾ in. × 3½ in. × 25 in.
• 4 side rails	¾ in. × 3½ in. × 11 in.
• 4 front and back stiles	¾ in. × 3½ in. × 20 in.
• 4 side stiles	¾ in. × 2¾ in. × 20 in.
• 2 long cleats	¾ in. × 1 in. × 30½ in.
• 2 short cleats	¾ in. × 1 in. × 16½ in.
• 2 long top edging	¾ in. × ¾ in. × 33½ in.
• 2 short top edging	¾ in. × ¾ in. × 18¾ in.

BIRCH PLYWOOD

- 2 front and back panels $\frac{1}{2}$ in. × $11\frac{3}{4}$ in. × $25\frac{3}{4}$ in.
- 2 side panels $\frac{1}{2}$ in. × $11\frac{3}{4}$ in. × $11\frac{3}{4}$ in.
- 1 bottom $\frac{1}{2}$ in. × 15 in. × $30\frac{1}{2}$ in.
- 1 top lid $\frac{3}{4}$ in. × $17\frac{1}{4}$ in. × 32 in.

HARDWARE AND GLUE

- $1\frac{1}{4}$-in. finish nails
- $1\frac{1}{4}$-in. all-purpose screws
- 2 butt hinges, $\frac{3}{4}$ in. × $2\frac{1}{2}$ in.
- 1 right-side toy box lid support for 35–40 in. lb.*
- 1 left-side toy box lid support for 35–40 in. lb.*
- Wood glue
- Two-part epoxy cement

*Available from Walmart®, item N208686 (right side) and item N208660 (left side)

Make the Frames

You'll begin this project by making two pairs of identical frames: One pair will make the front and back of the chest, and the other pair will be the sides.

Cut the stiles and rails

Cut the stiles and rails from nominal 1×4s to the lengths listed in "What You'll Need." For speed and accuracy, use a stop block on a hand or power miter saw to cut parts to the same length (1). The stop shown in the photo is made from two 5-in. × 7-in. scraps of plywood glued and screwed together. The dimensions of the scrap aren't important, as long as the stop piece is wide enough to extend above the saw table so the workpiece can butt into it and the bottom piece is wide enough to clamp securely to the bench. Clamp the miter saw to the bench, measure and cut the first piece, and then use that piece as a gauge to set the stop the proper distance from the sawblade.

Nominal 1×4s are already $3\frac{1}{2}$ in. wide, so there is no need to rip the rails or the front and back stiles. On the tablesaw, rip the side stiles to $2\frac{3}{4}$ in.

To give our toy chest a jauntier stance, we cut the ends of all the stiles at a 45° angle to form feet. Now is the time to choose the best face of each stile to face out in the finished chest. If you are using clear pine and will be

1   **CUT THE STILES AND RAILS. Clamp the miter saw and a stop to the bench to cut pieces precisely to the same length. You can also make these cuts with a power miter saw.**

TIP   It's common to taper feet on cases or chests. Table legs are often tapered, too. Tapering the vertical members adds visual interest to the piece, but there is also a practical reason to do it: By reducing the area of contact with the floor, you reduce the chance that irregularities in the floor surface will cause the piece to rock.

TOY CHEST

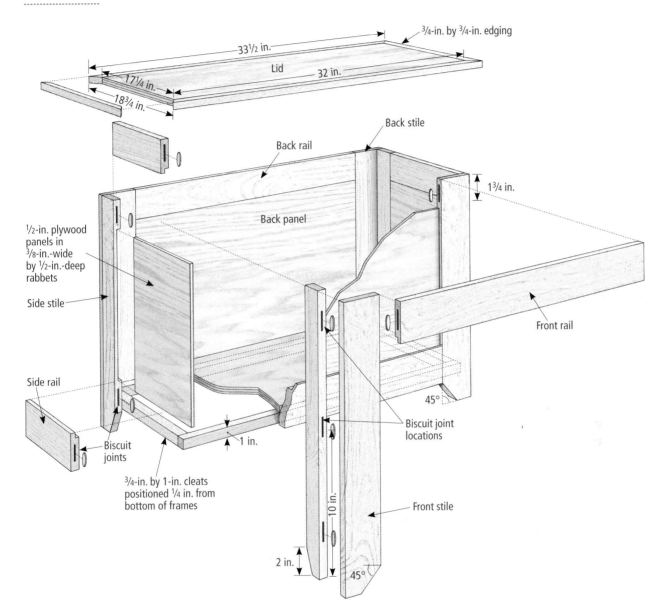

¾-in. by ¾-in. edging

33½ in.

Lid

32 in.

17¼ in.

18¾ in.

Back stile

Back rail

1¾ in.

Back panel

½-in. plywood panels in ⅜-in.-wide by ½-in.-deep rabbets

Side stile

Front rail

Side rail

45°

Biscuit joint locations

Biscuit joints

¾-in. by 1-in. cleats positioned ¼ in. from bottom of frames

1 in.

10 in.

Front stile

2 in.

45°

 LAY OUT THE STILE FEET. Use a square to mark the 45° cuts at the bottom of the stiles.

3 **LAY OUT BISCUIT JOINTS FOR THE FRAMES.** Mark the biscuit joints for the frames using a combination square set to 1¾ in.

painting the project, this probably won't matter, although even pine sold as clear sometimes has small knots on one side. If you plan to use a clear finish on the chest, choose the grain pattern you like best. Assign each stile a position—left front, left front side, etc., and mark them accordingly.

To lay out the foot on each stile, measure 2 in. up from the bottom inside edge and use a square to lay out a 45° cut down to the bottom edge **(2)**. Make these cuts with a miter saw.

Lay out the biscuit joints

The rails and stiles for each frame are joined with one #20 biscuit centered at each joint. Put each set of frame pieces in position on your bench. Set a combination square to 1¾ in. and use it to locate the mating biscuit slots on each joint **(3)**.

As shown in the drawing on p. 159, the front and back stiles cover the edges of the side stiles. The stiles are joined at each corner with three biscuits—one centered 1¾ in. from the top and bottom and one centered across the length of the stiles. To lay out the biscuit positions, clamp each pair of stiles against each other and mark them together **(4)**. Then transfer the mark to the outside edge of the stiles.

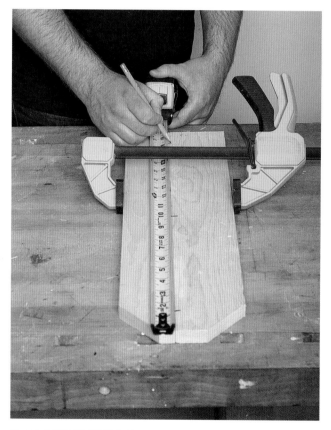

4 **LAY OUT THE CORNER BISCUIT JOINTS.** Clamp each front stile to its mating side stile to mark the parts together for biscuit joints.

Cut the biscuit slots

Set the biscuit joiner for #20 biscuits and set the fence to center the slots in the edge of the side stiles. Cut the biscuit slots in the ¾-in. edges of the side stiles. When cutting slots on the inside faces of the front and back stiles, place them in a vise flush on top with another 3½-in.-wide piece **(5)**. The second piece is to provide more bearing for the joiner fence so it doesn't wobble during the cut.

Put glue in each biscuit slot and on the adjoining surfaces. Insert biscuits and assemble the frames with clamps across the top and bottom of each one **(6)**.

5 **CUT THE BISCUIT SLOTS IN THE STILES.** Secure each front and back stile in a vise to cut biscuit slots where its inside edge will join a side stile. An extra piece of stock in the vise provides more surface for the joiner fence to bear on.

TIP Put waxed paper under the joints when you glue up frames to protect the bench from glue squeeze-out.

6 **ASSEMBLE THE FRAMES.** Use glue and two clamps to assemble the biscuit-joined frames.

1 **ROUT THE PANEL RABBETS. To allow the router bit to scoop cleanly, move the router in a clockwise direction as you make the rabbets in the frames.**

2 **GLUE AND CLAMP EACH PANEL. To assemble the frame and panel, set the panel in the frame and place narrow scraps along the panel over the rabbets. Then clamp boards across the strips to get clamping pressure where you need it.**

Make and Insert the Panels

The panels will be glued into rabbets along the inside of the frames. You'll cut the rabbets first, then check measurements between rabbets before cutting the plywood panels to fit.

Rout the panel rabbets

Put a ³/₈-in. piloted rabbeting bit in the router and set it to cut ½ in. deep. Place two pieces of ¾-in. scrap under a frame to raise it off the bench and make room for the router bit pilot bearing nut. Position the scrap back from the inside edges of the frame so it doesn't interfere with the pilot bearing, and clamp the scrap and frame to the bench. Move the router clockwise as you rout the rabbet **(1)**. Square the corners of the rabbets with a sharp chisel.

Cut the panels and glue them in place

The panel sizes are listed in "What You'll Need," but it's always a good idea to check the actual dimensions now that the frames are built. Measure across the rabbets in the frames in case you need to adjust the size of the panels slightly from the dimensions in the parts list.

If you are starting with a full sheet of plywood, see "Rough-Ripping Plywood" on p. 21. In the case shown here, the panels are cut from a 24-in. x 48-in. quarter sheet of ½-in. birch plywood available at home centers. Rip the panels to width on the tablesaw, and then use the rip fence to cut them to length. Alternately, you can crosscut the panels to length as shown in "Making a Crosscutting Jig" on p. 22

Unless you have wide-mouth clamps, they won't reach the panels. To get around this, cut two pieces of narrow scrap to about 25 in. for the front and back panels and two pieces to about 11 in. for the side panels. Also have on hand two wider pieces of scrap that are longer than the width of your bench. Put glue in the rabbets, insert the panel, and place the narrow scraps along the panel over the rabbets in the rails. Put the longer scraps across the narrow ones and clamp them to the sides of the bench **(2)**. You don't need a lot of pressure—stop tightening the clamps before the boards begin to bend.

TIP Quick clamps like the black and yellow DeWalt® models used in the photo on the facing page come with pads that prevent the clamp faces from denting the wood. Older-style pipe clamps like the ones at the bottom don't have pads, so you need to use a scrap pad of wood or plywood under each clamp face. (Note that the pipe clamps are used at the bottom so the pads can't slip out—just one less thing to worry about during glue-up.)

Assemble the Box

With the frame and panels made, you are ready to assemble them and then cut and install the bottom and make the top.

Test-assemble and glue up the chest

Begin by inserting biscuits into all the slots you made in the stiles. Test-assemble the box with four clamps to get your clamps preadjusted and to make sure everything fits properly. Use a framing square to make sure the box is square. When it is, tack-nail a length of scrap across the top diagonally from front to back. Mark which end of the scrap is at front. Then pull the scrap off and disassemble the box. Pull the tack nails up until they protrude just slightly from the scrap piece.

Now put glue in the biscuit slots, insert the biscuits, and reassemble the box. As soon as you clamp the box, put the front nail back in its original hole and tack it down. If the back nail finds its hole, the box is square **(1)**. If not, quickly loosen or, if necessary, remove the clamps and pull on opposite corners of the box until you can insert the back nail in its hole. Tack the second nail in to help keep the box square.

Router Direction

When routing against a fence, with the router between you and the fence, always move the router from left to right. Here's why: Router bits rotate clockwise and if you move left to right, the bit's cutter will scoop into the wood, cutting cleanly and pulling the router against the fence. If you move right to left, the bit will try to climb out of the cut, making the router hard to control and likely resulting in an imperfect cut. The same principle applies if you are using a piloted bit. Keep in mind though, that if you are routing rabbets inside a frame, left to right means moving clockwise. If you are routing outside a frame, left to right means counterclockwise.

1 **TEST-ASSEMBLE THE CHEST. After** squaring the dry-assembled box, affix a temporary diagonal brace with a finish nail at each end. During glue-up, if both nails on the diagonal brace find the holes they made during test assembly, you'll know the box is square.

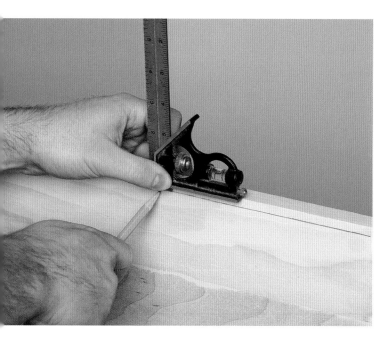

Lay out the cleats

The four cleats will be installed around the inside perimeter of the box to support the bottom. On the tablesaw, rip stock for the cleats to 1 in. wide. The cleats will be positioned ¼ in. from the bottom of the frames—use a combination square set to ¼ in. to draw a layout line around the perimeter **(2)**.

Cut the long cleats to fit between the stiles, and predrill countersunk holes for five 1¼-in. screws. Use a clamp to hold each cleat in position as you drill **(3)**. Glue and screw the long cleats in place, then measure, cut, predrill, and install the short cleats with three screws into each.

Cut and install the bottom

With the perimeter cleats installed, you now can fit the box bottom. Measure the width and length of the inside of the box in case the dimensions vary a bit from those in the parts list. Cut the bottom to fit, and install it with glue and 1¼-in. finish nails **(4)**.

2 **LAY OUT THE CLEATS. With the box upside down on your bench, use a combination square set to ¼ in. to lay out the positions of the cleats on the bottom of the box.**

PLAN VIEW

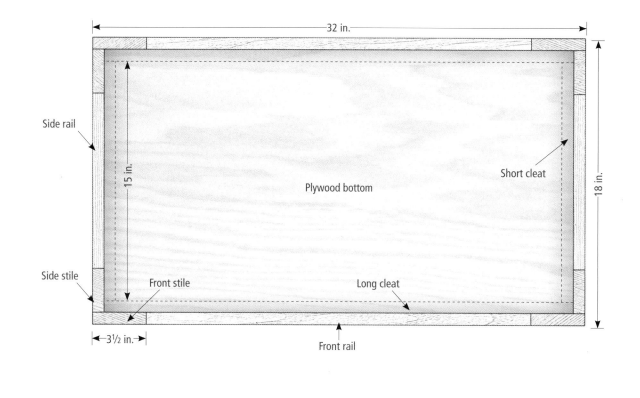

Side rail

15 in.

32 in.

18 in.

Short cleat

Plywood bottom

Side stile

Front stile

Long cleat

3½ in.

Front rail

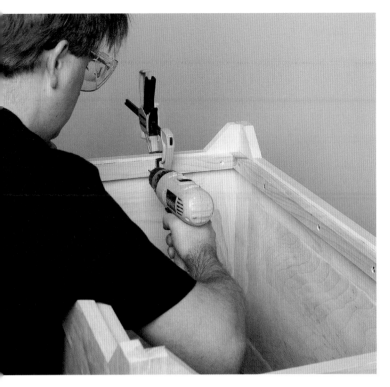

Make the top

Cut the plywood for the top to the dimensions listed in "What You'll Need." Rip ¾-in. x ¾-in. stock for the top edging. Cut a 45° miter on one end of a piece of stock, put it in position on one side of the top, and use a utility knife and square to mark the position of a miter cut on the other end **(5)**. Make the cut and attach the piece with glue and 1¼-in. finish nails. Cut, fit, and install the front edging the same way. Cut and fit the edging for the other side and the back before installing both these pieces.

TIP	If you will be attaching wooden letters to spell the toy chest owner's name, paint the project, including the letters, before gluing the letters to the box—it's virtually impossible to separate the colors neatly if you try to do it after the letters are in place. If your panel fields will be a different color than the frames, see "Cutting in" on p. 31 for advice on how to crisply separate the colors.

---

3 **ATTACH THE CLEATS.** Hold each cleat in position with a clamp while you predrill holes before gluing and screwing the cleats in place.

4 **INSTALL THE BOTTOM.** Set the bottom in place on top of the cleats and then secure with glue and 1¼-in. finishing nails.

5 **LAY OUT MITERS ON THE EDGING.** Use a combination square to scribe the miter cuts on the top edging.

Install the Lid Hardware

Place the lid on the chest, flush to the back and with equal overhang on both sides. For each hinge location, measure in 2 in. from the outside corner of the box and mark the lid and the box at the same time for the outside edge of the hinge **(1)**.

Cut the hinge mortises

Extend the hinge layout marks to the top back edge of the chest and the back of the inside face of the lid. Put a hinge leaf in position and use a utility knife to scribe the leaf's footprint on the box and the lid **(2)**.

You can chop out the mortises with a chisel as described in "Cutting Hinge Mortises" on p. 26.) But this method will be tougher than usual because part of the mortise will

TIP An easy way to set the router bit depth to cut hinge mortises is to set two mortises on a flat surface and then place the router base on the hinges. Now just drop the bit until it hits the surface.

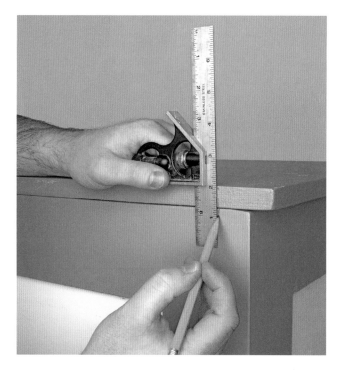

1 **LAY OUT THE HINGE POSITIONS.** Set the lid in place and mark hinge positions on it and the box.

Add the Owner's Moniker

If you choose to emblazon the toy chest with the owner's name, you can find wooden letters in varying sizes at a craft store. You'll have to consider the number of letters in the owner's name, of course, when deciding on the size of the letters. "Ethan" is a short name, so we were able to use bold 5-in.-high letters.

Attach the letters with two-part epoxy glue. It's a good idea to cut spacers to exactly register the positions of the letters as you glue them down. We decided to center the letters top to bottom and the name left to right on the 11-in. x 25-in. front panel. To make a height spacer, we subtracted 5 in. from 11 in. to get 6 in. Dividing that in half, we ripped a piece of scrap to 3 in. wide and then cut it to 25 in. long.

We decided a ½-in. space between letters looked good, so we cut four pieces of ½-in. plywood scrap to roughly 5 in. long. The five letters with the four spacers between measured 21 in. Dividing the

remaining 4 in. of panel length by 2 told us to make a mark on the height spacer 2 in. from the left. Now all we had to do was put the height spacer in place, glue the "E" to the right of the mark, and use the ½-in. spacers to position the letters as we glued them in place.

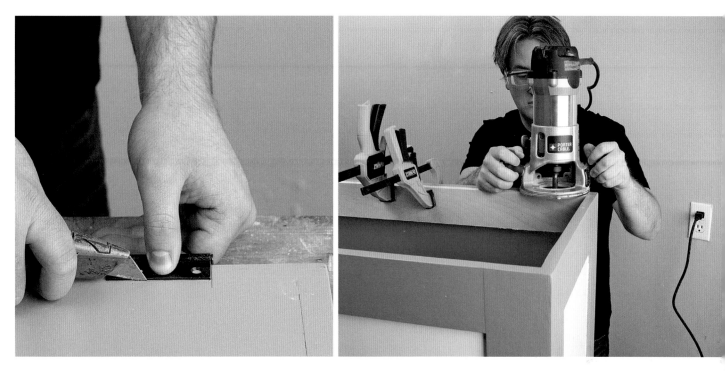

2 **LAY OUT THE MORTISES.** Use a hinge leaf and a utility knife to scribe the hinge mortises on the inside of the lid and the back top edge of the box.

3 **CUT THE MORTISES.** Use a ½-in. bit in the router to remove most of the waste from the hinge mortises. A scrap clamped flush to the top adds stability.

be in the end grain of the chest stiles. An easier method is to put a ½-in. bit in a router and set it to cut to the depth of a hinge leaf. Carefully rout out the hinge area, stopping a bit short of the perimeter and then clean up and square the corners with a chisel. For the mortises in the box, clamp a ¾-in. or wider scrap flush to the top edge to prevent the router from tipping **(3)**.

Install the hinges and the lid supports

Install the hinges in their mortises with the screws provided. Lay out and predrill screw holes for the lid support, positioned as shown on the hardware package. Install the lid supports with the screws provided **(4)**. The supports shown are just one model you can use. A similar support designed to do the same job is available from Rockler Woodworking and Hardware (sold in pairs as item #33027).

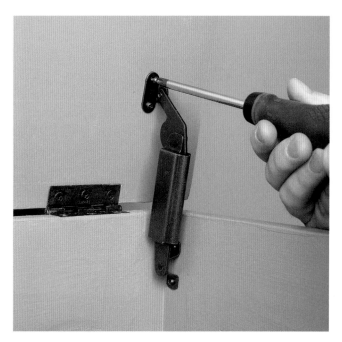

4 **INSTALL THE LID SUPPORTS.** After predrilling holes, screw the lid supports into place on the lid and inside back corners of the box.

CHAPTER SIX

THE MUDROOM

THE FRONT DOOR MAY BE THE GRAND ENTRANCE to your home, but the mudroom entrance is the one that gets used every day. As such, it needs to be attractive and functional.

There are a few essentials every mudroom needs, including a place to hang coats and hats, a place to stow gloves and scarfs, a place to sit while removing shoes and boots, and a place to stow that footwear. If there's a door between the mudroom and the rest of the house, consider adding a waist-high shelf for setting down packages while you open that door.

Beyond that, you need to think about your family's lifestyle. Do you need a place to store sports equipment, such as hockey sticks, basketballs, tennis rackets, perhaps even cross-country skis or snow shoes?

Together, the Cubbies with Coat Hooks and the matching Boot Bench with Storage Bin projects that follow will suit the needs of many families. If you have room for more storage, consider adapting the Closet Tower project on p. 142. The open adjustable shelving system with pull-out baskets can work perfectly in a mudroom.

CUBBIES WITH COAT HOOKS

Here's a family's worth of coat-and-hat hooks with cubbies for stuff like hats, gloves, and scarves. It's a weekend project that's a classic storage solution for any mudroom or foyer. Make it alone or to complement the Boot Bench with Storage Bin on p. 182.

The cubby is made from solid-pine boards, a material that is very easy to cut, nail, and sand and that looks great when painted. The design makes efficient use of nominal 1×10 boards, which actually measure ¾ in. × 9¼ in. The cubby shown here is 4 ft. long, but you can make yours any length you like, adding additional cubby dividers and hooks to accommodate the needs of your family.

WHAT YOU'LL NEED

- 1 top   ¾ in. × 9¼ in. × 48 in.
- 1 bottom   ¾ in. × 8½ in. × 45¾ in.
- 2 sides   ¾ in. × 8½ in. × 16⅝ in.
- 2 dividers   ¾ in. × 8½ in. × 10⅜ in.
- 1 cleat   ¾ in. × 2½ in. × 45 in.
- 1 hook board   ¾ in. × 5½ in. × 45 in.

HARDWARE

- 4d finish nails
- 3 wood screws, #10 × 2½ in.
- 4 all-purpose screws, 1¼ in.
- 5 utility hooks, available from Rockler Woodworking and Hardware, item P27120-PB
- Wood glue

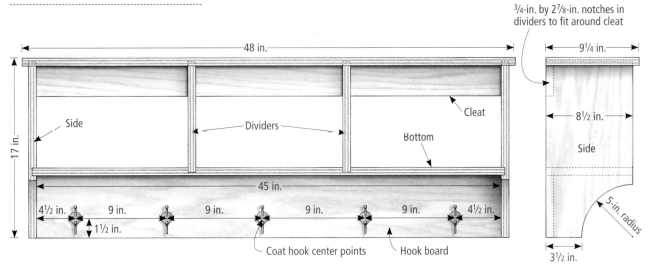

3/4-in. by 2 7/8-in. notches in dividers to fit around cleat

48 in.

9 1/4 in.

Cleat

Side

Dividers

Bottom

8 1/2 in.

Side

17 in.

45 in.

4 1/2 in.   9 in.   9 in.   9 in.   9 in.   4 1/2 in.

1 1/2 in.

5-in. radius

Coat hook center points   Hook board

3 1/2 in.

Make the Parts

Because the parts are made of pine boards that are no wider than 9 1/4 in., cutting the parts to size is simple. Once everything is cut to width and length, you'll lay out and cut dadoes. Later, you will cut the simple curves at the bottom of the sides.

Cut the top, bottom, sides, and dividers

All the parts except the cleat and hook board are made from two 8-ft.-long nominal 1x10s, as shown in the "Cutting Diagram" on p. 172. Use a circular saw with the crosscutting jig to cut the pieces to the lengths listed in "What You'll Need" (see "Making a Crosscutting Jig" on p. 22). Set the workpiece atop a sacrificial piece of plywood on the bench and use a square to lay out the crosscut. Align the outside edge of the jig's base to the layout line and clamp everything in place. Set the circular saw to the combined depth of the workpiece, the jig base, and half the thickness of the sacrificial plywood and make the cut (1). Because the stock is actually 9 1/4 in. wide, you don't have to rip the top piece. Set the tablesaw fence to 8 1/2 in. and rip the bottom, sides, and dividers to width.

1 **THE CUBBY PARTS are too wide for most miter saws, so use a circular saw with a crosscutting jig to safely and accurately cut the cubby pieces to width. The block of 3/4-in.-thick scrap in the foreground under the clamp and jig keeps the jig level with the 3/4-in.-thick workpiece.**

CUTTING DIAGRAM

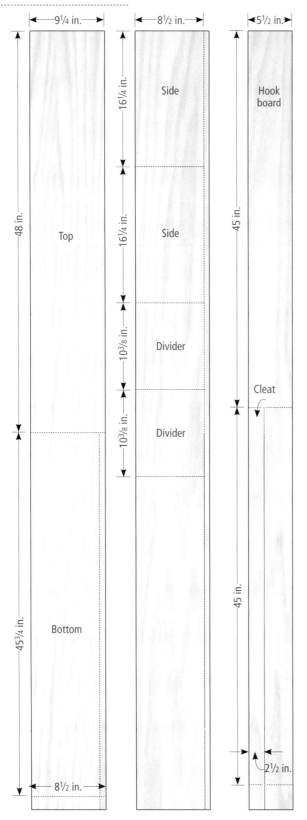

9¼ in.

48 in.

Top

45¾ in.

Bottom

8½ in.

8½ in.

16¼ in.

Side

16¼ in.

Side

10⅜ in.

Divider

10⅜ in.

Divider

5½ in.

45 in.

Hook board

Cleat

45 in.

2½ in.

2 **LAY OUT THE DADOES.** Clamp the top and bottom pieces together to lay out the dadoes. The top gets four dadoes, the bottom two dadoes.

Lay out the top and bottom dadoes

The sides and dividers are housed in four dadoes in the top. The top overhangs ¾ in. at the front and sides, adding some visual interest plus a little extra storage space on top. To accommodate this detail, the dadoes in the top stop ¾ in. from the front. The two dadoes in the bottom that house the dividers and the dado in each side that houses the bottom are not stopped.

Clamp the top and bottom side-by-side and lay out the dadoes as shown in "Dado and Curve Layouts" on the facing page. Draw Xs to indicate which side of the lines the dadoes will be on **(2)**. Leave the boards clamped together.

Position the dado fence for the common dadoes

You'll cut each of the two dadoes in the bottom piece in the same pass as the opposing dado in the top. Add another clamp at one end, with its pad spanning both boards as shown in the photo above to help hold the board down on the bench.

To use as a fence, prepare a straight piece of ¾-in.-thick scrap long enough to span your bench. Use the dado gauge block (see "Making a Dado Gauge Block" on the facing page) to position the fence across the top and bottom pieces. Place a ¾-in.-thick clamping block on the bench against the side of the top piece and another against the side of bottom piece. Clamp both ends of the fence to the bench with blocks underneath, using the gauge block to check the spacing and making sure the fence is square to the workpieces **(3)** (p. 174).

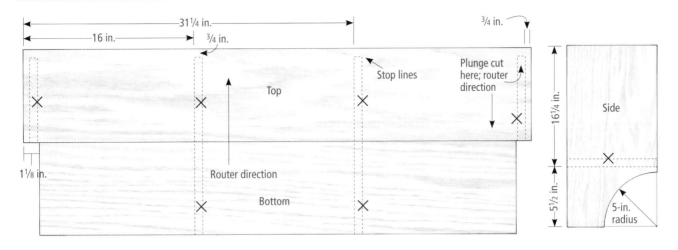

Making a Dado Gauge Block

1. CUT A DADO IN THE GAUGE BLOCK.

2. SCRIBE A LINE WHERE THE FENCE CROSSES THE GAUGE BLOCK.

When cutting dadoes, the fence needs to be offset from the layout line by the distance from the outside edge of the router bit to the guiding edge of the router base. You can measure to set the fence offset, but it's quicker and more accurate to use a gauge block.

Make the block from a ¾-in.-thick scrap that's 2 in. or 3 in. wide and long enough to clamp to the bench without interfering with the router. Clamp a fence squarely across the block, put the router against the fence, and cut a dado in the block as shown in photo **1** at left.

Before unclamping the fence, scribe a cutline on the block where it meets the fence as shown in photo **2** at left. Use a miter saw or the miter gauge on a tablesaw to cut along this line. Draw an arrow to indicate which side of the block goes against the fence and extend lines on both edges indicating the width of the dado. Finally, cut the non-gauge side of the block to a convenient length.

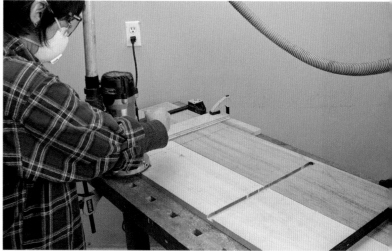

3 USE THE GAUGE BLOCK TO POSITION THE FENCE.
To check for square, run the block along the fence to make sure the fence is properly aligned along its length. Double-check for square with a framing square.

4 CUT THE COMMON DADOES FIRST. Move the router from left to right against the fence as you rout the common dadoes.

Cut the dadoes

Cut the common dadoes in the top and bottom first **(4)**. Set a ¾-in.-dia. bit in the router to a depth of ⅜ in. As you make each dado, move the router from left to right against the fence as indicated in "Dado and Curve Layouts" on p. 173. This way, the router will be pulled against the fence as the bit scoops wood instead of trying to climb out of the cut.

Now prepare to rout the end dadoes in the top. Remove the bottom piece (with the through dadoes) and clamp the top piece (with the stopped dadoes) to the bench. Use the dado gauge block to set the fence **(5)**. Note that for the side shown in the photo and noted in "Dado and Curve Cut Layouts," the fence must be set to the right of the dado, rather than to the left as with all the other dadoes—otherwise, the router wouldn't ride on the board. As a result, for this one dado you will need to plunge at the stop in order to rout from left to right against the fence. Rout both end dadoes.

5 CUT THE END DADOES IN THE TOP. Use the dado gauge block to set the fence for the dadoes on the ends of the tops. Check that the fence is square to the top.

> **TIP** If, after clamping, you find that the fence is a tiny bit out of square, you might not have to unclamp and start over. Often a light tap or two on the fence with a hammer will nudge the fence the tiny bit you need.

Use a ¾-in. chisel to chop square each of the stopped dadoes in the top **(6)**. When chopping the end dadoes, cut the sides first so you are cutting across the grain. Then chop the front as shown in the photo. This will prevent splitting the end of the board.

The final dadoes to cut are those in the sides. Each side gets one dado to receive the bottom (5½ in. up from the bottom of the side). As you did for the top and bottom, clamp the sides together to lay out the dadoes. Then use the dado gauge block to set the fence and rout the dadoes **(7)**.

Cut the hook board and cleat

The hook board and cleat can be made from a single nominal 1x6, as shown in the "Cutting Diagram" on p. 172. Measure the distance between the outermost dadoes on the top piece in case it varies a bit from the 45 in. specified for the length of the hook board and cleat in "What You'll Need." Use a power or hand miter saw to cut the hook board to length **(8)**. Because the stock is actually 5½ in. wide, you don't need to rip the hook board. Rip the cleat to 2½ in. and then crosscut it to length with the miter saw.

6 **SQUARE THE STOPPED DADOES. To prevent splitting, chop first along the sides of the dadoes and then at the front.**

7 **ROUT A DADO IN EACH SIDE. Clamp the sides together to lay out and rout the dadoes to receive the cubby bottom.**

8 **CUT THE HOOK BOARD AND CLEAT. Use a miter saw to cut the hook board and the cleat to length.**

1 **LAY OUT THE CURVES IN THE SIDES.** For each side piece, set a compass for a 5-in. radius, place the point on the outside bottom corner, and draw a curve.

2 **LAY OUT THE NOTCHES IN THE DIVIDERS.** Clamp a divider to the bench so it won't slide around, then use a combination square to lay out the notch that the cleat will pass through.

Cut the Decorative Curves and Notches

Now that all the parts are cut to length (and width as appropriate), you can cut the curves in the two sides and the notches to accommodate the cleat in the dividers. Set a compass to a 5-in. radius. For each side piece, place the compass point at the bottom outside edge and draw a 5-in. radius **(1)**, as shown in "Dado and Curve Layouts" on p. 173. Clamp each piece to the bench and cut the curves with a sabersaw.

The dividers need to be notched to fit over the hanging cleat. Set a combination square to ¾ in. and use it to lay out ¾-in. x 2⅞-in. notches in the dividers **(2)**. Cut the notches with the sabersaw. It's easiest to sand all the parts now before assembling them. Round over all the edges that will be exposed and make the curves in the sides smooth and fair.

> **TIP** Use a thin, fine-toothed blade to cut curves with the sabersaw. Save the wider blade for when you need to make unwavering straight cuts.

1 **GLUE THE CLEAT TO THE TOP.** Glue and clamp the cleat along the back edge of the top piece.

2 **PREDRILL THE DIVIDERS.** Before glue-up, put the dividers in place, make sure they are square to the cleat and the top, and predrill countersunk holes for the 1¼-in. screws.

Assemble the Cubby

First, test-assemble the whole project to make sure everything fits. Then put glue on one long edge of the cleat and clamp it to the back of the upside-down top with the clamps extending under the bench **(1)**. Before you tighten the clamps, make sure the ends of the cleat are flush to the end dadoes and the cleat is flush to the back of the top.

Install the dividers

When the glue sets, remove the clamps except for one at each end to hold the assembly on the bench. Put the dividers in place in their dadoes without glue. Clamp a square against a divider to keep it square to the bottom, then predrill two countersunk holes through the cleat into the divider **(2)** (see "Countersinking and Counterboring" on p. 27). Predrill the other divider in the same way. Remove the dividers. For each one, put glue in the dado and in the notch. Replace the divider and secure it with a 1¼-in. screw in each hole.

Flip the assembly up and use a square to draw light pencil marks indicating the centerline of the dadoes below. You'll draw these lines whenever you are nailing through a piece into a dado. Drive three 4d nails through the top into each divider **(3)**. Be careful to drive the nails straight down. Set the nails.

3 **NAIL THE TOP TO THE DIVIDERS.** After gluing and screwing the dividers in place, add three nails through the top into each divider.

4 **ATTACH THE SIDES.** Assemble the sides to the bottom with three finish nails into each joint.

5 **NAIL THE SIDES TO THE CLEAT.** After gluing and nailing the sides into the dadoes in the top, add two nails through each side into the cleat.

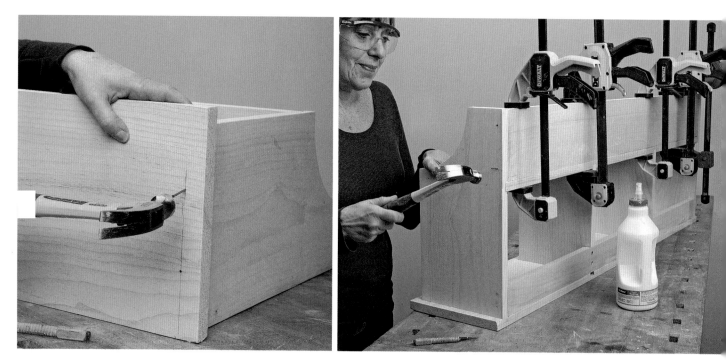

6 **NAIL THE TOP TO THE SIDES.** Add two nails through the top into each side.

7 **ATTACH THE HOOK BOARD.** After gluing and clamping the hook board to the bottom, secure it to each side with two nails.

Attach the sides to the bottom

Put glue in the dadoes in the sides and attach them to the bottom with three 4d nails on each end **(4)**. Use a rubber mallet if necessary to tap joints together or align them at the front before you nail. Always check for square after nailing a joint in case you have to pull on a piece a bit to make it square. Set the nails.

Finish the cubby assembly

With the top upside down on the bench, put glue in the end dadoes and on the ends of the dividers. Put the bottom-and-sides assembly in place, and drive three 4d nails through the bottom into each divider. Drive and set two nails through each side into the ends of the cleat **(5)**.

Finish by nailing the top to the sides **(6)**. Use just two 4d nails to make each of these connections, keeping the nails well away from the front and back.

Attach the hook board

The final piece to install is the hook board, which runs between the two sides below the cubby bottom. Put glue on one long edge and both ends of the hook board and clamp it in to the bottom, making sure it is flush to the back of the bottom and sides. (You can use 4d nails through the bottom if you are short on clamps.) Drive

two 4d nails through the sides into each end of the hook board **(7)**.

When the glue sets, remove the clamps, fill the nail holes, and do a final sanding to make all adjoining surfaces perfectly flush. Prime the project and sand lightly with 80 grit. Add another coat of filler to any nail holes that need it and sand them flush. Then apply two coats of paint.

Attach the coat hooks

The number of hooks you install depends on the overall width of the cubby. For this 48-in.-wide cubby, five hooks are about the most you'd want to use without crowding the coats.

Begin by laying out the center points for the five coat hooks (as shown in the drawing on p. 171). Set a combination square to 1½ in. and use it to gauge the distance from the bottom of the hook board while using a tape measure to mark each point **(8)**. As you locate each point, use the square to scribe a line about ½ in. to each side of the point. You will use these lines to locate the two screw holes in each hook.

Center each hook over a center point, and adjust its height until you can see the layout line centered across each screw hole. Install with the screws provided with the hooks **(9)**.

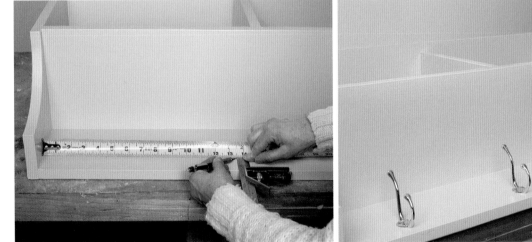

8 **LAY OUT THE POSITION OF THE HOOKS. Use a tape measure in conjunction with a combination square set at 1½ in. to lay out the center points for the coat hooks.**

9 **INSTALL THE HOOKS. Place each hook on its center point with the layout line centered across each hole, then install with the screws provided.**

Hang the Cubby

The project will be mounted to three studs in the wall with three 2½-in. #10 screws through the cleats. Decide on the height you want for the top shelf of the cubbies—about 80 in. works well. Subtract 2 in. to get the height of the screws.

Locate the attachment points

For this installation, we wanted the cubby to be centered over the 5-ft.-long boot bench (see p. 182). The boot bench will be placed in a corner—due to baseboard molding, it will be about 1½ in. from the wall. Since the boot bench is 12 in. longer than the cubby, it will extend past the cubby by 6 in. on each side. Adding in the 1½ in. for baseboard, we made a mark 7½ in. from the corner and 80 in. from the floor.

Use a 4-ft. level to draw a level line from this mark **(1)**. Then use a stud finder to locate three studs along the line (see "Finding Wall Studs" on p. 28). Predrill the center hole.

Locate the screws on the cleats

Measure the distance from the corner to each hole you drilled in the wall. From each of these measurements, subtract the distance the top shelf will be from the wall— 7½ in. in this case. Now set the cubby across a pair of sawhorses with the back facing up. Hook your tape on the side of the cubby and mark the distances on the back of the cleats **(2)**. Then use a combination square to transfer these points to the front of the cleats, 1¼ in. from the bottom of the cleats.

Counterbore holes for #10 screws through the front of the cleats **(3)**. Increase the diameter of the holes with a ³⁄₁₆-in. bit.

Mount to the wall

Poke a screw through the hole near the middle of the cleat so that it protrudes slightly from the back. Put the cubby up on the wall, and insert the protruding screw into the center hole on the wall. Drive in the center screw. Level the project with a 4-ft. level on the top shelf, then drive screws through the two remaining holes in the cleats **(4)**.

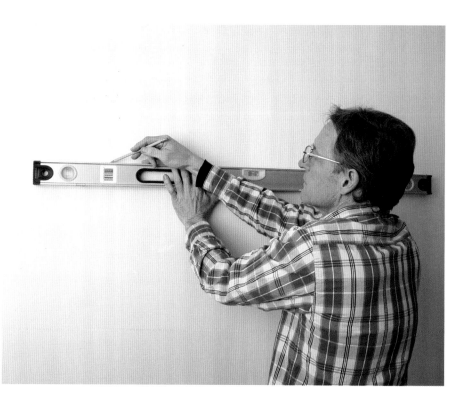

1 **LOCATE THE ATTACHMENT POINTS. Use a 4-ft. level to mark the height of the three attachment screws, then use a stud finder to locate three studs along the line.**

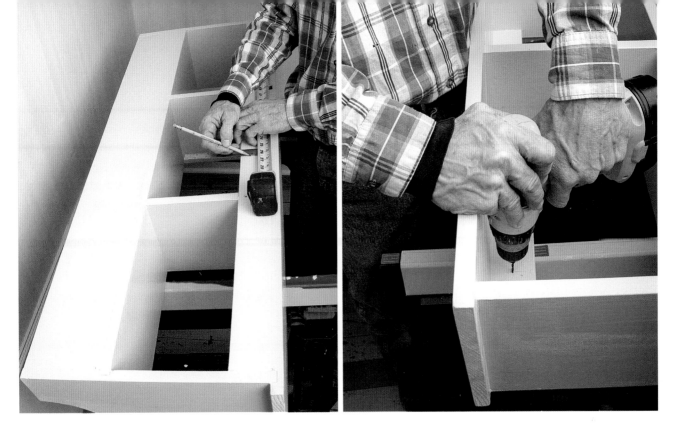

2 **LOCATE THE SCREW HOLES ON THE CLEAT.** Use a tape measure to locate the screw holes on the back of the cleat, then use a combination square to transfer the measurements to the front of the cleat.

3 **COUNTERBORE AND PREDRILL THE SCREW HOLES.** Countersink the screw holes in the cleats, then enlarge them with a 3/16-in.-dia. bit.

4 **ATTACH THE CUBBY TO THE WALL.** Insert the middle screw (not visible here), then level the project on the wall before installing the two remaining mounting screws.

BOOT BENCH WITH STORAGE BIN

It's not always practical to build in a project, but you can still customize it for your needs and to coordinate with the décor. This mudroom boot bench is a good example. It is freestanding so that it can easily be pulled away from a plumbing access panel behind it, yet it appears built-in. That's because it is sized to fit the space and painted to match the room trim. Also, like a closet door beside it, the front and the exposed side have faux panels covered in the same wallpaper as the walls. The "panels" are actually mitered molding attached to the face of the plywood front and side. You can paint them to match your wall or trim color, or, for a slicker look, you can skip them altogether.

This 5-ft.-long bench is built in two sections—a 2-ft.-long enclosed bin with a lid that opens for stowing gear, and a 3-ft.-long section that's open in the front for stowing boots. The sections are built separately in the shop and then screwed together on site. This makes the project easy to transport and install. It also makes it adaptable to your needs. You can build just the boot bench or just the storage bench. And, of course, it's a simple matter to adapt the length of either or both sections to your needs. It works perfectly as a companion to the other mudroom project: the Cubbies with Coat Hooks.

WHAT YOU'LL NEED

STORAGE BIN

- 1 front panel — ¾ in. × 15¼ in. × 24 in., birch plywood
- 1 mitered side panel — ¾ in. × 15¼ in. × 15¼ in., birch plywood
- 1 side panel — ¾ in. × 14¾ in. × 15¼ in., birch plywood
- 1 rear panel — ¾ in. × 15¼ in. × 22½ in., birch plywood
- 1 bottom panel — ¾ in. × 13¾ in. × 22½ in., birch plywood
- 2 side cleats — ¾ in. × ¾ in. × 13¾ in., pine

- 2 front and rear cleats   ¾ in. × ¾ in. × 21 in., pine
- 1 lid   ¾ in. × 14¾ in. × 23¼ in., birch plywood
- 2 front and rear lid edging   ¾ in. × ¾ in. × 24¾ in.
- 2 side lip edging   ¾ in. × ¾ in. × 16 in.
- 2 front horizontal face molding   ⅜ in. × 1⅛ in. × 19 in., preprimed
- 2 side horizontal face molding   ⅜ in. × 1⅛ in. × 10¼ in., preprimed
- 4 front and side vertical
  face molding   ⅜ in. × 1⅛ in. × 10¼ in., preprimed

BOOT BENCH

- 1 rear panel   ¾ in. × 15¼ in. × 34½ in., birch plywood
- 2 side panels   ¾ in. × 14¾ in. × 15¼ in., birch plywood
- 1 bottom panel   ¾ in. × 13¾ in. × 34½ in., birch plywood
- 1 box rail   ¾ in. × 1¼ in. box rail × 34½ in., plywood
- 1 front bottom cleat   ¾ in. × ¾ in. × 34½ in., pine
- 2 side bottom cleats   ¾ in. × ¾ in. × 13 in., pine
- 1 rear bottom cleat   ¾ in. × ¾ in. × 33 in., pine
- 2 face-frame stiles   ¾ in. × 1½ in. × 15¼ in., clear pine
- 2 face-frame rails   ¾ in. × 1½ in. × 33 in., clear pine
- 1 seat   ¾ in. × 14¾ in. × 34½ in., birch plywood
- 2 front and rear seat edging   ¾ in. × ¾ in. × 36 in.
- 2 side edging   ¾ in. × ¾ in. × 16¼ in.

FEET

- 4 foot sides   ¾ in. × 2 in. × 1¾ in., clear pine
- 4 foot sides   ¾ in. × 2 in. × 2½ in., clear pine
- 2 center-foot sides   ¾ in. × 2 in. × 13 in., clear pine
- 4 foot bases   ¾ in. × 1¾ in. × 1¾ in., plywood
- 1 center-foot base   ¾ in. × 1½ in. × 13 in., plywood

HARDWARE

- #20 joinery biscuits
- #0 joinery biscuits
- 1¼-in. pocket-hole screws
- 1¼-in. all-purpose screws
- 1½-in. finish nails
- ¾-in. brads
- 2 pairs 1½-in. × 2½-in. butt hinges
- 1 lid support*
- 5 utility hooks

*Available from Rockler Woodworking and Hardware, item number 66649

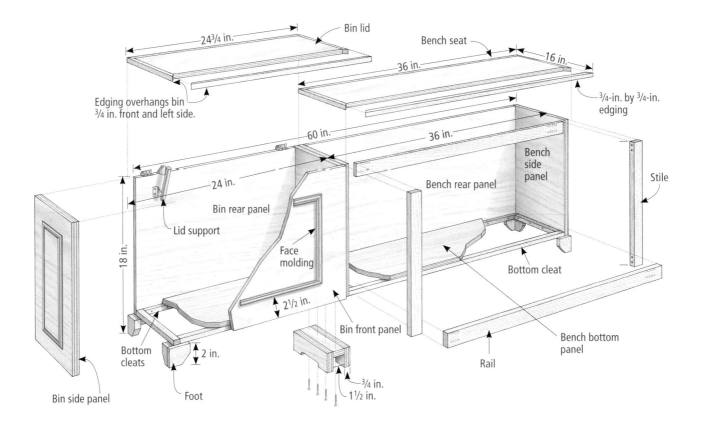

Bin lid

24³⁄₄ in.

Bench seat

36 in.

16 in.

Edging overhangs bin
³⁄₄ in. front and left side.

³⁄₄-in. by ³⁄₄-in.
edging

60 in.

36 in.

Bench
side
panel

Stile

24 in.

Bin rear panel

Bench rear panel

Lid support

Face
molding

18 in.

Bottom cleat

2½ in.

Bin front panel

Bottom cleat

Bottom
cleats

2 in.

Bench bottom
panel

Foot

³⁄₄ in.

Rail

1½ in.

Bin side panel

Cut the Plywood Parts

The first step is to cut all the plywood parts to dimension. You'll first rip plywood sheets to the width of the widest parts, then crosscut the parts, and finish by cutting the narrower plywood parts to final width.

Make the first rips

All the plywood parts can be cut from a single 4-ft. x 8-ft. sheet of plywood, as shown in the "Plywood Cutting Diagram" on the facing page. Unless you have a professional-size tablesaw with an outfeed table, the best strategy is to use a circular saw to rough-rip the sheet at 31 in. to give you two manageable pieces before cutting those pieces to the precise dimensions you need. Do the cutting on the floor with "sacrificial" lumber or plywood underneath as shown in "Rough-Ripping Plywood" on p. 21.

After making the rough rip, set the tablesaw fence to 15¼ in. Make sure you have 8 ft. of space in front of the saw and behind the saw and that you have rollers, a table, or a helper in position to catch the rips as they come off the saw. Make two rips from the piece you rough-ripped at 31 in **(1)**.

Make the square-edged crosscuts

You'll make the crosscuts now because shorter pieces are easier to rip on the tablesaw. Use a crosscutting jig with the circular saw (see "Making a Crosscutting Jig" on p. 22) to make all the square-edged crosscuts shown in the "Plywood Cutting Diagram." The bin front panel and bin side panel will meet with a miter. For this reason, cut them each ½ in. longer than final length—you'll trim them to final length when you make the miter cuts.

PLYWOOD CUTTING DIAGRAM

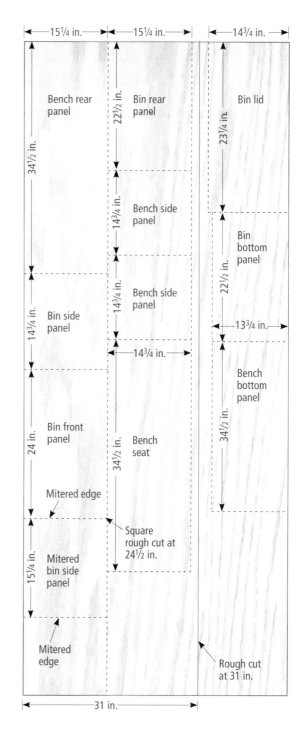

- 15¼ in.
- 15¼ in.
- 14¾ in.

Bench rear panel

22½ in.

Bin rear panel

Bin lid

23¼ in.

34½ in.

Bench side panel

14¾ in.

Bin bottom panel

22½ in.

Bench side panel

14¾ in.

Bin side panel

14¾ in.

- 14¾ in.

- 13¾ in.

Bench bottom panel

34½ in.

24 in.

Bin front panel

Bench seat

34½ in.

Mitered edge

Square rough cut at 24½ in.

15¼ in.

Mitered bin side panel

Mitered edge

Rough cut at 31 in.

- 31 in.

1 **CUT THE PLYWOOD PARTS TO WIDTH.** When ripping the full-length pieces of plywood on the table-saw, make sure you have adequate clearance at the front and rear of the saw and that the workpieces will be supported by roller stands, as shown here, or by an outfeed table or a helper.

2 **MAKE THE SQUARE-EDGED CROSSCUTS.** Use the circular saw with the crosscutting jig to cut the square-edged pieces to final length.

Place a piece of sacrificial plywood on the workbench with the workpiece on top and clamp both pieces to the bench. Use a square to lay out the crosscut line. Align the base of the jig to the layout line and clamp the jig to the workpiece. Set the saw depth to the combined thickness of the workpiece and the base of the jig plus ⅛ in., then make the cuts **(2)** (p. 185).

Make the miter cuts

The bin side panel and the bin front panel are wide enough to crosscut safely using the tablesaw, if the fence on your saw can be set far enough from the blade. If not, you can do the job by making a crosscutting jig as described in "Making a Crosscutting Jig" on p. 22, with one

> **TIP** When laying out the crosscuts, always make them square to a factory edge or the edge you cut on the tablesaw—not the rough cut.

difference: Set your circular saw to 45° to cut the jig's base to width.

If you'll be making these cuts on the tablesaw, measure and mark the final length, then use a combination square to lay out the 45° cut from this mark on the edge of each piece. It is a good idea to extend the line across the top of the workpiece, just to monitor that you're cutting parallel to the fence.

Set the tablesaw blade to 45° and align the layout mark to the mark. Adjust the fence to meet the workpiece and make the cut **(3)**.

Make the final rips

At this point, some pieces are already at their final width of 15¼ in. (as shown in the "Plywood Cutting Diagram"). Return the tablesaw blade to 90° and set the fence to 14¾ in. to rip the bench side panels, the bench seat, and the bin lid to final width. Finally, set the fence to 13¾ in. to cut the bin bottom panel and the bench bottom panel.

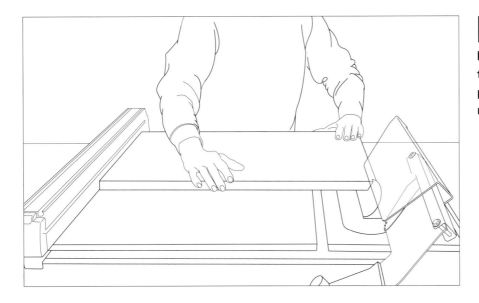

3 **MAKE THE MITER CUTS.** Lay out the miter cuts on the bin front and side panels; use the layout line on the side of the piece to set the rip fence and make the cut.

> **TIP** When using the tablesaw to make final-dimension rips, never place the rough-ripped edge against the fence. To ensure straight rips, guide cuts with the factory edge or an edge that has previously been ripped on the tablesaw.

Lay Out and Cut the Biscuit Joint Slots

The side, front, and rear panels for both the bench and the bin are assembled with biscuit joints. Begin by laying out the butt joints.

Lay out the butt joints

With the outside faces of the panels on the bench, align each pair of edges that will be butt-joined. Mark them together for five equally spaced biscuit slots. Make marks about 2 in. from the top and bottom edge, a center mark, and two more marks approximately centered between the edge and center marks **(1)**. Identify the mating joints by writing the same letter on each.

Cut the edge slots

You'll be cutting slots into the edges of both back panels and the front edge of the bin right side panel. Remove the fence from the biscuit joiner for this operation and the next step. Rather than clamping each piece to the bench to make the cuts, you can save time by clamping a scrap across the workbench. Now you can place each workpiece outside face down against this stop **(2)**. Hold the workpiece down on the bench while you cut the slots.

Cut the face slots

All four side panels get slots along the back of their inside faces. To help make these joints, make an L-fence from two 5-in.-square scraps of ¾-in. plywood. Screw the pieces together to make a flush corner. (This is the same fence that was used in the Toy Chest project; see p. 157.)

Clamp the workpiece to the work surface with the face to be slotted facing up and overhanging your workbench about 6 in. Use a combination square to extend the layout marks into lines to make them easier to see. Hold the L-fence firmly against the bottom and edge of the workpiece, put the base of the joiner against the L-fence, and plunge down to make slots **(3)**.

1 **LAY OUT THE BISCUITS FOR THE BUTT JOINTS. Place adjoining square edges together to lay out the** biscuit slot locations.

2 **CUT THE EDGE SLOTS. Clamp a stop across your bench to make quick work of cutting biscuit** slots in the panel edges.

3 **USE AN L-FENCE TO CUT THE FACE SLOTS. With the panel clamped to and overhanging the edge of** the work surface, hold an L-fence firmly against the bottom and edge as you make slot cuts in the panel faces.

4 **LAY OUT THE MITERED SLOTS.** Mark the mitered corner of the bin for seven biscuit slots.

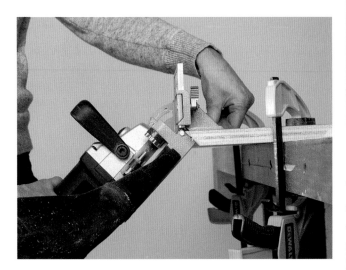

5 **MAKE THE MITERED BISCUIT SLOTS.** Set the biscuit joiner fence at 45° and cut the slots in the mitered edges.

Lay out and cut the mitered slots

The left front corner of the bin is the only miter joint because it is the only place where a butt joint would expose a plywood edge. To prevent cutting through the face of the workpieces while making the slots, you need to use seven smaller #0 biscuits to make this joint. Mark the outside edge of one workpiece for slots 1⅝ in. from each end and every 2 in. between. Then stand the pieces up with the mitered edges together and transfer the slot locations to the other piece **(4)**.

Set the biscuit joiner fence to 45° and the cutting depth stop to #0. Clamp the bin side or front to the workbench with the mitered edge overhanging. Hold the joiner's fence firmly on top of the workpiece as you cut the slots from underneath **(5)**.

Biscuit-Joint Alignment

One of the things that makes biscuit joinery so easy to work with is that the design of the biscuits makes the joinery both precise and forgiving. Mating outside surfaces will automatically be precisely flush, whether you are making corners as in the Boot Bench or joining pieces edge-to-edge as in a tabletop. At the same time, the football shape of the biscuits means that mating biscuit slots do not need to be precisely aligned along their length. You can adjust the joint along its length a bit during glue-up—for example, to get the top and bottom edges of the bin panels perfectly flush.

Glue Up the Panels

With all the parts cut and slotted for the biscuits, it's time to glue up the panels. Here, we assemble the bench panels first, but it doesn't matter if you start with the bin panels.

Assemble the bench panels

Put the bench bottom panel on the work surface. You won't be attaching it now; it's just there to help you square the side panels to the back panel. The back panel sits inside the side panels. Test-assemble the three panels to make sure everything fits properly and to get four clamps adjusted to the length you need. Put glue in all the biscuit slots and assemble the panels **(1)**. Apply clamps across the bottom at the back and front, across the top of the back, and finally across the middle of the back. Check the corners for square, top and bottom.

Assemble the bin panels

Now test-assemble the four sides of the bin. Remember, the front left corner is a miter joint, the back panel sits inside the two side panels, and the front panel runs past the side panel on the right corner (this is a butt joint, but the plywood edge won't be visible as it will be covered by the left side of the bench).

1 ASSEMBLE THE BENCH PANELS. Check for square after assembling the bench sides to the back with biscuits, glue, and three clamps. Use the bottom panel to help square the assembly—don't glue it in place yet.

2 ASSEMBLE THE BIN PANELS. Use six clamps with glue and biscuits to assemble the bin sides to the front. Check for square as you tighten clamps.

You'll need six clamps—one at top and one at bottom spanning the length of the bin and one at top and one at bottom spanning the width. Use an additional clamp on each side spanning from the front to the back—this will help pull the miter joint together while putting equal pressure on the other side **(2)**.

will allow you to disassemble the bench from the bin for transport and then screw the two back together through these holes on site.

Make the Face Frame

Now it's time to turn your attention to the face frame for the bench.

Rip stock for the face frame

Rip stock for the stiles and rails to 1½ in. Place the bin and bench against each other and use a piece of face-frame stock to make sure the face frame will be flush to the bin front panel. (The plywood is probably a bit thinner than the ¾-in. pine stock—this tiny offset won't matter at the back.) Clamp the bin and bench together. Countersink a 1¼-in. screw in each corner through the bench side panel into the bin side panel, keeping the screws at least 2 in. from the bottom so the holes won't be covered when you install the bottom panel **(1)** (at right). (See "Countersinking and Counterboring" on p. 27.) This

1 ASSEMBLE THE BIN TO THE BENCH. Use a piece of face-frame stock to make sure the bin and bench are flush at front. Hold the sides in position with a clamp as you counterbore and screw the bench to the bin.

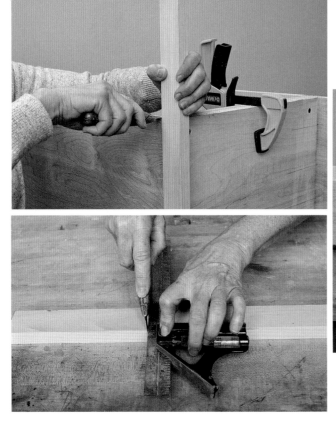

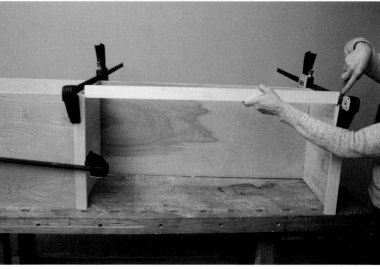

3 **SCRIBE AND CUT THE RAILS TO LENGTH.** Clamp the stiles in place so you can scribe the length of the rails.

2 **MARK THE LENGTH OF THE STILES.** Hold the stock in place flush with the front of the bin and use a utility knife to scribe the length of the stiles. Use a square to score across the front of the stile.

Cut the stiles and rails to length

With a piece of stile stock in place against the front of the bench, butted into the side of the bin, use a utility knife to make a notch as shown in the top photo above **(2)**. Then, with the knife in the notch, put a square against the blade and score across the piece. Cut both stiles to this length with a power or hand miter saw.

The rail lengths are listed in "What You'll Need," but it's always best to scribe parts in place in case any measurement has changed slightly. Clamp the stiles in place with two clamps across the top and one across the front of the bin, pulling the stiles tightly against the bin as shown. Then scribe and cut one rail to fit **(3)**. Cut both rails to the same length.

Assemble the face frame

The rails are joined to the stiles with pocket screws. Use a pocket-hole jig to drill two pocket holes for 1¼-in. pocket-hole screws in the end of each rail **(4)**. With the jig shown here, adjust the spacing of the holes to be as close together as the jig will allow. Center the workpiece in the jig's clamp.

4 **CUT POCKET HOLES IN THE RAILS.** Drill holes for 1¼-in. pocket screws in the ends of the rails.

Place a stile in the workbench vise, put glue on the end of a rail, and clamp the rail to the stile. Insert the screws and repeat the process to attach the other rail. Put the other stile in the bench and attach the rails to it **(5)**.

5 **ASSEMBLE THE FACE FRAME.** With one stile in the vise, assemble the rails with glue and pocket screws. Then attach the rails to the other stile.

TIP When nailing the bottom rail into the side of the bottom panel, it's important to nail straight so the nails don't come through either face of the bottom. It's easier to nail straight down than to nail horizontally, so tip the bench on its side to nail the rail.

Install the Bottoms

Now it is time to install the bottoms, which are supported by cleats attached around the perimeter of the bin and bench.

Cut and install the cleats

Disassemble the bin from the bench. Rip stock to ¾-in. x ¾-in. for all the bottom cleats for the bin and the bench.

Install the bin side cleats first. Hold a piece of overlong cleat stock in place and use a utility knife to scribe a cut for a cleat to fit between the front and back. Cut two cleats to this length with a power miter saw or hand miter saw. Put the side cleats in place, making sure they are

flush to the bottom, and drill countersinks for three ¼-in. screws. Glue the back face of the cleats and screw them in place. Now repeat the process to cut and attach the front and back cleats with four screws each **(1)**.

Use the same method but a different sequence to install the cleats in the bench: First, install the front cleat with five screws, then the side cleats with three screws each. Finally, install the back cleat with five screws.

Glue and nail the bottoms into place

Apply glue to the top of the bench cleats and also along the inside of the bottom rail **(2)**. Set the bottom panel in place and secure it with two 1¼-in. finish nails into each side cleat and three into the front and rear cleats. Then add three nails through the bottom rail into the side of the bottom panel. Set the nails.

TIP When installing cleats in a box, the box will be stronger if the cleat joints are offset from the box joints. In other words, if a side panel butts into a front panel, the side cleat should butt into the front cleat.

1 **CUT AND INSTALL THE CLEATS.** Scribe and drill countersinks for each bottom cleat before gluing and screwing it into place.

2 **PREPARE TO INSTALL THE BOTTOM PANEL.** Put glue on the inside of the bottom rail as well as the top of all the cleats before installing the bottom panel.

Make and Install the Feet

The feet add a nice design touch to the project but also serve a practical purpose: Few floors are perfectly flat, and since the boot bench is freestanding it would probably rock if the entire bottom were in contact with the floor.

Lay out and cut the corner-foot parts

On the tablesaw, rip about 4 ft. of ¾-in. clear pine to 2 in. wide. This is enough stock for the corner feet and the recessed center foot.

Each corner foot is made of a 2½-in.-long front piece, a 1¾-in.-long side piece, and a 1¾-in.-square base, as shown in the drawing "Foot Construction" at right. Because the feet are small, the safest way to get a good grip on the stock while keeping your fingers away from the sawblade is to lay out the first piece, make the angled cut **(1)**, then square-cut the piece off the board. Repeat the process to make all the pieces. Still working with the 2-in.-wide stock, cut two 13-in.-long pieces for the recessed center foot. Save any 2-in.-wide offcuts you have—they will come in handy later when you cut hinge mortises.

To complete the parts for the corner feet, reset the tablesaw and rip a piece of plywood to 1¾ in. Then use a miter saw to cut it into four 1¾-in.-square-foot bases.

FOOT CONSTRUCTION

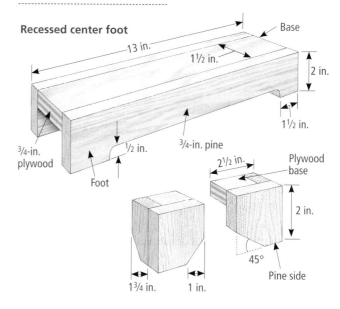

Glue up the corner feet

When gluing up the feet, you want to make sure that the angle cuts will oppose each other on each side. For best appearance, you also want the wider pieces at front. To make this happen, arrange the pieces as they will be oriented on the project as you glue them up with one clamp per assembly **(2)**.

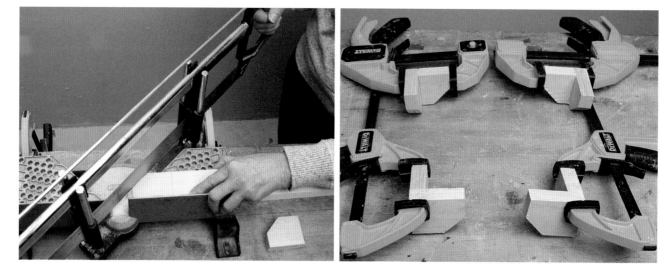

1 **CUT THE PARTS FOR THE CORNER FEET. To keep your fingers safely away from the miter saw blade while cutting the feet parts, make each angled cut before square-cutting the part to length.**

2 **GLUE UP THE CORNER-FOOT SIDES. Orient the angled foot pieces in their installed positions to ensure you are gluing the correct sides together.**

Once the glue has set, remove the clamps from the corner-foot sides and use glue and two clamps to attach a base flush to the top of each one **(3)**.

Make the recessed center-foot parts

The center foot is made from two long pine sides with a plywood base between them. On the tablesaw, rip a piece of ¾-in. plywood to 1½ in. wide for the center-foot base, then use a miter saw or the miter gauge on the tablesaw to crosscut it to 13 in. long.

Using a sabersaw, make the cuts on the bottom of the 13-in. pine pieces to form feet as shown in the drawing "Foot Construction" on the facing page. These cuts make it less likely that unevenness in the floor will cause the bench/bin assembly to rock. The cuts need not be exact— you can draw the curves freehand **(4)**.

Use four clamps as shown to glue the center feet to the sides of the center-foot base. Make sure the parts are flush at top **(5)**.

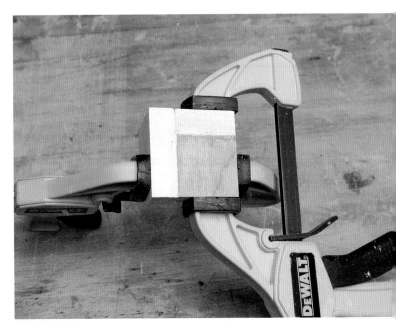

 ATTACH THE CORNER-FOOT BASES. Use two clamps to glue a base block to each foot assembly.

 CUT THE RECESSES IN THE CENTER-FOOT SIDES. Use a sabersaw to form feet on the bottom of the center-foot sides.

5 **GLUE UP THE CENTER FOOT. Use four clamps to glue the center-foot sides to the base.**

Install the feet

Clamp a corner foot in position on the bin or bench. Drill countersinks into the cleats for two 1¼-in. screws **(6)**. Remove the clamp and attach the foot with glue and screws. Install the other three corner feet in the same way.

Next, clamp the center foot in position on the bottom of the bench flush to the back and the side cleat. Countersink holes for four 1¼-in. screws into the bottom of the bench side **(7)**. Remove the clamp and glue and screw the foot in place.

Now you need to drill center-foot attachment holes in the bottom of the bin. Put the bench and bin on their sides and join them by reinserting screws through the four holes you made earlier through the bench side. Countersink four holes through the center-foot base into the bin side **(8)**. Detach the bin from the bench again.

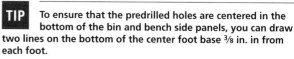

TIP To ensure that the predrilled holes are centered in the bottom of the bin and bench side panels, you can draw two lines on the bottom of the center foot base ⅜ in. in from each foot.

6 **INSTALL THE CORNER FEET. Counterbore for two screws into the base of each corner foot before** attaching them to the bin and the bench.

7 **INSTALL THE CENTER FOOT. Countersink four holes before gluing and screwing the center foot to** the bottom of the bench.

8 **DRILL CENTER-FOOT ATTACHMENT HOLES IN THE BOTTOM OF THE BIN. After screwing the bin and** bench side panels together again, countersink four holes for attaching the center foot to the bin.

Install the Wallpaper Frames

As shown in the photo on p. 182, the front and the left side of the bin have framed wallpaper panels. The frames are made of mitered pieces of molding glued and nailed in place.

Lay out and cut the frames

To lay out the frame perimeters, set a combination square to 2½ in. and use it to guide a pencil as you draw the outside perimeter of the wallpaper frames **(1)**.

Use a hand or power miter saw to cut a 45° angle on one end of a piece of molding. Place the molding along one side of the perimeter layout with the long end of the miter at the corner. Mark for the outside of the miter on the other end **(2)** and make that cut. Tack the first piece in place with two nails driven in partway.

Install the molding

Cut a miter on one end of another piece of molding, put it in position against the first piece, and mark for the miter on the other end. Make that cut and tack the second piece in place with one nail near the second cut. Lay out and cut miters on the final two pieces **(3)**; there's no need to tack-nail them.

1 **LAY OUT THE WALLPAPER FRAMES. Use a combination square set to 2½ in. to lay out the outside perimeter of the wallpaper frames on the front and side of the bin.**

2 **MARK THE FIRST PIECE OF MOLDING. Miter one end of the first piece of molding and use the perimeter layout to mark the outside of the opposing miter.**

3 **CUT THE MOLDING TO LENGTH. After cutting the first two pieces of molding and tacking them in place, fit and cut the remaining two pieces.**

4 **REATTACH THE FIRST TWO PIECES OF MOLDING.** Leave the nails protruding through the molding as you apply glue, then relocate the nails in their holes to quickly reposition the first two pieces before nailing them in place.

5 **INSTALL THE REMAINING MOLDING.** Secure each piece of molding with glue and three finish nails. Wipe up glue squeeze-out as you go.

6 **INSTALL THE EDGING.** Use a combination square and utility knife to scribe miters as you cut, fit, and install edging on the bin lid and bench seat.

Now pull the two tacked pieces of molding off the bin, leaving the nails in the molding. For each of these pieces, put glue on the bottom (being careful not to catch your finger on the protruding nails), then align the nails back into their original holes **(4)** and hammer them in. Secure each of these pieces with a total of three nails.

After putting glue on each piece of molding, attach it with three 1¼-in. finish nails and set the nails **(5)**. Install the molding for the other wallpaper frame in the same way. You'll install the wallpaper after the project is painted (see "Installing Wallpaper in the Frames" on p. 199).

Install the edging on the lid and seat

The lid of the bin and the bench seat have exposed plywood edges on all four sides. You'll need to cover these edges with ¾-in. edging. On the tablesaw, rip pine to ¾ in. x ¾ in. to make edging for the bin lid and bench seat. Use a combination square and utility knife to scribe miter cuts to fit **(6)**.

The sequence is similar to installing the wallpaper frame molding: Miter the end of one piece, scribe and cut the other end, then attach it with glue and three 1½-in. finish nails. Miter the second piece to fit against it, then scribe and cut the other end. Glue and nail the second piece in place. Fit and cut both the third and fourth pieces before you glue and nail them both in place.

1 **GLUE AND NAIL THE SEAT TO THE BENCH.** Secure the seat to the bench with glue and three nails on the front and back and two nails in each side.

2 **LAY OUT THE HINGE MORTISES.** Use two pairs of business cards to gauge a gap between the bench seat and the bin lid as you mark for hinge mortises on the lid and bin.

Attach the Seat and Bin Lid

To prepare to attach the bench seat, set it in place and make sure it is flush to the back and the side that will be against a wall. (The seat should also be flush at the side that will meet the bin, but if there is a slight discrepancy there, it won't matter.) Put glue on the top edges of the bench and secure with three 1½-in. finish nails into the front, three into the back, and two into each side **(1)**. Note that the nails will go into the edging on the sides and back but behind the edging at front.

Lay out the hinge mortises

Reattach the bench to the bin once more. This time, you need only insert two screws through the two upper holes you made earlier in the sides. Put the bin lid in place flush to the back, and use two sets of two business cards to gauge a space between the lid and bench seat—you need a slight gap so the lid won't hit the bench seat when you open and close it. Mark the backs of the lid and the back of the bin for the outside of mortises located 2 in. in from both sides of the bin **(2)**.

Place a 2-in.-wide piece of scrap under the footless side of the bin to level it, then clamp the bin to the work surface. Put the hinges in position on the top of the bin and scribe their perimeters with a utility knife **(3)**. Then trace with a pencil to make the scribe lines easier to see.

3 **SCRIBE THE HINGE MORTISES.** Use a utility knife to scribe the perimeter of the hinges on the bin and the lid.

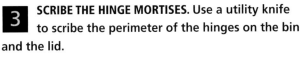

4 **SET THE ROUTER BIT DEPTH.** Set the router base on the hinges on a flat surface and drop the bit until it contacts the surface.

5 **ROUT THE MORTISES. Clamp a straight scrap to the inside of the bin to prevent the router from tipping as you cut the mortises.**

6 **ROUND OVER THE EXPOSED EDGES. Attach the lid to the bin and screw the bench and bin together so you can sight along the front edge to sand a flush roundover.**

Rout the mortises

Because of plywood's alternating grain direction, it would be difficult to use a chisel to cut mortises in the edges of the plywood. But it's easy to do with a router fitted with a ½-in.-dia. straight bit. To set the cutting depth, place the router base on the hinges as shown in photo **(4)** on p. 197 and then set the bit to contact the surface.

Clamp a straight scrap of ¾-in. or wider stock to the inside of the bin to prevent the router from tipping as you rout the mortises **(5)**. Clean and square the corners of the mortise with a chisel.

Sand and paint

Attach the lid to the bin with the hinges. Now round over the front edges of the bin lid and the bench seat at the same time so they are flush to each other **(6)**. Detach the bin from the bench to complete sanding, rounding over all exposed edges. Also detach the bin lid and remove the hinges so you don't get paint on them. Paint the project, except for the sides where the bench and bin will meet and the top of the center foot.

Install the lid support

The lid is held in place by a lid support (the one used on this project is the Easy-Lift Lid Support available from Rockler). First, reinstall the hinges. Place the lid support 3 in. from the outside of the bin **(7)**. You can place it on either side of the box—we chose the side that meets the bench.

The distance between the two attachment plates on the lid support is adjustable so that the tension on its spring will

7 **INSTALL THE LIP SUPPORT. Attach the hinges and the lid support with the screws provided.**

match the weight and size of the lid. This lid weighs about 5½ lb., so the screw being installed in the photo must be 3¹¹⁄₁₆ in. from the hinge barrel. The screw opposing it inside the bin must be ¹¹⁄₁₆ in. from the hinge barrel. (The instructions that come with the support include a helpful diagram.)

When you get the bin and bench on site, assemble them with screws into the predrilled holes in the sides and the center foot.

TIP Before priming and painting the bin, apply a light coat of wood filler to the top edge and sand it smooth. This will fill any voids and hide the layers of plywood.

Installing Wallpaper in the Frames

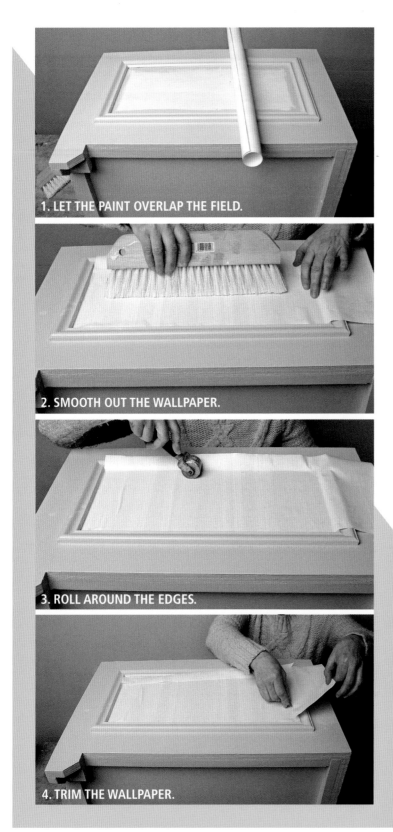

1. LET THE PAINT OVERLAP THE FIELD.

2. SMOOTH OUT THE WALLPAPER.

3. ROLL AROUND THE EDGES.

4. TRIM THE WALLPAPER.

The panel fields on this bin are wallpapered to match the room. If your room is not wallpapered, you can just paint the fields or skip the frames altogether.

If you decide to apply wallpaper, paint the project first. Prime the wallpaper fields, but there is no need to paint them—just let the paint overlap the fields when you paint the frames as shown in photo **1**.

Cut a piece of wallpaper that's a few inches wider and longer than the field you'll be covering. Use a framing square so the cut will be square to one side of the paper, and make the cut with a new single-edged razor blade. Wet the piece and butt the square edge into adjacent sides of the frame as shown in photo **2**. Smooth out any air bubbles with a wallpaper brush.

Use a wooden wallpaper seam roller to secure the wallpaper around the perimeter of the frame as shown in photo **3**. Trim the wallpaper against the inside of the frame (photo **4**).

CHAPTER SEVEN

THE GARAGE AND THE ATTIC

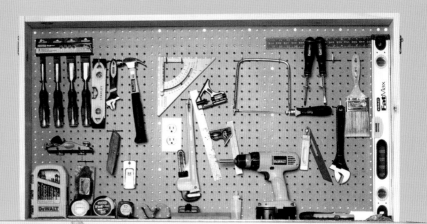

WE ASK A LOT OF OUR GARAGES. We use them as a place to do home projects, and we store lots of stuff in them. And, yes, we'd like to park our cars in there, too, though all too often the garage is so filled with tools, recreational equipment, extra furniture, and so on that the auto is relegated to the driveway.

The attic also tends to be an inefficiently used space. We just toss stuff up there, making it hard to move around and find anything if and when we need it again.

The key to a successfully multitasking garage and an efficient attic is to get the stuff off the floor, and this chapter offers easy-to-build projects to help you do just that. You'll find two utility-shelf projects: One is a freestanding unit that will work in a garage or basement or even against the gable end wall of a big attic. The other is designed to be built into the rafters of a sloped attic roof. Also for the garage, there is a generous overhead unit, a simple wall rack for garden tools, and a fold-up worktable/cabinet.

And, of course, manufacturers have come up with lots of storage systems you can buy, from cabinets to hoists for ladders and bicycles to wall systems with movable shelves and specialized clips to hold all kinds of tools and sports equipment. We show you a sampling of commercial storage solutions in this chapter. You can find a lot more with a trip to a home center or an online search. Welcome back, family auto!

UTILITY SHELVES

Looking for sturdy shelving that's inexpensive and quick and easy to build? All you need is a pile of 2×4s and a sheet of CDX plywood—a sturdy grade of plywood that's most commonly used for house sheathing. The shelves are 48 in. long to make efficient use of the plywood sheet. You can easily adapt the plan to fit your space by making the unit shorter or changing the depth of the shelves. And if you have lots of stuff to store, it won't take much more time to assemble two or three of these while you are at it.

WHAT YOU'LL NEED

• 5 shelves	¾ in. × 16 in. × 48 in.
• 10 long rails	1½ in. × 1½ in. × 48 in.
• 10 side rails	1½ in. × 1½ in. × 13 in.
• 4 stiles	1½ in. × 3½ in. × 77 in.
• 4 bottom spacers	1½ in. × 3½ in. × 6 in.
• 16 spacers	1½ in. × 3½ in. × 15 in.

HARDWARE

- 2½-in. all-purpose screws
- 1¼-in. all-purpose screws

UTILITY SHELVES

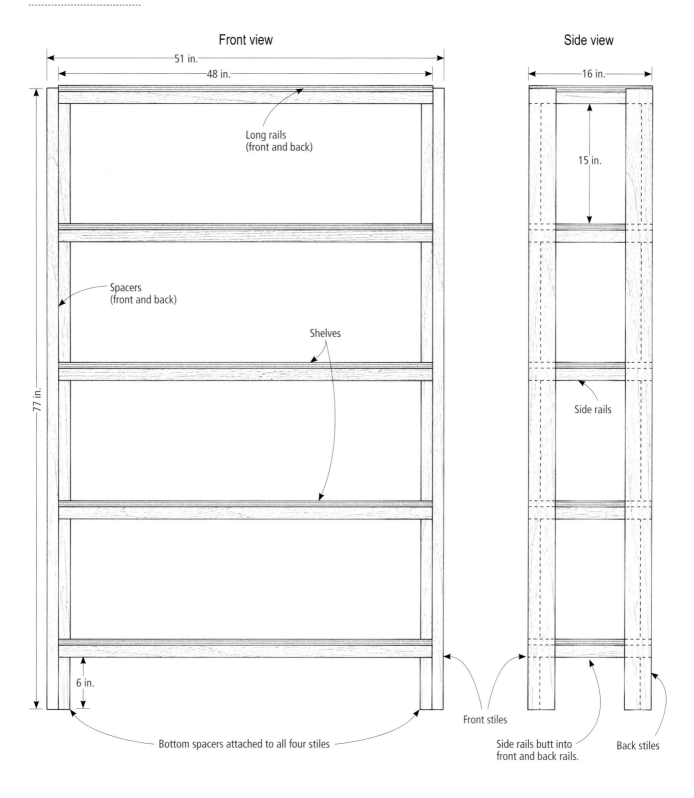

Front view

51 in.

48 in.

Long rails
(front and back)

Spacers
(front and back)

Shelves

77 in.

6 in.

Bottom spacers attached to all four stiles

Side view

16 in.

15 in.

Side rails

Front stiles

Side rails butt into
front and back rails.

Back stiles

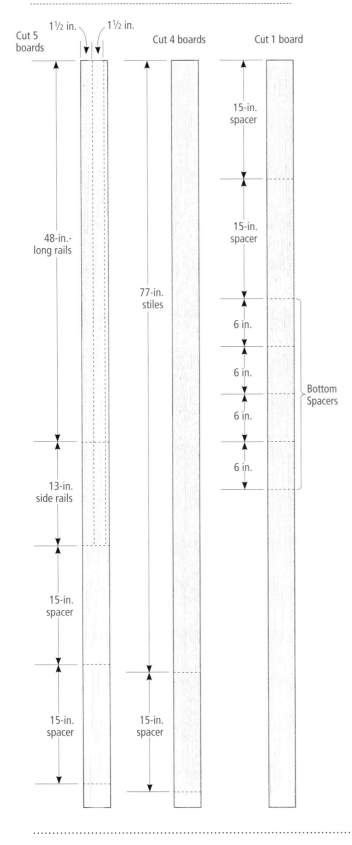

Cut 5 boards

1½ in.　1½ in.

Cut 4 boards

Cut 1 board

48-in.-long rails

13-in. side rails

15-in. spacer

15-in. spacer

77-in. stiles

15-in. spacer

15-in. spacer

15-in. spacer

15-in. spacer

15-in. spacer

6 in.

6 in.

6 in.

6 in.

Bottom Spacers

Cut the Parts

Cut the plywood shelves first and then cut 2x4s for the lumber frame.

Put the plywood for the shelves on the floor with scraps of plywood underneath and lay out the first crosscut at 16 in. Set the blade on your circular saw to cut through the plywood and into the scrap without cutting into the floor **(1)**. Lay out and cut the rest of the shelves.

The "Cutting Diagram" at left shows how to get all the frame parts from ten 8-ft. 2x4s. First, make all the crosscuts. When cutting four or five boards to the same length, clamp them together flush at the ends and make each cut in one pass **(2)**.

Use a tablesaw to rip all the 48-in. pieces and all the 13-in. pieces into 1½ x 1½ rails. Be sure to use a push stick when making these cuts **(3)**.

> **TIP** If you don't have a tablesaw to rip the rails, you can purchase 8-ft. 2x2s (actual 1½ in. x 1½ in.) at a lumberyard or home center.

1 **CUT THE PLYWOOD. Use a circular saw to crosscut plywood for the shelves (with a sacrificial scrap of plywood below).**

2 **CROSSCUT THE LUMBER PARTS TO LENGTH.** Clamp 2x4s together on top of a sacrificial piece of plywood to cut them to the same length in one pass.

3 **RIP THE RAILS TO WIDTH.** Carefully guiding each workpiece with a push stick, rip the rails to width on the tablesaw.

Assemble the Unit

Once you've cut all the parts, get ready to assemble the unit. All the lumber connections are made with 2½-in. screws. Begin by attaching a bottom spacer to each stile with two screws **(1)** (below); these four spacers will support the bottom shelf.

Place two stiles on edge and position a long rail between them. Attach with two screws on each end—one through the stile and one into the bottom spacer **(2)** (below). Next, put a side rail in place butting into the long rail and secure it with one screw through the stile and one into the bottom spacer **(3)** (below).

2 **ATTACH A LONG RAIL.** With the stiles on edge, attach a long rail to the stiles and the bottom spacers.

3 **ATTACH A SIDE RAIL.** Screw a side rail to the stile and to the bottom spacer.

1 **ATTACH THE BOTTOM SPACERS.** Attach the bottom spacers to the stiles with 2½-in. screws. Use a clamp to help hold the spacer in position while you drive the screws.

4 **COMPLETE THE BOTTOM FRAME. Stand up** the stile/rail assembly and attach the other stiles and the remaining bottom rails.

5 **INSTALL THE LOWEST SHELF. Attach the bottom** shelf with 1¼-in. screws.

Stand up the stile/rail assembly you made and clamp it to the side of your workbench or have a helper hold it upright. Put the other two stiles and a long rail in place. Screw the rails to the bottom spacers and stiles **(4)**. Then screw the second side rail into place.

Put the bottom shelf in place and attach it to the rails with 1¼-in. screws spaced about every 6 in **(5)**.

At each corner, put a spacer down against the shelf you just installed and secure it to the stiles with four 2½-in. screws **(6)**. Repeat the process for adding rails, shelves, and spacers until the unit is complete.

6 **ADD SPACERS AND COMPLETE THE UNIT. Screw four** spacers into place above the installed shelf, then continue adding rails, shelves, and spacers until the unit is complete.

TIP When securing a 1½ x 1½ rail to a spacer, pre-drill the hole to prevent splitting the end of the rail. You may want to predrill all the holes for the 2½-in. screws, just to make it easier to drive them. To select the right size drill bit, hold the screw behind the bit—if you can see the screw threads but not the body of the screw, you have the right bit.

Commercial Wall Storage Systems

Getting stuff off the floor and up on the wall is an essential part of any garage storage scheme. There are lots of wall systems you can buy to help you achieve this goal. You'll find hooks designed to hold various items—from garden hoses to garden tools to bicycles or ladders. There are metal grids to which you attach various hooks, baskets, and shelves at different heights.

If you want the option of easily changing your wall storage layout, channels are a great way to go because hooks, baskets, and shelves can be snapped in or removed in seconds. Some channel systems are designed to cover whole walls. Or, you can purchase individual lengths of channel. The channel system shown here uses 48-in.-long channels. The end caps are sold separately so you can line up the channels for lengths in any 48-in. increment. You screw the channels into studs, and then you snap in the accessories of your choice.

OVERHEAD STORAGE

This storage rack, constructed of 2×4s and plywood, is a great way to gain storage while sacrificing zero floor space. It is extremely sturdy thanks to the use of lag screws, joist hangers, and L-angles.

The simple design is easily adapted to many garage situations. The 30-in.-deep version shown here is installed in a garage with 10-ft. ceilings, leaving plenty of room to walk beneath. If your ceiling is lower, you can make a shallower unit, or you can reduce the width or length to suit as long as you space the joists 4 ft. or less on center.

WHAT YOU'LL NEED

- 1 ledger   1½ in. × 3½ in. × 8 ft.
- 1 front joist   1½ in. × 3½ in. × 8 ft.
- 1 ceiling cleat   1½ in. × 3½ in. × 8 ft.
- 5 hanger boards   1½ in. × 3½ in. × 30 in.
- 5 joists   1½ in. × 3½ in. × 45⅛ in.
- 1 floor   ¾ in. × 4 ft. × 8 ft., CDX plywood

HARDWARE

- 12 lag screws, ¼ in. dia. × 3 in.
- 2½-in. all-purpose screws
- 17 L-angles for 2×4 construction
- 6 joist hangers for 2×4s
- 1½-in. joist hanger nails
- 8d joist hanger nails
- 1¼-in. all-purpose screws

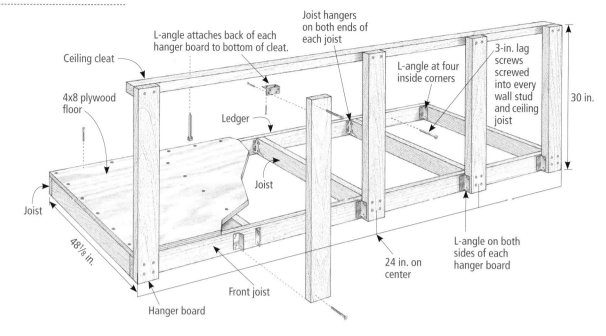

L-angle attaches back of each hanger board to bottom of cleat.

Joist hangers on both ends of each joist

Ceiling cleat

3-in. lag screws screwed into every wall stud and ceiling joist

L-angle at four inside corners

4x8 plywood floor

Ledger

30 in.

Joist

Joist

48⅛ in.

L-angle on both sides of each hanger board

24 in. on center

Front joist

Hanger board

Install the Ledger

The first step is to lay out the joist and hanger board locations on the three 8-ft.-long 2x4s. Clamp the three 2x4s together, with edges up and ends flush. Starting from your left, strike lines at 23¼ in., 47¼ in., and 71¼ in. Make an X to the right of each line **(1)**. On two of those boards, extend the lines and Xs to one face; label these boards as the ledger and the front joist. Extend the lines to the other face of the front joist. Label the third board as the ceiling cleat.

Now use a 4-ft. level to draw an 8-ft.-long level line along the wall 30 in. from the ceiling **(2)**; this line represents the bottom of the ledger. Next, find the studs along the line. If your garage isn't painted, you can easily identify stud locations by the vertical rows of nails or screws. Otherwise, use a stud finder to mark where your layout line crosses each stud (see "Finding Wall Studs" on p. 28).

1 **LAY OUT THE JOIST AND HANGER BOARD POSITIONS.** Clamp the ledger, front joist, and ceiling joist together to lay out positions for the joists and hanger boards.

2 **LAY OUT THE LEDGER.** Lay out an 8-ft. level line 30 in. from the ceiling.

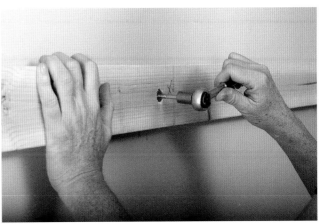

3 POSITION THE LEDGER. Use 2½-in. screws to hold the ledger in position.

4 SECURE THE LEDGER. Secure the ledger to the studs with lag screws.

TIP A full sheet of plywood is used for the floor of this overhead storage rack. If you don't have a way to transport 4-ft.-wide sheets, have the lumberyard or home center cut the sheet in half along its length. The seam won't matter in the finished project.

With a helper holding one end, align the bottom of the ledger to the layout line with the X marks to your left. Drive a 2½-in. screw through the ledger into the stud closest to one end of the board **(3)**. Check for level, then drive a screw into the stud closest to the other end.

To secure the ledger, predrill and install one lag screw with washer into each stud along the length of the ledger **(4)**. If a screw falls over an X, you'll need to counterbore the screw hole so the screw head will be below the surface where it won't interfere with the joist. Make the counterbore with a ¾-in. spade bit, then predrill the screw hole through the counterbore.

Install the Ceiling Cleat and Hanger Boards

To lay out the ceiling cleat, first use a 4-ft. level to make a plumb mark on the ceiling above each end of the ledger. Use a framing square to make a line on the ceiling square to each end. Then use a chalkline to extend these lines 48⅛ in. from each end. (That extra ⅛ in. will make it easier to slide the plywood floor into place.) Snap a line parallel to the wall between the ends of the two lines **(1)** (p. 210).

Use a stud finder to mark where the line crosses joists in the ceiling.

Now install the ceiling cleat. With a helper, align the ceiling cleat to the inside of the line, with Xs to your right as you face the wall. Hold the cleat in place with a screw into a joist at each end. Predrill, then install one lag screw into each joist **(2)** (p. 210).

Using a circular saw or power miter saw, cut the five hanger boards to length. Position each board along its layout line, covering the X and butting into the ceiling, then attach it to the cleat with a 2½-in. screw **(3)** (p. 210). Check for plumb, and then add a second screw.

What if the Joists Run Parallel to the Ceiling Cleat?

This project assumes that the ceiling joists in your garage run perpendicular to the ceiling cleat. If the joists run parallel to the cleat, you have two choices: You can adjust the width of the storage unit to the nearest joist. Or you can make five 2x4 cross-cleats to span two joists. Use 3-in. lag screws to attach the cross-cleats through the ceiling into the joists. Then lag-screw the ceiling cleat to the cross-cleats.

1 LAY OUT THE CEILING CLEAT. Snap a line on the ceiling 48⅛ in. from the wall.

 TIP Use the 3-4-5 method to check if your chalkline is square to the wall. Make a mark on the chalkline 3 ft. from the wall. Along the top of the wall, make another mark 4 ft. from where the chalkline meets the wall. Measure diagonally between the two marks you just made. If the measurement is 5 ft., the chalkline is square to the wall.

2 INSTALL THE CEILING CLEAT. Use lag screws to attach the ceiling cleat along the inside of the layout line.

3 INSTALL THE HANGER BOARDS. Attach the hanger boards covering the Xs on the side of the ceiling joist. Check for plumb as you add the second screw.

4 REINFORCE THE JOINTS. Install an L-angle wherever a hanger board meets the ceiling cleat.

Install the Joists and Floor

All that now remains is to install the front joist and the floor joists and floor. First, you need to reinforce the unit by installing L-angle hardware where the hanger boards meet the ceiling cleat. Use an L-angle with 1¼-in. screws to attach the back face of each hanger board to the bottom of the ceiling cleat **(4)** (facing page).

Install the front joist

To prepare to install the front joist, install three joist hangers on the ledger and three on the front joist positioned so that the joist ends will cover the X at the three inner layout lines **(1)**. It's important to install the hangers before you install the front joist because the hanger boards are not yet stable enough to hammer against. Use a scrap of 2x4 as shown in photo 1 below to make sure the hangers are properly positioned.

Now install the outer L-angles. Strike a line 1½ in. from each end of the ledger (the thickness of each joist) and the front joist. Install an L-angle at each end of the ledger and the front joist **(2)**. With a helper, position the front joist, aligning both ends of the joist with the bottom outside edges of the outermost hanger boards; clamp the joist in place **(3)**. Clamp the front joist to another hanger board. Check that the joist is level and then make the connection with four 2½-in. screws. Clamp and screw each connection **(4)**.

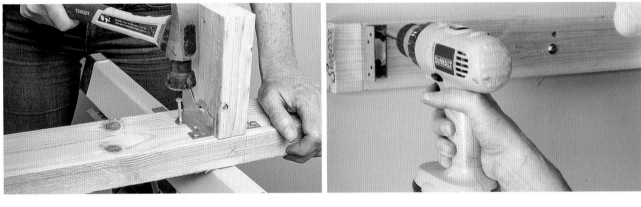

1 **INSTALL THE JOIST HANGERS. Using 1½-in. joist hanger nails, install the joist hangers on the front joist before the front joist is installed.**

2 **INSTALL THE OUTER L-ANGLES. Locate L-angles 1½ in. from the ends of the ledger and screw them in place.**

3 **POSITION THE FRONT JOIST. Clamp the front joist to the hanger boards at each end.**

4 **ATTACH THE FRONT JOIST. Use four screws to connect each hanger board to the front joist.**

Install the remaining joists and the floor

Cut the five joists to 45⅛ in. long. Then slip three of the joists into their joist hangers and secure them with 8d joist hanger nails into the angled hole on each side of each joist hanger **(5)**. Put the outer joist against the L-angles and secure with 1¼-in. screws. Then install the remaining L-angles. Use 1¼-in. screws to secure each side of each hanger board to the front joist **(6)**.

Finish the unit by installing the floor. Set the plywood in place, climb aboard, and snap lines to locate the joists below at 24 in., 48 in., and 72 in. **(7)**. Secure the plywood with 1¼-in. screws about every 12 in. into the ledger, front joist, and joists.

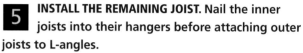

5 **INSTALL THE REMAINING JOIST.** Nail the inner joists into their hangers before attaching outer joists to L-angles.

6 **INSTALL THE REMAINING L-ANGLES.** Add L-angles to both sides of each hanger board.

7 **INSTALL THE FLOOR.** Snap lines on the floor to locate the joists below before screwing the floor in place.

Hoist It Out of the Way

There are several methods available for stowing bulky items like bikes or ladders in the garage. There are simple ceiling hooks and wall hooks, overhead racks for ladders, and even a "claw" for bikes. You screw the claw to the ceiling and it grabs the rim when you bump a wheel against it.

A hoist is a convenient way to get moderately heavy stuff up out of the way without having to muscle it over your head. You'll find hoists designed for bikes and similar systems designed for ladders, kayaks, or canoes.

GARDEN TOOL RACK

In less than an hour, you can get that jumble of long-handled yard tools neatly stored in this simple rack. The best part is that the rack will be customized to exactly the tools you want to store. You can place it at any convenient height, as long as there is enough room for the tool handles to hang below. All you need is a length of 1x6 lumber, two 5-in. x 6-in. metal brackets, six 1½-in. screws, and two ⅝-in. screws.

Prepare the Rack

The first step is to decide on the length. Lay your long-handled garden tools side by side with about 2 in. of clearance separating each tool from the next **(1)**. Measuring across the point where the handle meets each tool, determine the distance from the middle of one handle to the middle of the next and write down these measurements.

Now cut the rack to length. Add 12 in. to the sum of your handle measurements and cut a 1x6 to that length. Use a combination square to draw a line along the length of the board, ¾ in. from one edge **(2)**. Mark 6 in. along that line for the first tool and then make marks for the rest of the tool handles, adding 6 in. to each measurement you noted.

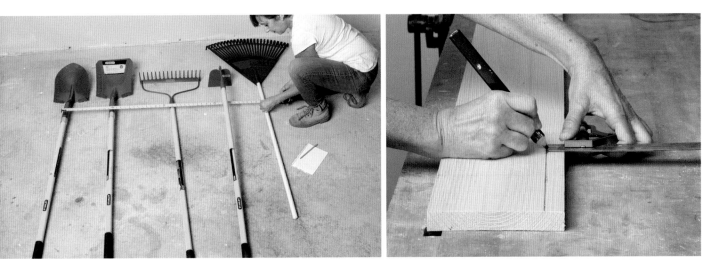

1 **DECIDE ON THE LENGTH.** Lay out your tools on the floor to determine how long you want your tool rack to be.

2 **LAY OUT THE TOOL HOLES.** Draw a line along the board ¾ in. from one edge before marking positions for the tool holes along the line.

To prepare to drill the tool holes, clamp the board to your bench with at least 2 in. overhanging along the length. Center a 2-in. hole saw over each mark and drill a hole **(3)**. The saw will overlap the edge of the board creating a slot for the handles. If you want to paint or finish the rack board, now is the time to do it.

3 **DRILL THE TOOL HOLES.** Use a 2-in. hole saw to drill the holes that will hold the tools.

Install the Brackets and Rack

Use a 4-ft. level to draw a line on the wall at your chosen height. Find the two studs that fall closest to where you want the ends of your rack to be (see "Finding Wall Studs" on p. 28). Center the brackets over the studs and with the line passing through the top holes of each bracket's long leg. Mark for the screw holes **(4)**. Predrill and attach the brackets with 1¼-in. screws.

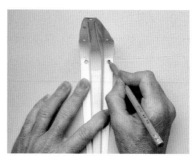

4 **LAY OUT THE BRACKETS.** Use a bracket to mark for screw holes along a level line on the wall.

Center the rack across the brackets, adjusting if necessary to prevent a slot from falling over a bracket. Mark for screw holes. Take the rack down to predrill, then secure it to the bracket with ⅝-in. screws **(5)**.

5 **ATTACH THE RACK.** After marking and predrilling for holes, screw the bracket to the rack.

Quick Garden Storage Solutions You Can Buy

If you're not in the mood to make your own garden tool rack, there are plenty of commercially available alternatives. Shown at far left is a system of 16-in.-long interlocking plastic rails that you screw into wall studs—three sections are used here. Tools are supported by metal hooks that slip into slots or plastic pegs that snap into holes. If you have lots of tools and don't mind devoting a little floor space, you can pick up the freestanding rack shown at near left that snaps together in a minute or two.

FOLD-UP WORKTABLE/ TOOL CABINET

You long for a convenient workstation with a good-sized table, a place with your tools and fasteners organized and right at hand. But you still need to get your car in the garage. Here's the solution. This project features a fold-up worktable with pegboard above and a cabinet below. Open the doors, slip on the removable feet, drop the table, and you have a rock-solid work surface. Close it up, and everything is hidden and protected in a unit that protrudes just 7 in. from the wall.

This worktable/tool cabinet is built from AC plywood. Use the clear "A" side for the faces of the doors and the work surface of the table. The shelves and trim pieces are #2 pine, which has some knots. The table work surface is protected with two coats of wipe-on polyurethane.

WHAT YOU'LL NEED

- 2 side furring   ¾ in. × 2½ in. × 25¼ in., pine
- 2 top and bottom furring   ¾ in. × 2½ in. × 43 in., pine
- 2 middle furring   ¾ in. × 2½ in. × 20¼ in., pine
- 1 pegboard   25¼ in. × 48 in.
- 2 sides   ¾ in. × 5½ in. × 61 in., pine
- 1 top   ¾ in. × 5½ in. × 48 in., pine
- 1 pegboard bottom   1½ in. × 5½ in. × 48 in., pine
- 1 center post   ¾ in. × 5½ in. × 33½ in., pine

(Continued on p. 216)

- 7 shelves $\quad$ ¾ in. × 5½ in. × 23⅝ in., pine
- 8 dividers $\quad$ ¾ in. × 5½ in. × 7¼ in., pine
- 6 dividers $\quad$ ¾ in. × 5½ in. × 9¹⁵⁄₁₆ in., pine
- 4 bottom shelf cleats $\quad$ ¾ in. × 5½ in. × 1½ in., pine
- 2 stiles $\quad$ ¾ in. × 1½ in. × 34¼ in., pine
- 2 doors $\quad$ ¾ in. × 23⅛ in. × 32¾ in., plywood
- 1 worktable $\quad$ ¾ in. × 25¼ in. × 48 in., plywood
- 2 door foot bottoms $\quad$ ¾ in. × 2¼ in. × 5 in., plywood
- 4 door foot sides $\quad$ ¾ in. × 1½ in. × 5 in., plywood
- 2 levelers $\quad$ ¾ in. × 5 in. × 5 in., plywood
- 2 side table edging $\quad$ ¾ in. × ¾ in. × 25¼ in.
- 1 front table edging $\quad$ ¾ in. × ¾ in. × 49½ in.
- 1 table cleat $\quad$ ¾ in. × 10 in. × 45 in., plywood

HARDWARE

- 4 hinges $\quad$ ¾ in. × 2½ in.
- 1 continuous hinge $\quad$ 48 in.
- 2 hooks and eyes $\quad$ 2½ in.
- 1 swivel hasp $\quad$ 4½ in.
- 1¼-in. screws
- 1½-in. screws
- 2½-in. screws
- 4d finish nails
- 8d finishing nails

Install the Pegboard and Frame

The first step is to locate the pegboard that goes above the worktable. Find the center of the stud nearest to where you want to locate the left side of the pegboard (see "Finding Wall Studs" on p. 28). Then find the center of the next three studs to the right. To locate the left side of the pegboard, measure 1¼ in. to the left of the center of the stud. Use a 4-ft. level to make a plumb line from the floor up to 60¼ in. Draw another plumb line 48 in. to the right to locate the right side of the pegboard. Connect the top of the lines with a level line for the top of the pegboard **(1)**.

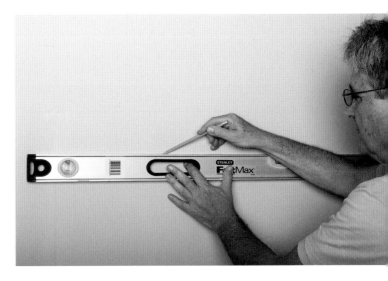

1 **LOCATE THE PEGBOARD AND FURRING.** After locating studs and the sides of the cabinet, draw a level line to indicate the top.

FOLD-UP WORKTABLE/TOOL CABINET

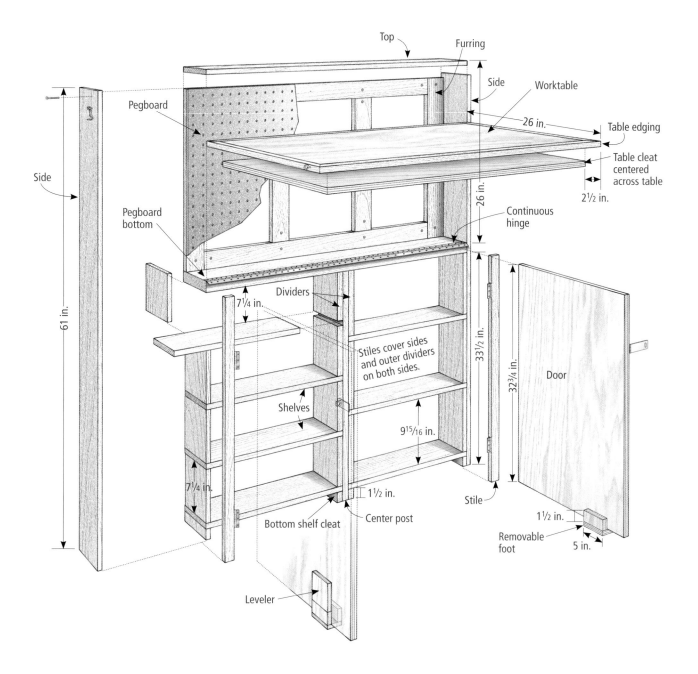

Top

Furring

Side

Worktable

Pegboard

26 in.

Table edging

Side

Table cleat centered across table

2½ in.

Pegboard bottom

Continuous hinge

26 in.

61 in.

Dividers

7¼ in.

33½ in.

32¾ in.

Stiles cover sides and outer dividers on both sides.

Door

Shelves

9¹⁵/₁₆ in.

7¼ in.

1½ in.

Stile

Bottom shelf cleat

Center post

1½ in.

Removable foot

5 in.

Leveler

The pegboard is "furred out" from the wall to allow room for the tool hangers. Cut the outside furring strips to the dimensions listed in "What You'll Need," then attach them with 2½-in. screws. Next, cut and install the horizontal furring strips with 2½-in. screws every 6 in. into studs. To catch the studs, toe-screw the horizontal strips into the vertical strips **(2)**. Finally, cut and install two middle vertical strips centered over the studs.

Use a circular saw with a jig to crosscut the pegboard to 25¼ in. (see "Making a Crosscutting Jig" on p. 22). Put the pegboard on the floor with a sacrificial piece of plywood underneath and lay out a crosscut at 25¼ in. Set the blade on your circular saw to cut through the pegboard and into the sacrificial piece without cutting into the floor **(3)**.

Attach the pegboard to the furring strips with 1¼-in. screws into the corners and every sixth hole along the perimeter and the middle strips **(4)**.

2 **CUT AND ATTACH THE FURRING.** Screw the furring strips to studs, toe-screwing the horizontal strips to catch the studs.

3 **CUT THE PEGBOARD.** Set the pegboard on the floor (on top of a sacrificial scrap of plywood), and make the cut using a circular saw with the crosscutting jig.

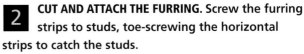

4 **INSTALL THE PEGBOARD.** Use a screw into every sixth hole to attach the pegboard to the furring strips.

5 **CUT AND INSTALL THE SIDES AND TOP.** Install the sides, then attach the top with screws through the sides and down into the furring.

TIP Wood can easily split when you drive screws close to ends and edges. To prevent splitting, drive the screws just flush; don't bury them. Predrilling holes also helps.

Now cut and install the sides and top. Cut the sides to the dimensions in the parts list. Attach them to the side furring strips with 1¼-in. screws. Cut the top to fit between the sides, and attach it with two screws through each side and screws down into the furring **(5)**.

Cut a piece of 2x6 to 48 in. With a helper holding it in place, attach the piece with 2½-in. screws up into the furring **(6)** and then drive two screws through each side.

6 **CUT AND ATTACH THE PEGBOARD BOTTOM.** Attach the 2x6 with screws up into the furring.

Extend an Outlet

What if the pegboard covers an electrical outlet? Lucky you! It's handy to have power at your workstation. All you need is a box extender. Turn off power to the outlet. Take off the cover plate and measure to locate one corner of the box. Trace the extender on the pegboard. Cut the hole with a sabersaw. Pull the receptacle through the hole before you attach the pegboard. Slip the extender over the receptacle, and secure the receptacle through the extender with the longer screws provided. Replace the cover.

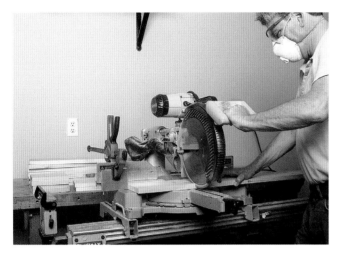

Install the Shelves

The 1x6 shelves will butt into each side of the cabinet and the center post and will be positioned and supported by the 1x6 dividers. Cut the center post to fit between the 2x6 pegboard bottom and the floor. Cut the seven shelves, the eight left-hand dividers, and the six right-hand dividers to the lengths in the parts list. For quick accuracy, make the cuts using stops on a power miter saw as shown **(1)**. Otherwise, a circular saw will do fine.

To install the center post, temporarily put two shelves up against the 2x6 with the center post fitted between. This will position the center post while you secure it with two 2½-in. screws through the 2x6 **(2)**. Then remove the shelves.

Working on the left-hand side of the cabinet first, install a pair of short dividers with four 1¼-in. screws, clamp a shelf in place, and secure it with two 2¼-in. screws on each end. Repeat for all four left-hand shelves and their dividers **(3)**. Extend lines around the outside of the cabinet as you go to ensure that your screws don't miss the shelves.

1 CUT THE SHELVES AND DIVIDERS. Use a stop block with a miter saw to quickly and accurately cut shelves and dividers to length.

2 INSTALL THE CENTER POST. Shelves placed temporarily against the underside of the 2x6 position the center post as you screw it in place through the 2x6.

3 INSTALL THE LEFT-HAND SHELVES AND DIVIDERS. Working from the top down, install the left-side shelves with dividers between.

Install the top two right-hand shelves and their dividers as you did on the left, but this time use 2½-in. screws through the left-hand dividers and the center post into the shelves **(4)**. You won't have access to the inside end of the final shelf, so predrill holes for toe-screws into the divider and secure with 1½-in. screws as shown **(5)**.

To support each bottom shelf, you need to install a pair of short cleats. For both ends of both bottom shelves, scribe cuts on pieces of 2x6 to fit snugly underneath **(6)**. Cut the pieces and tap them into place with a hammer; there's no need for fasteners or glue.

The final step before installing the doors is to cut and install the stiles. Rip pine to 1½ in. wide for the stiles, and cut them to reach from the floor to ¾ in. below the bottom of the 2x6 pegboard bottom. Install them with glue and 8d finish nails **(7)**.

6 **CUT AND INSTALL THE BOTTOM SHELF CLEATS.** Scribe the height of the bottom shelf cleats before cutting them to length and tapping them into place.

4 **INSTALL THE RIGHT-HAND SHELVES.** Install the top two right-hand shelves with dividers.

5 **INSTALL THE BOTTOM SHELF.** Toe-screw through predrilled holes to attach the lowest right-side shelf.

7 **INSTALL THE STILES.** Use glue and 8d finish nails to attach the stiles.

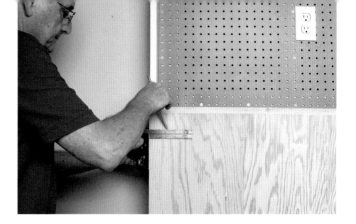

1 **DOUBLE-CHECK THE DOOR DIMENSIONS.** Measure the height and width of the opening before cutting the doors to size.

2 **MARK THE HINGE LOCATIONS.** Use a square to mark the hinge locations on the front of the doors and the stiles.

3 **SCRIBE THE MORTISES.** Use a combination square set to the depth of a hinge to scribe the depth of the mortises.

4 **CUT THE MORTISES.** After chopping the sides of the mortises, slice them to depth.

TIP When chopping mortises, place the chisel on the scribe line with the flat side toward the outside of the mortise. Tap the chisel with a mallet or hammer until it cuts to the scribed hinge depth.

Make and Install the Doors and Worktable

Before cutting the two doors, check your door dimensions—they may vary a bit from the dimensions listed in "What You'll Need." For the height of the doors, measure from the bottom of the shelves to the top of the stiles **(1)**. For the width, measure between the inside of the stiles, divide in half, and subtract 1/16 in. for each door.

Using the same technique as for the pegboard (see p. 218), crosscut a plywood sheet to the door height. Then rip the doors to final width on the tablesaw or with the circular saw and jig. Use the circular saw and jig to crosscut the worktable to 25 1/4 in.

To prepare to hang the doors, mark hinge locations on the front of the doors 2 in. from the top and bottom **(2)**. Put each door in position and shim it flush to the top of the stiles. Then transfer the hinge locations onto the stiles.

Scribe the outline of each hinge mortise on the outside edge of each door and the inside of the stiles. Set a combination square to the thickness of a hinge leaf and use it to scribe the mortise depth on the faces of the stiles and doors **(3)**.

Chop the sides of the mortises and then slice them out to depth **(4)**. Attach the hinges to the doors and then to the stiles.

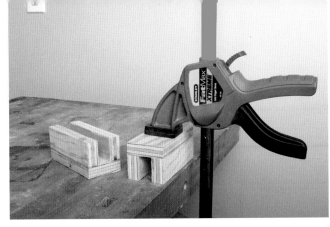

5 **MAKE THE DOOR FEET. Assemble each door foot with glue and a clamp.**

6 **INSTALL THE FOOT LEVELERS. Glue and clamp each foot leveler to the door using a door foot to gauge its height.**

7 **MARK THE TABLE EDGING TO LENGTH.** Hold each piece of ¾-in.-square table edging in place to scribe its length.

TIP It's a good idea to protect the working surface of the worktable with a couple of coats of polyurethane. You can brush it on or, easier, use the wipe-on variety.

8 **INSTALL THE CONTINUOUS HINGE. Predrill and screw the continuous hinge in place where the worktable meets the 2x6 pegboard bottom.**

Make the door feet and levelers

The removable door feet supply solid bearing for the worktable when it is supported by the open doors. When not in use, you can stow them in the cabinet. Cut the foot base and sides to the dimensions in the parts list. Assemble each foot with glue and a clamp, placing the sides flush to the edges of the base **(5)**.

Now cut and install the foot levelers. The levelers compensate for any irregularity in the level of your garage floor. Cut them to the dimensions in the parts list. At the bottom of each door face, make a mark ½ in. in from the outside edge. Open a door until it is perpendicular to the 2x6—use a framing square to check. Put a foot in place, put glue on the back of the leveler, and push the edge of the leveler firmly against the foot as you clamp the leveler in place **(6)**. Now, even if your garage floor isn't level, the

door feet will fit snugly under the levelers, firmly supporting the worktable.

Make and install the worktable

The two sides and front of the plywood worktable are finished with ¾-in. x ¾-in. edging to give the edges of the table a cleaner look. Use a utility knife and square to scribe cuts in place as shown **(7)**. First, cut the side edging pieces so that they will fit flush with the front and back of the worktable. Install the pieces with glue and 4d finishing nails. Cut the front edging to cover the ends of the side edging and install with glue and nails.

Put the worktable in place on the open doors with feet in place. Center the continuous hinge over where the tabletop abuts the 2x6 pegboard bottom. Predrill and screw the hinge in place **(8)**.

9 **INSTALL HOOKS AND EYES.** Install eyes on the edges of the worktable, then locate and install the hooks on the side of the cabinet.

10 **MARK THE POSITION OF THE WORKTABLE CLEAT.** Scribe lines where the cleats will meet the inside of the doors.

Install an eye on each side edge of the tabletop, then raise the tabletop and insert the hook into the eye to locate where to screw in the hook **(9)**. Attach the hooks.

Next, mark the position of the worktable cleat, which stiffens the worktable and provides stops for the doors. Open the doors square to the cabinet. Scribe lines where the inside of the doors meets the bottom of the worktable **(10)**.

Now you're ready to install the cleat. Raise the worktable and insert the hooks into the eyes. Scribe a line on the bottom of the worktable 2½ in. from the front edge. Put glue on the cleat and have someone help you position it while you secure it with 1¼-in. screws **(11)**. Use five columns of three screws.

Finish by installing the swivel hasp and smoothing exposed edges. A swivel hasp is a sturdy latch that will allow you to padlock the cabinet if you wish. Position it 3 in. from the top of the door and install with the screws provided **(12)**. Round exposed edges of the project, especially the plywood, to prevent splinters.

11 **INSTALL THE CLEAT.** Have a helper hold one end of the worktable cleat in place while you attach the other end.

12 **INSTALL THE SWIVEL HASP.** Position the two parts of the hasp 3 in. from the top of the door and install with the screws provided.

ATTIC SHELVES

These shelves are an economical and quick-to-build way to make the most of your attic storage space by getting items up off the floor. The shelves, suspended from the rafters, are made of 2×4s and CDX plywood, a sturdy grade of structural plywood that's most often used to sheathe houses. Have the plywood ripped into three 15⅞-in.-wide pieces at the lumberyard or home center.

The rafters shown here slope at 45°. Carpenters call that a "12 on 12" roof, meaning that the roof rises 12 in. for every 12 in. of horizontal run. As the drawing on p. 226 shows, that's convenient because it means that if the front of a shelf is 16 in. down from the bottom of the rafter, the horizontal distance from the front of the shelf to the bottom of the rafter will also be 16 in. Likewise, the top of a 32-in.-wide shelf will be 16 in. from the top of the

16-in. shelf. Keep in mind, though, roof framing is rough carpentry—rafter slopes and dimensions may not be exact and rafters can sag over time. So the dimensions in the parts list are useful only as a guide. The procedure here shows you how to measure as you go so your shelves will fit your rafters.

You can easily adapt the project to roofs of different slopes: If your roof slope is less steep than 45° and you allow 16 in. between shelves, there will be a little space behind the 32-in. bottom shelf. If your roof slope is steeper, you'll need to re-rip one piece of plywood on the tablesaw because the space for the bottom shelf will be narrower. Alternately, you can increase the distance between top and bottom shelves to create 32 in. of width below.

WHAT YOU'LL NEED

- 4 short cross-supports   1½ in. × 3½ in. × 29½ in.
- 4 long cross-supports   1½ in. × 3½ in. × 45 in.
- 4 uprights   1½ in. × 3½ in. × 44¾ in.
- 4 blocks   1½ in. × 3½ in. × 6 in.
- 3 shelf sections   ¾ in. × 15⅞ in. × 80 in.

HARDWARE

- 2½-in. deck screws
- 1¼-in. all-purpose screws

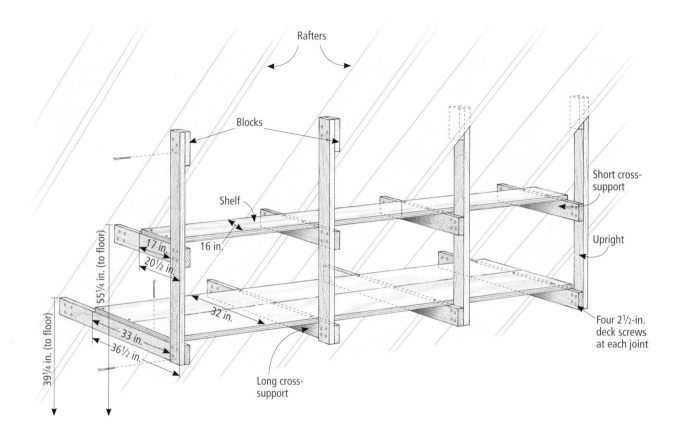

Rafters

Blocks

Shelf

17 in.

16 in.

20½ in.

55¼ in. (to floor)

39¼ in. (to floor)

33 in.

36½ in.

32 in.

Long cross-support

Short cross-support

Upright

Four 2½-in. deck screws at each joint

Lay Out the Shelves

Begin by marking the shelf height on the rafters. When choosing the height you want for the bottom shelf, bear in mind that you want to allow enough room below the shelf for accessible storage space on the floor. For the shelves shown here, the measurements are 55¼ in. and 39¼ in., putting the top of the ¾-in. shelves at 56 in. and 40 in. from the floor of the attic. Measure from the floor to mark the shelf bottom heights on the bottom of the rafters **(1)**.

TIP A couple of safety tips when working in an attic: First, watch out for nails protruding through the roof sheathing—they can give you a nasty gash. Wear a hat as added protection. Second, if your attic has no floor, nail down ¾-in., plywood before starting this project. In addition to letting you work safely, having a floor will create much more useful storage space.

1 **MARK THE SHELF HEIGHT.** Measure from the floor to mark the height of the shelf bottoms on the bottom of a rafter.

Cut and Install the Framework

The shelves are suspended from a framework of 2x4 cross-supports and uprights. Measure and install the crosspieces first and then the uprights and spacer blocks.

Install the cross-supports

Draw a level line from the back of the rafter to one of the height marks. To determine the length of the short cross-supports, add the length of this line plus 16 in. (the width of the shelf plus ⅛ in. of wiggle room) plus 3½ in. (the width of the uprights). Then add another 1 in. because the top of the shelves will meet the rafters a little farther out **(1)** (right). In the attic shown here, the level line across the rafter measures 9 in. long. So, for the short cross-support, 9 in. + 16 in. + 3½ in. + 1 in. = 29½ in.

Use the same formula for the long cross-supports, except that you need to add 32 in. for the shelf width instead of 16 in. Use a circular saw to cut one short cross-support and one long cross-support to length.

Mark the top of the short cross-support at 20½ in. and the top of the long cross-support at 36½ in. Start two 2½-in. deck screws into one end of each crosspiece. Hold a cross-support against the rafter with the bottom of the support along the layout line on the rafter. Move the support back or forth until the mark on the top of the support aligns with the bottom of the rafter. Drive in one screw. Use a 2-ft. level to check that the crosspiece is level, then drive in the other screw **(2)**. Add two more screws to the connection. Attach the longer cross-support in the same way.

Extend the Shelves

Want a longer run of shelves? A full-length rip of plywood will, of course, give you a shelf that's up to 8 ft. long—just add one or two support assemblies, depending on your rafter spacing. If you want to continue the shelves beyond 8 ft., you'll need additional rips of plywood. Cut the plywood so that joints will fall over a support with each plywood piece lapping the support by ¾ in. so you can screw down both pieces at the joint.

1 **DETERMINE THE LENGTH OF THE CROSS-SUPPORTS.** Strike a level line on a rafter at the height of the shelf bottoms, then measure across the line. Add that measurement to the width of the shelf plus the width of the uprights plus 1 in.

2 **ATTACH THE CROSS-SUPPORT.** Place a cross-support along the level line on the rafter and drive in one screw. Check for level and drive in three more screws at the connection.

Install the uprights

With the cross-supports cut, now it's time to cut the uprights and spacer blocks to length. Use a square to draw plumb lines 3½ in. from the outside end of each cross-support. Along these lines, measure from the top of the rafter to the bottom of the long crosspiece **(3)**. Cut an upright to this length. Also cut the four spacer blocks.

Place a 4-ft. level against the ends of the cross-supports, extending up to the rafter **(4)**. Place a spacer block against the level and mark its position on the rafter. Predrill four holes in the block to prevent splitting, then screw it to the rafter.

Clamp the upright to the bottom cross-support and the spacer. Use a 4-ft. level to check that it is plumb. Secure the upright to the spacer and both cross-supports with four 2½-in. screws at each connection **(5)**.

> **TIP** When you adjust the cross-supports to make them level to each other, you may notice that some may end up slightly above or below the bottom of their upright. That may be due to rafter sag and is no problem—the important thing is that the shelves will be level.

3 **MEASURE THE LENGTH OF THE UPRIGHTS. Draw plumb lines 3½ in. from the ends of the cross-supports to indicate the inside of the upright. Measure along these lines from the bottom of the long cross-support to the top of the rafter to determine the length of the upright.**

4 **MARK THE POSITION OF THE SPACER BLOCKS. Place a 4-ft. level against the ends of the cross-supports, put the block against the level, and mark its position on the rafter.**

5 **SCREW THE UPRIGHT INTO PLACE. Clamp the upright to the spacer block and rafter and to the bottom cross-support. Then make each connection with four 2½-in. screws.**

6 INSTALL THE REMAINING SUPPORTS. With one support assembly installed, you can clamp the parts together for the next assembly and make sure it is plumb and level before screwing it together.

Install the remaining supports

Now that you have confirmed the lengths of the cross-supports and uprights, cut all the remaining parts to length. Mark the short cross-supports at 20½ in. and the long cross-supports at 36½ in. as you did previously. Clamp two cross-supports, a spacer block, and an upright to the next rafter. Use a 4-ft. level to check that the cross-supports are level across the front **(6)** and a 2-ft. level to check that they are level along their length. When everything is level, drive four screws into each connection.

Plumb Enough

Framing lumber, whether it is the 2x4s you are using to build this project or the rafters in the attic, is not always perfectly straight. As a result, your uprights might not be plumb. If an upright is twisted, you can pull it into plumb, or nearly plumb, later when you screw the shelves in place—it doesn't need to be perfectly plumb. If the problem is slight, you can just pull on the upright as you screw in the shelves. If the problem is more severe, you can screw the shelves to the neighboring upright so it will be fixed in place, and then use a long clamp at the bottom between the neighbor and the twisted upright. Tighten the clamp until the twisted upright is as plumb as you can get it.

Cut and Install the Shelves

Measure across the uprights. Use a framing square to lay out a line at that length on the plywood shelves. Clamp the plywood to the sawhorses and cut them to length with a circular saw **(1)**.

To install the shelves, first mark the top of each bottom cross-support at 16 in. from the inside of the uprights. Put the back shelf piece in place along these marks and attach it with three 1¼-in. all-purpose screws into each cross-support **(2)**. Screw the other bottom shelf piece into place, then screw the top shelf into place.

1 CUT THE SHELVES TO LENGTH. With all the support assemblies in place, measure across the uprights and then cut the shelves to length.

2 INSTALL THE SHELVES. Screw the lower back shelf piece into place first while it is easy to reach.

RESOURCES

For the Window Seat
(pp. 77–99)

Accuride model 7434 22-in. full-extension plus 1-in. slides: available from CabinetParts.com, 1-800-857-8721

For the Rolling Kitchen Cart
(pp. 102–117)

1½-in. x 25-in. x 36-in. prefinished solid maple cabinet top, model H9687: available from Grizzly Industrial Inc., Grizzly.com, 1-800-523-4777

Locking wheels item number 350-75-BEBL-BL-TS-NB; available from CoolCasters.com, 1-800-394-8502

For the Closet Tower
(pp. 142–156)

Accessories including sliding baskets, tie/scarf rack, and valet rod: available from Rev-A-Shelf, Rev-a-Shelf.com, 1-800-626-1126

For the Toy Chest
(pp. 157–167)

Right and left box lid supports for 35 to 40 in. lb., item numbers N208686 (right side) and N208660 (left side): available from Walmart, www.walmart.com

For the Boot Bench with Storage Bin
(pp. 182–199)

Lid support, item number 66649: available from Rockler Woodworking and Hardware, Rockler.com, 1-800-279-4441

METRIC EQUIVALENTS

INCHES	CENTIMETERS	MILLIMETERS	INCHES	CENTIMETERS	MILLIMETERS
1/8	0.3	3	13	33.0	330
1/4	0.6	6	14	35.6	356
3/8	1.0	10	15	38.1	381
1/2	1.3	13	16	40.6	406
5/8	1.6	16	17	43.2	432
3/4	1.9	19	18	45.7	457
7/8	2.2	22	19	48.3	483
1	2.5	25	20	50.8	508
1 1/4	3.2	32	21	53.3	533
1 1/2	3.8	38	22	55.9	559
1 3/4	4.4	44	23	58.4	584
2	5.1	51	24	61	610
2 1/2	6.4	64	25	63.5	635
3	7.6	76	26	66.0	660
3 1/2	8.9	89	27	68.6	686
4	10.2	102	28	71.7	717
4 1/2	11.4	114	29	73.7	737
5	12.7	127	30	76.2	762
6	15.2	152	31	78.7	787
7	17.8	178	32	81.3	813
8	20.3	203	33	83.8	838
9	22.9	229	34	86.4	864
10	25.4	254	35	88.9	889
11	27.9	279	36	91.4	914
12	30.5	305			

INDEX

If you like this book,
you'll love *Fine Homebuilding*.

Read *Fine Homebuilding* Magazine:

Get eight issues, including our two annual design issues, *Houses* and *Kitchens & Baths*, plus FREE tablet editions. Packed with expert advice and skill-building techniques, every issue provides the latest information on quality building and remodeling.

Subscribe today at:
FineHomebuilding.com/4Sub

Discover our *Fine Homebuilding* Online Store:

It's your destination for premium resources from America's best builders: how-to and design books, DVDs, videos, special interest publications, and more.

Visit today at:
FineHomebuilding.com/4More

Get our FREE *Fine Homebuilding* eNewsletter:

Keep up with the current best practices, the newest tools, and the latest materials, plus free tips and advice from *Fine Homebuilding* editors.

Sign up, it's free:
FineHomebuilding.com/4Newsletter

Become a FineHomebuilding.com member:

Join to enjoy unlimited access to premium content and exclusive benefits, including: 1,400+ articles; 350 tip, tool, and technique videos; our how-to video project series; over 1,600 field-tested tips; monthly giveaways; tablet editions; contests; special offers; and more.

Discover more information online:
FineHomebuilding.com/4Join